May 1992

HOW TO OPEN AND OPERATE A BED & BREAKFAST HOME

"A must for anyone who has ever toyed with the idea of becoming a B&B host. . . . Warm and witty."
—*Mid-Atlantic Country*

"The many owners who wish to become involved in the growing bed-and-breakfast trend could not find a better source of information on the topic than this thorough, authoritative guide."
—*ALA Booklist*

"May well be the best book on the subject. Stankus . . . is an excellent researcher. . . . Stankus has filled her book with the personal impressions and voices of innkeepers across the nation. She also contributes her own special ideas in an immensely readable and engaging style."
—*America's Bed & Breakfast Report*

"Covers everything from the basic question of whether you should jump into the field, to pricing and making a memorable breakfast, to bidding your guests farewell. There is also a handy resource guide listing B&B hosts who will help newcomers; tourist offices; and [reservation] services."
—*The San Diego Union*

"One of the most readable and well organized of this genre we've come across. . . . It covers everything you need to know."
—*Country Living*

". . . a refreshingly realistic picture of what it's like to 'rent' your spare bedroom(s) to weary travelers. It supplies most of the information you'll need to prepare for a B&B host home career—from what you can claim on your income tax forms to whether or not you should hug your guests when they check out."
—*Innsider* magazine

"If you like the idea of earning a few extra dollars while entertaining interesting folks, operating a B&B may be for you. . . . Read more about it in *How to Open and Operate a Bed & Breakfast Home*."
—*Better Homes & Gardens*

HOW TO OPEN AND OPERATE A BED & BREAKFAST HOME

Second Edition

by Jan Stankus

The Globe Pequot Press

Chester, Connecticut

Library of Congress Cataloging-in-Publication Data

Stankus, Jan.
How to open and operate a bed and breakfast home / by Jan Stankus. — 2nd ed.
p. cm.
Includes index.
ISBN 0-87106-527-4
1. Bed and breakfast accommodations. 2. Hotel management. I. Title.
TX911.2.S73 1989
647.94—dc20 89-32603
CIP

Manufactured in the United States of America
Second Edition/First Printing

Contents

Foreword ix
Preface xi

1. Should You Become a Bed and Breakfast Host? 1

Would You Make a Good Host? 1
The Right Reasons 4
Meeting interesting people 4
Unused space 6
The right skills 10
A home-based business 13
A community service 15
Extra income 17

2. What Does It Take to Run a Successful Bed and Breakfast? 22

Location 22
Comfort 28
Noise 28
Children 31
Pets 32
Smoking 32
Temperature and ventilation 33
Neighborhood 34
Atmosphere 34
Cleanliness 35
Lifestyle 40
The Working Host 44

3. Getting Started 50

The Basics 50
Bedroom basics 50
Bathroom basics 60

The Amenities 66
Pricing Your Bed and Breakfast 74

4. Getting Connected 78

Reservation Service Organizations 78
What assistance does the RSO offer new hosts? 80
What kind of ongoing assistance does the RSO provide? 81
How does the RSO publicize its services to potential guests? 82
Is the RSO affiliated with any organizations? 84
Does the RSO encourage communication among its hosts? 85
Does the RSO keep in touch with former guests? 86
What obligations does an RSO have to its hosts? 87
What obligations does a host have to his or her RSO? 88
Does the RSO require a host contract? 89
What fee is paid to the RSO for its services? 90
Special-Focus B&B Groups 91
National Bed and Breakfast Groups 94
The American Bed and Breakfast Association 94
The National Bed and Breakfast Association 95
Tourist House Association of America 95
Inn Reference 95
Regional Bed and Breakfast Groups 96
The Helping Hands Network 99
Resources 101
Newsletters 101
Real Estate 102
Consultants and workshops 103

5. Publicizing Your Bed and Breakfast 106

Creating Your Literature 107
Your B&B brochure 107
Your B&B's image 107
Choosing colors and paper 108
Cutting costs 108
Naming your B&B 109
Using artwork effectively 109
Locating illustrations 110

Doing it yourself 112
The content 113
Your B&B stationery 114
Distributing Your Literature 116
How to Use Your Community Resources 118
How to Get Listed in B&B Guidebooks 120
Bed and breakfast booklist 122
How to Get Press Coverage 129
Advertising Your Bed and Breakfast 131
Creative Marketing for Off-Season Business 132

6. The Perfect Guest **134**

Screening Your Guests 134
Meeting your guests' needs 134
Meeting your own needs 137
Confirming a reservation 140
The role of the RSO 141
One-Night Guests 147
Single Travelers 148
Hosting Children 152
Four-Legged Guests 156
Hosting Foreign Visitors 160
An Accessible B&B 162

7. The Perfect Host **167**

The Welcome 167
Orientation 174
Guest Letter 178
Welcome 178
Breakfast 179
Food and drink 179
Keys 179
Lights 179
Quiet hours 180
The telephone 180
House and grounds 181
Care of the room 181
Check-out time 181
Smoking 181
Alcohol 182

Laundry 182
Pets in residence 182
Emergencies 182
The closing 183
The Visit 184
The Farewell 190
Guest Comments 193
Memories 195
What's in a name? 196
Remember me? 197
Your own newsletter 200
A thousand words 200
A book exchange 201
Holiday greetings 202
The Neighbors 203

8. A Memorable Breakfast 206

Scenic Settings 206
The centerpiece 208
Especially for children 211
The Coffee 213
For tea drinkers 217
The Food 217
Especially for children 225

9. The Business of B&B 227

Zoning 228
Insurance 230
Safety Precautions 232
Taxes 236
Keeping Records 240

Appendix I: The Helping Hands Network 246
Appendix II: Reservation Service Organizations in North America 254
Appendix III: State and Local Tourist Offices 271
Index 293

Foreword

Bed and breakfast hosting seems like the most natural home occupation in the world . . . and it really is. On first thought, one would think that anyone who has managed a home, entertained guests, or chatted with strangers at a social gathering could become a successful B&B host without any further training. Those of us in the business know that this is not quite true, and Jan Stankus has provided a much-needed training manual for current and prospective hosts.

A B&B home must provide quality accommodations and genuine hospitality to its guests. To do this, it must be managed by "professional" hosts whose attitudes and expectations are in line with the realities of the business. *How to Open and Operate a Bed & Breakfast Home* offers the reader a complete course on the nuts and bolts of hosting, including all the pitfalls as well as the many joys and benefits.

I am delighted to finally have a truly comprehensive text to recommend to all my hosts. This thoughtfully researched book includes valuable personal checklists, detailed financial information, and up-to-date resource lists. It's a pleasure to read, full of anecdotes and examples, and it is a much-needed addition to the growing library of bed and breakfast literature.

Arline Kardasis
President
Bed and Breakfast
The National Network

To Robyn and Tom,
who have shared
some of the best moments
of my life.

Preface

A book like this had to happen, and it had to happen now. That much was clear from the many, many letters coming into my office at the Traveler's Information Exchange from people who want to become bed and breakfast hosts but don't know where to begin. There are questions that need to be answered, and the answers should come from the people who are in the best position to give them. Who knows more about bed and breakfast than the hosts who open their homes to guests, the people who travel the B&B way, and the managers of reservation service organizations (RSOs) that help hosts and guests get together?

I'm very proud of this book. It is a product of the combined knowledge, experience, and advice of several hundred hosts and RSO managers from across North America, and guests who have enjoyed their hospitality. Together, they offer the basis for a comprehensive guide to opening and operating a bed and breakfast home; individually, they show the personal style that makes each B&B a unique experience. All of the people who contributed information to make this book possible have done so freely, with the hope that what they know can help a new host get started.

What exactly is bed and breakfast? This question is at the top of the list for people who are thinking about starting their own B&B but still aren't quite sure what it's all about. Many people are familiar with bed and breakfast as it exists in Europe, where B&B has long been a tradition. Or they've read about it in magazines, newspapers, or guidebooks. Or they've heard about it from friends or acquaintances who have stayed in bed and breakfast homes during their travels as an alternative to hotels. By now, we've all heard about "bed and breakfast" somewhere or another. In fact, the term has become so commonplace that it's applied to all sorts of things, and that's part of the problem. Some large hotels now offer what they call a "bed and breakfast" package. No wonder there's confusion about what B&B is all about! One of the growing pains of an emerging industry is that it must seek definition—what it is and what it is not.

This book makes these distinctions: A *bed and breakfast home* (also called a *host home* or *homestay*) is a private residence or other structure on a homeowner's property (such as a guest house or cabin) that is used to accommodate paying guests overnight. Breakfast (either continental or full) is provided. B&B offers guests a good old-fashioned dose of hospitality in a world that is sometimes a little too impersonal. A bed and breakfast home is not a rooming house. It is not a hotel or a motel. It is not a restaurant. And it is not a bed and breakfast inn or a country inn, although they have some important characteristics in common, including a commitment to providing the best in hospitality. Rather, inns are small commercial enterprises (usually having four to twelve guest rooms) in which breakfast is usually part of the deal, just as it is in a bed and breakfast home. But a bed and breakfast home is in a class by itself.

Is bed and breakfast too good to be true? Some people fear that it is. Right now, bed and breakfast is a relatively new industry in North America, little more than a decade "old." We're still in our honeymoon phase, where everything is pretty terrific. It's hard to believe that something this wonderful can exist, so we want to protect what we've got. We're afraid that too-rapid growth will make B&B too commercialized, but if we protect it too much we run the risk of smothering what we have. It's a delicate balance, but one we must work to keep. We have to try to attract the right kind of people to hosting, for the right reasons. That's why this book was necessary.

Who should use this book? If you're thinking about operating a bed and breakfast home, you will benefit from the gold mine of information contained here. It will help you figure out if bed and breakfast is right for you. It will help you start up and run a bed and breakfast home. It will put you in touch with reservation service organizations that can help you. It will outline your responsibilities as a host. And it will show you where you fit into the B&B industry as a whole in North America.

If you already operate a bed and breakfast home, this book allows you the opportunity to compare notes with other people who share your interests. There is no need to be out there all alone. If you wish, you can use the book to get personally connected with other hosts across the country through the exclusive Helping Hands network. The more we work together, the better able we'll be to shape the future of bed and breakfast.

In addition, those who operate reservation service organizations can use the information here as an easy reference. The book will make their job easier by providing a useful tool for their work.

Finally, an owner of a bed and breakfast inn or a country inn can also take advantage of the information here. Anyone who loves offering the best in hospitality will find a wealth of ideas from the bed and breakfast hosts who share that love.

What comes next? The bed and breakfast industry is still evolving in North America. Even as this book goes to press, changes are taking place that will eventually affect all of us, for better or worse. A book like this must evolve with the industry. For this reason, I invite readers to get in touch with new developments that will benefit the readers of future editions. Please write to me at The Globe Pequot Press, 138 West Main Street, Chester, Connecticut 06412.

Acknowledgments

This book is a product of the time, efforts, and support of many people. Special thanks go to all the bed and breakfast hosts, managers of reservation service organizations, and B&B guests for filling out those long, long questionnaires. (To Jim and Greg at Printer's Ink for printing those long, long questionnaires.) To the American Bed & Breakfast Association for inviting me to attend an important B&B conference where vital issues were dealt with in detail. To Bed and Breakfast of Rhode Island for organizing a conference that was a perfect opportunity for all in attendance to network and get to know the people behind the names in the B&B industry. To Brigita Veisbergs of the Boston Tourist and Convention Bureau for information about the role of the tourist bureau. To Lee Riethmiller, director of the Intercontinental Foreign Language Program, for straightening out the *thees* and *thous* in The Host Commandments and The Guest Commandments. To Liza Roman, owner of Roman Numerals bookkeeping firm, for record-keeping pointers and tax-filing information. To Doctor of Veterinary Medicine John Bujalski, my cat's favorite doctor, for advice on hosting pets. To Jean at the Career Services Department of the Women's Educational & Industrial Union for resources on home-based businesses; to Jill in WEIU's restaurant for tips on attractive presentations of food. To Anna Fiorino, owner of Helping Hands Typing Service, for lending hers when I really needed it. To the Body Language Dancers for putting up with me when I missed rehearsals and classes to work on this important project. To Mom and Dad for keeping an eye out for resources that helped in developing this book.

1

Should You Become a Bed & Breakfast Host?

Many of us toy with the idea of becoming a bed and breakfast host after a wonderful visit at a B&B during a vacation or business trip, or after hearing about how much others have enjoyed this unique type of accommodation. The life of a host seems so easy, so pleasant, so glamorous.

But before getting completely caught up in the fantasy, it's a good idea to look a little more closely at what it really takes to be a good bed and breakfast host. The following quizzes will help to prepare you for the realities of bed and breakfast hosting that are discussed later.

Would you make a good host?

For each of the following questions, choose the one answer that most closely describes your life at the moment, or what you would do in each situation if you were a bed and breakfast host.

1. What do you like to serve for breakfast?
   a. Eggs Benedict
   b. Blueberry waffles made from your own special recipe
   c. Granola with chilled yogurt and strawberries, topped with honey
   d. Leftover chili from last night's poker game

2. What kind of a bed is in your guest room?
   a. An antique four-poster double bed with a new, firm mattress
   b. A queen-sized platform bed (made of natural pine) and a futon

c. A king-sized waterbed with adjustable heat control
d. An army cot that's been in the attic since World War I

3. What is the oldest item in your refrigerator?
a. Fruit salad left over from this morning's breakfast
b. Marinated mushrooms for tomorrow's lunch
c. An unopened jar of homemade raspberry preserves
d. The corsage from your junior prom

4. What type of wastebasket do you have in the guest room?
a. A wicker basket that matches the writing table and the chair near the window
b. A brightly polished metal container lined with tissue paper that complements the wallpaper
c. A large, handcrafted ceramic urn made by the same artist who also created the lamp base and ashtray in the room
d. A paper bag that says "A&P" on it

5. When did you buy the shower curtain in the bathroom that your guests will use?
a. It's brand new
b. Six months ago
c. One year ago
d. It came with the house

6. A guest arrives at your door after a long, difficult trip that involved missed connections and lost luggage. How do you greet him?
a. You show him to his room immediately
b. You take his coat, offer him a seat in the living room, and bring him a glass of wine
c. You point out the nature trail behind your home that goes through a beautiful wooded area to a peaceful lake
d. You yell, "Come on in!" from your prone position on the couch in front of the TV

7. You have to leave for work a half hour before your guests plan to be up. How do you handle their breakfast?
a. You put a quiche and homemade muffins in the oven on "warm"
b. You prepare a "cold tray" with a selection of fresh fruit, croissants, butter, and jam
c. You leave a coffee cake ready to pop into the oven
d. You throw a box of cornflakes on the kitchen table and hope that your guests will find the milk and sugar

Okay, I admit that this quiz is a bit on the light side. Nevertheless, two major points should have become clear as you looked over the possible answers to each serious question.

The first point is that there is no one "right" answer or solution that makes someone a "good" host and someone else not. Each host is an individual with a unique personal style and brand of imagination. A host should be able to rely on his or her own good sense of hospitality and grace—and common sense, too—to make sure that guests feel welcome and comfortable.

The second point is that there are some things that are clearly unacceptable. I truly hope that you did not, in good faith, choose the letter "d" as the answer to any of the questions. If you did, bed and breakfast hosting is probably not for you. But if you chose a, b, or c as answers for any of the questions, you're ready to try the *real* quiz, which follows.

For each of the following questions, choose "yes" or "no" as the answer. Remember: This is the *real* test for what it takes to become a bed and breakfast host.

1. Do you like meeting all kinds of people?
   a. yes
   b. no

2. Is your house located in an area that attracts visitors?
   a. yes
   b. no

3. Do you keep your home clean and neat?
   a. yes
   b. no

4. Do you like to cook?
   a. yes
   b. no

5. Do you currently have a regular income?
   a. yes
   b. no

6. Do you have an extra room that isn't being used?
   a. yes
   b. no

7. Do you consider yourself a cheerful person?
   a. yes
   b. no

8. Do you enjoy entertaining visitors in your home?
   a. yes
   b. no

If you found that you answered "yes" to all or most of the preceding questions, it's possible that you are just the kind of person who would enjoy being a bed and breakfast host. Both quizzes cover the major qualities that a bed and breakfast host should have. They are outlined well here by Lauren Simonelli, president of Greater Boston Hospitality: "We look for what we like to call 'The Three C's'—Cleanliness, Comfort, and Congeniality." Combine these qualities with a good location, and you could very well have a successful bed and breakfast a short time from now.

The right reasons

Before reading any further, get a pencil and write down the reasons why you want to become a bed and breakfast host.

Done? Now put a big star next to your main reason. Then decide which reason is the second most important and mark it with a number "2" and so on down the line until each reason has been rated in importance. Now we're ready.

Meeting interesting people

"I love people!" Does your first reason sound something like this? It should. Anyone who has been a bed and breakfast host will tell you that a genuine love of people is first and foremost in this business. "You must be a 'people person,' " says Marjorie Amron, who runs a bed and breakfast called Trade Winds in Philadelphia. This is true, and it means that a host must honestly enjoy all kinds of people—and I mean *all* kinds. Through bed and breakfast, you will meet people from the far reaches of the earth, with different customs, traditions, philosophies, religions, lifestyles, vocations, fashions. They come in all shapes, sizes, and colors. It takes a special person to welcome all types into one's own home with open arms. You need a good blend of curiosity, tolerance, trust, and respect for others.

The variety of people you will meet should be one of the major rewards of your bed and breakfast. "Life is never humdrum," say the hosts of Valley View Farm in Mathias, West Virginia; "there are always new people to talk to and share what each contributes to the others' culture." Edna and Ernest Shipe have hosted hundreds of visitors from all over the world—most European countries, Bolivia, Chile, Haiti, Hong Kong, Japan, China, "and most states in the good old U.S.A." They make a point of saying that such enjoyable educational exchanges are possible only if you are the kind of person who can "accept people who are much different from what you are."

Some people can't, and they will not make good hosts, plain and simple. They will be uncomfortable; their guests will be uncomfortable. The managers of several reservation service organizations report that they have had to turn away prospective hosts on this basis. Anyone with strong intolerances for certain people, for whatever reason, should not become a host. One reservation service organization, called The Traveler in Maryland, handles the issue through its contract with its individual hosts. The contract contains a warning to be read before signing the document. It says, "If you have any irreconcilable differences regarding race, creed, color, or national origin, we strongly advise you not to become a host."

Two hosts were dropped by a reservation service organization in Washington, D.C., not because they had strong prejudices, but because they just were not the kind of "people person" you've got to be in this business. "In both cases, they would call us and have some sort of complaint or other about the guests, and we felt B&B wasn't for them," says the manager of Bed 'n' Breakfast Ltd. "We have many hosts who really enjoy having guests, and those who find fault just aren't worth dealing with."

So yes, you must like people ("Even those you don't like," say the hosts of Friends We Haven't Met, a bed and breakfast in Westminster, California). But more than this, you must show it easily. Are you a warm person? "Our philosophy of bed and breakfast is that you become an honorary member of our family while you are with us," reads the brochure for Penury Hall in Southwest Harbor, Maine. Its owner, Prentice Strong, says that a host "must like people above all and be willing to treat them as family one has not seen for a year or two." Your guests will *feel* completely welcome only if they *are* completely welcome.

"I love activity and company," says one host in Eureka Springs, Arkansas. "I've never been married and didn't want to be a 'little ol' lady' with no kids or family coming to visit. Now I've created my own family. Each guest who comes through my door—in five minutes they're family."

Do you feel this way about the people who come to visit you now? This is a good test to see whether or not you will enjoy all the activity that goes with bed and breakfast. Do you love getting company and look forward to talking with friends and relatives who come to see you? Or do you usually find yourself sneaking a look at your watch, counting the minutes until they will leave you in peace?

If you live alone, are used to being alone, and *like* being alone, ask yourself if the presence of other human beings in your home will make you feel that your inner sanctum has been invaded by hostile forces. A person who really cherishes privacy should think twice about opening a bed and breakfast home. You will end up being uncomfortable in the place you love the most, and guests will sense the strain on you.

Take an honest look at your social skills. "I'm a naturally social being," says Janet Turley, who owns The House of Amacord in Buckland, Massachusetts. Can you say the same about yourself? Do you make friends quickly? Are you able to put strangers at ease immediately? Are you pleasant and polite, no matter what? And most important, is all of this easy and enjoyable for you?

"My folks had taken in tourists when I was growing up, and I thought it was entirely natural to have 'new friends' in and out of the house," says Ellen Madison, owner of Woody Hill Guest House B&B in Westerly, Rhode Island. That's exactly how hosting should feel to you—entirely natural.

Unused space

Do you have an extra room or two in your house? A suite? Perhaps an entire apartment? Or a separate guest house or cottage on the grounds? What about a boat or trailer that you use only a short while each year for yourself and your family? A barn? A shed? A lighthouse? All of these places were once "wasted space" for people who decided to put them to use for bed and breakfast.

"I had a vacant room after my children grew up and moved out," says a host who lives in Philadelphia. "It is attractive, and our home is pleasant. It seemed to be a great way to make a little extra money and to meet new people from all over the country and the world."

"It provided a way to maintain and share our landmark home," say Cynthia and Charles Whited, owners of Strawberry Castle in Penfield, New York.

"Our big country house just seemed ideal for a B&B, so we decided to try it," says the owner of Anchor Hill Lodge in Rogersville, Missouri.

"After my estranged husband left, it was a way of increasing my income (for legal fees), meeting new people, sharing my son's and my home, and deriving more utility from the house," says a Pennsylvania host.

Many of us find ourselves in this situation as our lives change over the years. The house that served us so well for so long no longer "fits." It's too big. Too hard to keep up. Moving may be out of the question for you because the place holds so many memories, or you just plain love it there! But how do you make that big old place run economically after the kids are gone, or maybe your once near-and-dear spouse has taken off for parts unknown? Bed and breakfast could be the answer. The mayor of a town in New England put it well during his address to a bed and breakfast conference convening in his area for the weekend: "When you have a fifteen-room house, bed and breakfast starts looking pretty good!"

Even some young people who have not yet started their families have turned to bed and breakfast. One single woman who lives in Boston grew tired of having a never-ending series of roommates come and go. Yet she wanted the stimulation of having other people around because she works at home. ("When you live alone and work alone, it's too much," she says.) Her solution was bed and breakfast. Now she can have the company of other people and put the second bedroom to good use, all without losing the extra income that having a roommate had provided.

A suite in your home is an added plus if you want to offer bed and breakfast. According to Bed & Breakfast of Rhode Island, a suite consists of a sitting room and one or more sleeping rooms. It usually has a private bath and may contain cooking facilities. Some guests prefer this enlarged space. Bob and Hattie Michalis, owners of Gull House in Avalon, California, have found that having a suite has opened up a market for them with honeymoon and anniversary couples looking for a special getaway.

If you have an extra apartment unit in your house, you might want to consider using it for bed and breakfast as an alternative to renting it to full-time tenants. (Be sure to check any rent-control ordinances that may apply before you do this.) "We had a large sixteen-room house and no longer want to be landlords. So we took out the apartments," says Robert Somaini of Woodruff House in Barre, Vermont. "This enables us to have use of the whole house and still have an income."

Apartment rentals to "long-term" guests (who stay a week or more) have been quite successful for Ashby Willcox and Susan Hubbard, coordinators of Bed and Breakfast of Tidewater, Virginia: "In big cities this can be a very good idea because of relocating executives who need a place for more than two or three nights and desire an apartment."

An apartment differs from a suite in that it typically provides a fully equipped kitchen along with the sitting room and one or more sleeping rooms. A suite may or may not have a private entrance; an apartment generally does, although there could be an exterior door as well that is shared with others in the building.

Other good spaces to use for bed and breakfast are any small buildings that might be on your grounds. These go by different names—cabin, bungalow, guest house, cottage. What they have in common is that they are located near enough to the main house (where you live) so that you can easily take care of your guests' needs. These small structures are equipped for housekeeping in themselves, according to Bed & Breakfast of Rhode Island. In other words, you can expect to see an accommodation that is self-contained, with a bathroom, cooking facilities, a sleeping room, and most likely a sitting room.

Using this kind of extra space for bed and breakfast has worked well for Phil and Joan Blood of Chinguague Compound in San Juan Pueblo, New Mexico. They say: "We have this lovely compound with guest houses on it and we thought, 'What a fun way to meet people and utilize the property at the same time!' " Their bed and breakfast by the Rio Grande features guest houses that are each equipped with a kitchen so that if guests prefer, they may "cook in," plus a library and television. "We have a small house behind our home that had always been rented on a yearly basis," says Carol Emerick of San Diego, California. "We decided to furnish the little house and offer it to travelers on a daily/weekly basis."

Keep in mind, though, that if you do have a guest house separate from the main house, or an apartment or suite set off from your own living space, you must work harder to establish a "bed and breakfast environment" for the guests. The aspect of bed and breakfast that many guests (and hosts) enjoy the most is the opportunity to meet and talk with one another. So make sure that any guests who are not sharing the same roof with you are invited into your living room for coffee or a glass of sherry and a visit at least when they first arrive.

And remember, too, that their experience is not "bed and breakfast" if there's no breakfast! Do-it-yourself is okay on occasion, if the host's schedule absolutely demands it or if that is what guests prefer and ask for, but as a general rule, your hospitality should include a continental breakfast at the very minimum. How to get it there is the problem; some hosts prepare the trays in the main house and carry them over to the guest houses. (You might have to adjust your breakfast menu to rule out the more sensitive delicacies—such as a soufflé—that would not survive the journey.) Or you could always invite guests to have breakfast with you back at the main house. That way you can easily prepare and serve everything from your own kitchen. (It also gives the guests more of a chance to get to know their hosts.) Try to find what works best for you, as long as you don't eliminate breakfast altogether! If you do this, you might as well just rent out your extra units as regular short- or long-term housing and forget about bed and breakfast!

Some people have gotten involved in bed and breakfast by making the decision to use their boats to accommodate guests. Host Homes of Boston, for example, has a forty-six-foot yacht available to guests. Moored in Constitution Quarters in Charlestown, it is only a short walk from the shops and restaurants of the nationally known Faneuil Hall Marketplace in Boston. It's an ideal spot for out-of-town visitors who want to balance dry land with ocean air. The manager of Pittsburgh Bed and Breakfast (a reservation service organization) says she's waiting for a few enterprising people who own boats to realize that they could use them to offer bed and breakfast to tourists who want to enjoy the beauty of the Three Rivers during their stay in the city.

Some hosts have renovated what used to be a barn, offering a rustic environment for guests. Another redesigned a shed into a cute little guest house for those with a bit of adventure in their souls. Still another went to work on an old unused lighthouse. Needless to say, these all took major-scale operations to convert the unused space into interesting, but comfortable, accommodations.

So if you identified "unused space" as one of the main reasons for your interest in bed and breakfast, evaluate what you've got and what it would take to make the area livable. You can't just put guests in the shed out back with the lawn mower, in the basement behind the hot-water heater, in the attic up against Grandmother's trunks, or in the barn in Bossie's old stall (may she rest in peace). Ask yourself if the space you have is appropriate and worth the time and expense necessary to transform it into a bed and breakfast facility.

For most of us who have just an extra room or two in our homes, the decision is a little easier because the work that needs to be done to prepare them for guests is not that extensive. (Although if you want to offer bed and breakfast as a full-time business, you've got your work cut out for you to prepare and maintain at least six guest rooms.) If you have attractive space that is now being wasted and you would like to get the most out of your property, bed and breakfast could be a good idea.

The right skills

"My husband says I'm a cross between Perle Mesta, Erma Bombeck, and Betty Crocker," says Lisa Hileman, discussing the reason she decided to become a bed and breakfast host. If you're like Lisa, who runs a bed and breakfast called Countryside in Summit Point, West Virginia, maybe you made a similar assessment of your personal skills and realized that they are well suited to bed and breakfast hosting.

The social skills are first and foremost. A love of people is a good start, but can you translate your natural love of humanity into hospitality, as Perle Mesta did? "It's the ultimate compliment to be compared to her," says Lisa. Perle Mesta arrived on the Washington social scene in 1941 and reigned as its most celebrated hostess for the next thirty years. Her elegant parties were attended by prominent political figures and other notables, including Harry S Truman (who even played the piano at one of her gatherings) and Dwight D. Eisenhower (who sang "Drink to Me Only with Thine Eyes"). Can *you* make people feel this welcome and this comfortable? "Antennae" is what host Crescent Dragonwagon of Dairy Hollow House in Eureka Springs, Arkansas, calls this ability. You've got to have that inner sense of what makes people comfortable.

Are you courteous and tactful, no matter what? There could be times when guests test your patience by inviting someone to breakfast without first clearing it with you, playing the television too loudly late at night, leaving their children unsupervised, trailing mud all over your priceless Oriental rug, or using your best towels to remove mascara. Are you able to talk to the guest about the problem calmly and politely, regardless of how angry you might be? If you lose your cool, even with justification, you could lose business. Peg Tierney, coordinator of Bed and Breakfast of Maine, says she rejected one host wishing to list with her reservation service organization for "lack of friendly hospitality."

City Lights Bed & Breakfast in New York City reports rejecting a host for the same reason: "not hospitable by nature." It's sometimes not easy to keep smiling, but in this business you have to.

Are you straightforward? Can you say what you have to say without making a big deal about it? "I wish he would give me some money soon!" said one host about her week-long guest. She needed at least a partial payment to buy groceries for breakfast all week and meet other expenses. Yet she had never mentioned payment directly to the guest because it made her uncomfortable. She just hoped he would take the initiative and pay before the day he checked out. This was a mistake that could have been easily avoided (by establishing a clear policy about payment) or corrected (by talking to the guest when he arrived). It need never have caused such distress. No matter how uncomfortable it might make you, if there's a problem, you have to be able to deal with it head on, or it will continue to bother you and possibly affect your treatment of a guest or of subsequent guests.

And what does Erma Bombeck, the well-known writer and syndicated columnist, have that a bed and breakfast host needs? A sense of humor. Being able to laugh in the face of adversity will get you through those times when the commode overflows, the furnace goes on the fritz, or the soufflé implodes. "Roll with the punches," advise Ashby Willcox and Susan Hubbard, coordinators of a reservation service organization called Bed & Breakfast of Tidewater, Virginia. Linda Feltman and Brent Peters, owners of an RSO in Pine Grove Mills, Pennsylvania, called Rest & Repast, say, "Be flexible and ready for surprises. This is an unpredictable business." A good laugh once in a while is sometimes all it takes to set things right again.

Then again, sometimes it's not enough. Are you handy around the house? Remember that the plumbing, the electrical system, and some of your appliances will be getting more of a workout because there will be more people using them. Imagine this: While you are cleaning the guest bathroom in preparation for visitors this evening, the water faucet comes off in your hands, and water shoots up like Old Faithful. Now what? It's Sunday and there's no way you can get a plumber. Would you know what to do as an emergency measure? Do you know how to cut off the water supply, tighten the offending screw, or replace the worn-out washer?

Or what about this: While replacing a burnt-out light bulb in the reading lamp in the guest room, you notice that the wires are frayed. You unplug it to take a closer look, but when you plug it back in again, sparks fly. Guests are arriving tomorrow morning—not enough time to take the lamp to the repair shop. Do you know how to repair the frayed wire temporarily (but safely) with electrical tape, or rewire the lamp yourself?

A host must be prepared to handle emergencies such as these. Bob and Hattie Michalis, owners of Gull House in Avalon, California, claim that the most difficult aspect of being a host is "doing battle with Murphy's Law"—if something can go wrong, it will. If you have the knowledge and training to take care of minor home repairs, all you need is a good tool box and some basic supplies, and you're ready for almost anything. For the rest of us, glory be that there are some simple, basic books on the market that take us, step by step, through the procedures for a variety of emergency repairs. Sometimes a Perle Mesta has to turn into a Mister Fix-It very quickly.

Do you like to cook, and are you good at it? What Carol Emerick, owner of The Cottage in San Diego, California, likes most about offering bed and breakfast is "being able to have a legitimate excuse for trying new recipes." A major part of a host's responsibility is preparing and serving breakfast. Is this *your* idea of a good time? No, you don't really have to be a Betty Crocker in order to become a host. There are plenty of easy-to-make dishes that will delight your guests. But if you do love spending time in the kitchen trying new recipes and whipping up old favorites to share with your guests, it will make hosting all the more enjoyable for you.

"Flair for creating an atmosphere" is a valuable skill for a host, says Elsa Dimick, owner of Longswamp B&B in Mertztown, Pennsylvania. It's important to try to make the environment as special as possible for your guests. This aspect of bed and breakfast appeals to Roy Mixon, who bought and renovated Rockland Farm Retreat in Bumpass, Virginia. He says he especially enjoys "showing off my decorating skills—we have a Fantasy Island plantation for those who wish to enjoy the fantasy." If you're like Roy and have a knack for developing a "look" for your bed and breakfast home, you can use that skill to attract guests looking for something special.

Robert Somaini, owner of Woodruff House in Barre, Vermont, adds this quality to his list of those needed by a host: "knowledgeable in local history." Remember that many of your guests could be visiting your area for the first time, wanting to explore what it has to offer and to learn all about it. If you've watched your neighborhood grow and change over the years, now's the chance to put that knowledge to good use. Your guests will also want and need information about the here and now. Host Carol Emerick says that a major advantage to her guests is her own "in-depth knowledge of what there is to do in San Diego—not just knowledge about the amusements and expensive attractions." These, visitors can find in any guidebook. Your value to them is what you can tell them about the things that do *not* appear in any guidebook.

Small-business skills are extremely important for a bed and breakfast host. If you don't have them, either get them somehow (basic books on small-business management, a course or two) or hire someone who has them. Nancy Jenkins, former owner of a reservation service organization in St. Helena, California, called the Bed & Breakfast Exchange, says that the biggest mistake that new hosts make is "not being well-enough prepared for the bookkeeping and accounting aspects of the business." You have got to be well organized so that you can keep straight who is coming and going, and when; how much money is coming in and going out; and what it all means when it's tax time. This involves keeping receipts, names, addresses, dates, and schedules. (See chapter 9, "The Business of B&B.") It's all paperwork that might seem as if it has little to do with hospitality, but it's this same paperwork that will tell you whether you have a viable bed and breakfast business.

A home-based business

What Ellen Madison, owner of Woody Hill Guest House B&B in Westerly, Rhode Island, likes most about being a host is "the fact that the world comes to me; I do not have to go to it." Did you note something like this on your list of reasons describing why you want to become a host? Many people who get involved in bed and breakfast do so because they prefer running their own home-based business to heading out each day to a nine-to-five job.

Parents of children who are not yet old enough to go to school find bed and breakfast a great way of bringing in some income while they stay at home with the family. Some retirees want a part-time venture that does not require going back to the kind of schedule they have happily left behind. Other people have physical disabilities that hinder a lot of travel outside the home. Still others have another home-based business (consulting, writing, farming) that easily makes room for a second business also run out of the home (see "The Working Host" in chapter 2). Then there are those of us who simply enjoy the freedom that comes with being our own bosses.

With bed and breakfast, you can arrange your own schedule, accepting guests, or not, as you wish. "We're all booked on New Year's Eve," one Boston host told a prospective guest over the phone. Actually, she wasn't. What she really wanted to do was spend New Year's Eve with her family attending the city's annual First Night celebration without having the responsibility of meeting the needs of any guests. Because she runs her own business, she could make that decision. Of course, it meant losing a booking for that night. But if business is generally good for a host, the trade-off for some personal enjoyment can be worth it. The point is that with a home-based business like bed and breakfast, you can make your own decisions.

Perhaps you prefer to work like crazy during the "season" (whatever it may be for you in your location—skiing, football, fun in the sun) and then take the other months off. One couple accepts guests only during the week so that their weekends are free. Or maybe you just want a few guests every once in a while, as its suits your own schedule. One busy New England writer does not publicize her bed and breakfast in any way; rather, she has a special agreement with her local reservation service organization that whenever she has the time to take guests, she calls the RSO to let them know. The RSO then refers guests to her for as long as she wishes. This way, the host does not have to spend her time and energy turning away the many guests that she could never accommodate throughout the year. These choices are all available to a bed and breakfast host.

The idea of running your own show from your own home attracts many of us, but it works best for someone who can honestly say that he or she is a "homebody." Do you love your home dearly? Do you love caring for it? And most important, do you love spending most of your time there and nowhere else? This is exactly where you'll be if you become a bed and breakfast host. If you don't absolutely love it, you'll soon get that cooped-up feeling. Give this fact due consideration. If you're the kind of person who usually relies upon your work to get you out into the world regularly, bed and breakfast should be, at most, an adjunct to another job that does just this.

If you're thinking about starting a home-based business for the first time, realize now that there is a major disadvantage to it—you simply can't punch the time clock at 5:00 P.M. and be done with it. With bed and breakfast, you live right in the middle of your business, and you have to be careful or you'll end up sacrificing too much of your private life in your effort to do well. This might not seem like an issue when you first begin, but as time goes on and you find yourself surrounded by more and more guests, you'll want to set aside a time and a space just for yourself or you'll feel like you're working twenty-four hours a day.

It's a good idea to decide on a place that is completely off limits except to you and your family, preferably a room other than your bedroom (the den, library, or family room). Whenever you show guests the house, show them only the rooms that they are invited to use, or show them this one as well with the comment "This is where I go when I need a little peace and quiet," so that they know this is *your* space. (Be warned that some guests won't take the hint and will come knocking at your door for the slightest reason. Most guests, though, are very considerate and will respect your privacy.) Then set aside some time each day that you can have just for yourself to relax, watch the soaps, read a book, or have coffee with a friend. It might take some time to establish a pattern of personal time for yourself, but you'll be glad you did. It will help you to better enjoy the advantages of having a home-based bed and breakfast business.

A community service

Some people get involved in bed and breakfast because they want to share their home with others as a service to the community and its economy. Perhaps you live in an area in which the only lodgings available for visitors are hotels and motels, or there is no public lodging at all.

Norma Grovermann, who runs the Prince George Inn B&B with her husband in Annapolis, Maryland, says that she became a host for the purpose of "providing an alternative to high-cost hotels to guests who enjoy and appreciate B&Bs."

Mary Decker, owner of Corner House in Rhinebeck, New York, was motivated to become a host by her "awareness of the shortage of rooms available to village visitors."

And Crescent Dragonwagon, owner of Dairy Hollow House in Eureka Springs, Arkansas, had been "wanting to invest locally, in something socially responsible." She decided on bed and breakfast "to create lodging in keeping with the historic nature of our town. Before us, there were only motels and one large hotel."

A number of hosts reach their decision to open a bed and breakfast after enjoying this kind of hospitality themselves. "I stayed in a B&B room and enjoyed it and wanted to do that with my house," says the owner of RMF Bed & Breakfast in Atlanta, Georgia. As a bed and breakfast guest, you can see firsthand how B&B can be an integral part of the business community, offering lodging where there was none, attracting visitors for a boost in the area's tourism trade, and providing a good old-fashioned dose of hospitality to those travelers who are looking for more of a connection with the area they are visiting and the people in it.

Because B&B is good for local economy, some chambers of commerce are getting into the act to encourage residents to open their homes. They invite speakers, run workshops, and provide advice. Steve and Nancy Richards, a Rhode Island couple, got involved when their local chamber of commerce started a bed and breakfast program. And in the hill towns of Massachusetts, chambers are actively reaching out to homeowners to consider bed and breakfast.

Margie Haas is the owner of Marjon Bed & Breakfast Inn in Leaburg, Oregon. A private home built in 1971 on the edge of the McKenzie River, Marjon was planned and constructed with the thought of sharing the beauty of nature for all who came to visit. Over the years, the home and its two acres of landscaped grounds became well known to visitors. In the spring, especially, people came to enjoy the parklike atmosphere as the 2000 azaleas and 700 rhododendrons blossomed. Many visitors suggested to Margie how much more enjoyable the place would be if there were overnight accommodations. "Because of so many requests, Marjon was opened in June 1982 as a bed and breakfast inn where hospitality is a way of life," says Margie.

Perhaps your home is such a showplace in your community that opening it as a bed and breakfast establishment, as Margie Haas did, would make a valuable contribution to your area. This is especially true if you live in a historic district, or if your home qualifies for the National Register of Historic Places. One Philadelphia woman who has a large home in a historic area eventually succumbed to what she calls "gentle pressure" applied by the local reservation service organization to open her home for bed and breakfast.

You must be absolutely sure that you want to share your home with others. For this, you must have an innate trust of your fellow human beings; otherwise, you'll be constantly worrying that your silverware is going to disappear. "If you are concerned only about having your priceless antiques stolen, do not be a host," says Irmgard Castleberry, owner of a reservation service organization in Seattle, Washington, called Pacific Bed & Breakfast. Another RSO known as Bed & Breakfast of

Southeast Pennsylvania reports that it rejected a host because "the hostess was too nervous about her 'treasures.' " And Ellie Welch Ramsey tells the story of one prospective host who applied to an RSO in Massachusetts called Bed and Breakfast Brookline/Boston. The woman had a magnificent home but couldn't bring herself to share it. "She wanted to serve breakfast to guests in their bedroom because she didn't want 'just anyone' in her dining room," Ellie recalls. Guests would have immediately felt her distrust, so Ellie turned her down.

Of course, you have every right to be concerned about your home and everything in it. Just don't overdo it. You must have an "acceptance that possessions are susceptible to mishap," says Mildred Snee of The House of Snee in Narragansett, Rhode Island. Things happen. But if you're going to worry about it, you'll make your guests uncomfortable. They can't help but notice if your main interest is your home and not your guests.

One couple from Pennsylvania stayed at a bed and breakfast home in the southwest. They had been originally attracted to this particular B&B because it was especially lovely and had advertised a swimming pool. But the two felt most uncomfortable there because of the host's demeanor. "We felt she really wasn't interested in the guests, only in showing off her home." To them, the bed and breakfast felt like a "showplace" that wasn't meant to be used. The home was all it was advertised to be, but the hospitality just wasn't there.

Think about this when you're making your own decision. You must be careful that you don't bend to community pressure to open your home for bed and breakfast when you know it's just not for you. The manager of Eye Openers Bed & Breakfast Reservations in Altadena, California, offers this advice to anyone considering the idea of bed and breakfast: "Be certain that you feel right about opening your home to guests and then act accordingly." Good advice.

Extra income

Perhaps you listed "extra income" as one of your reasons for wanting to offer bed and breakfast. This is a perfectly legitimate reason, but the key word here is *extra*. No one can state with complete certainty that it's impossible to make a living solely by using the extra space in your home for bed and breakfast, but it is highly unlikely. This is true even of those B&B homes that are well located, have more than one guest room, accommodate a steady stream of guests, and charge a room rate higher than the norm. Why? Because a bed and breakfast business is limited in two very important ways—the number of rooms in the home, and the number of nights per year they are in use.

First, let's consider how the number of rooms available for guests' use affects income. How many extra rooms do you have? Let's assume for the moment that you have one double room. And let's say that you charge $40 per night for this room. Your immediate inclination might be to multiply $40 by the number of nights there are in a year to come up with a figure of what kind of income you could expect. So $40 multiplied by 365 is $14,600. And with *two* double rooms available for guests in your home, that means $29,200. Not bad. *Three* double rooms, that's $43,800! And *four* is $58,400! Wow! Sounds great!

Unfortunately, it just doesn't happen this way. Ask any commercial innkeeper or hotel or motel manager. They will tell you that their establishments are completely booked at some times of the year, and practically empty at others. This will also be the case with your bed and breakfast. All of your rooms will not be filled each night, every night, for 365 nights of the year, no matter what you do.

So what, then, constitutes "success" for a bed and breakfast? Many consider 100 nights out of a year filled to capacity a good year. So if you have one double room to use for bed and breakfast guests, and you are "filled to capacity" (two people in the room) for 100 nights out of the year, at $40 per night, your income is $4,000. For you, this is success. But can you live on $4,000? Of course not. But for an extra income, it might sound just fine.

If you have more than one guest room, projecting your income gets a little more complicated, and a little more theoretical. The guideline of "100 nights at capacity" does not mean, literally, that every bed available in your bed and breakfast will be in use on the same 100 nights. What will happen is that guests will come and go throughout the year, more at some times, fewer at others. Perhaps one room will be in demand more than another. Despite these things, you can use the guideline to make an educated guess about the income you could expect at the *height* of your bed and breakfast business.

Understanding this, you can now use the Income Projection Worksheet provided here to give yourself a rough, but realistic, idea of what "success" would mean for you.

The figure you arrive at on the worksheet does not mean, necessarily, that you won't do better than this once your business gets going. One

Income Projection Worksheet

Here is a formula that will help you figure out a rough projection of income for your "successful" bed and breakfast, based on 100 nights filled to capacity. (See "Pricing Your Bed and Breakfast" in chapter 3 for a detailed explanation of how to price your rooms.) The sample here uses the average nationwide prices determined by results from a survey conducted as part of the research for this book, plus adjustment for inflation and cost of living since the survey was conducted.

Sample

2 double rooms × $60 per night =
$120 × 100 nights = $12,000

1 single room × $50 per night =
$ 50 × 100 nights = $ 5,000

1 suite × $100 per night =
$100 × 100 nights = $10,000

PROJECTED GROSS INCOME FOR 1 YEAR: $27,000

Your Bed and Breakfast

___ double room(s) × $60 per night =
$______ × 100 nights = $______

___ single room(s) × $50 per night =
$______ × 100 nights = $______

___ suite(s) × $100 per night =
apartment(s) $______ × 100 nights = $______
guest house(s)
cottage(s)

PROJECTED GROSS INCOME FOR 1 YEAR: $______

very successful bed and breakfast with four double rooms reports 130 nights filled to capacity.

Nor should you expect too much in your first year of operation; success is something you build toward. "I'm still waiting for my first guest," writes one host who advertised her bed and breakfast in a guidebook last year. Says another, "I had eight guests last year, but I hope for more next year." When you're just starting out as a host, you should be very modest about your financial expectations until you see, from experience, what's possible for a B&B in your area.

Keep in mind that the total amount you calculate on the worksheet represents the possible *gross* income of your bed and breakfast at its best—that is, before taxes and before expenses on breakfast, laundry, new sheets, a paint job in the guest rooms, new towels, fresh flowers, new mattresses, business cards, a new reading lamp, the commission to your reservation service organization, the cost of membership in the chamber of commerce . . . to name just some of the usual expenses that must be made to run a bed and breakfast.

One of the biggest misconceptions that some people have is that bed and breakfast is a sure-fire, get-rich-quick scheme. "Some expect to make a million dollars the first month," says Rita Duncan, the director of Blue Ridge Bed & Breakfast in Berryville, Virginia. They're wrong.

"Don't expect this to become a large income producer," cautions the owner of Northwest Bed & Breakfast, a reservation service organization in Portland, Oregon. Anyone attracted to hosting mainly for the money will be sorely disappointed. Guests will see this immediately and feel quite uncomfortable about it. A number of reservation service organizations report that they initially rejected, or later dropped, hosts because they were overly concerned with money.

"I do not accept hosts who are doing this just for the bucks. It has to be something that the host enjoys!" says Ruth Wilson, owner of a Dallas RSO called Bed & Breakfast Texas Style. How can you tell? It shows. A host once registered with Bed & Breakfast of the Florida Keys met guests in the driveway and asked for payment in full, right there and then! When the RSO found out about it, this host was listed no longer.

But the question remains: Can someone be involved in bed and breakfast for the *right* reasons and still make a living by doing it? What if you had four or five rooms to offer guests? Would that be enough? "You need at least six to make a living," says Marcia Whittington of Host Homes of Boston. And with a property of that size, we're usually talking about an enterprise the level of an inn, rather than just a bed and breakfast home with rooms to spare. An inn is definitely a full-time commercial venture—with expenses, taxes, and regulations governing its operation in a commercial category. Bed and breakfast homes are not in the same category. Trying bed and breakfast in your own home can give you an idea of what it might be like to run an inn, but it is most assuredly a different ball game.

"If a host wants to make a living at B&B, he or she must open an inn," says Susan Morris of Southern Comfort Bed & Breakfast in Baton Rouge, Louisiana. For those who want to operate a bed and breakfast home, "they must realize that by and large it is not a way of earning a living but a way of supplementing income and having a marvelous time meeting all sorts of interesting people and making many friends."

Ken Mendis of Bed & Breakfast of Rhode Island adds this footnote: "If you need money and don't like people, find another way to make the money."

2

What Does It Take to Run a Successful Bed and Breakfast?

Location

"Location! Location! Location!" No one can phrase it any better than this host did, or any more emphatically. Your success with bed and breakfast depends primarily upon where your home is located. People must have a reason to visit the area where you live or you simply won't get any guests, no matter how nice you are or how clean and comfortable your home may be. You must carefully assess the location of your home before making a decision to offer bed and breakfast.

If you live right in a major city, you're in a prime spot. "Where the people are is where the people want to be," says Lauren Simonelli of the reservation service organization called Greater Boston Hospitality. Cities draw visitors throughout the year for myriad reasons. Homes in pleasant, low-crime neighborhoods with easy access to different parts of the city (by walking or public transportation) are most certainly in demand.

First of all, cities attract tourists who come to explore, visit the museums, see the sights, do some shopping. Then there are those who come to see a special exhibit or attend a particular performance—Renoir at the Museum of Fine Arts, Baryshnikov at the Met, Charlie Daniels at the Grand Old Opry. Business travelers come for meetings, to make sales, to go to job interviews, to relocate the family. And some people come to visit friends or relatives who are undergoing medical treatment in a local hospital, or to have tests or outpatient treatment themselves.

Any city or town will have visitors coming in for weddings, graduations, funerals, and holiday celebrations of one sort or another. These are all potential guests for bed and breakfast hosts located in more densely populated areas.

Rural areas also have their attractions. One successful independent bed and breakfast is Valley View Farm, owned by Edna and Ernest Shipe in Mathias, West Virginia. It is located near Lost River State Park, so visitors here can hike, play tennis, go horseback riding, or swim—that is, if they get bored with the beautiful farmland and all the animals (even chinchillas) right out the front door.

Another possible source of people to stay in your bed and breakfast is any national or international corporation near your home. A large company with branch offices is likely to have personnel shuttling back and forth between its different locations. One New England host offers bed and breakfast solely for business executives associated with a computer company a short distance from her home. She has as many guests as she wants from just this one company.

Consider, too, that each year thousands of people make special trips to see where the Pilgrims landed, where Custer made his last stand, where Hawthorne once lived, and where Elvis Presley is buried. Proximity to any kind of tourist attraction is a plus for a bed and breakfast. A notable success story comes from Green Meadow Ranch in Shipshewana, Indiana, which is the location of one of the largest flea markets in the country (held twice a week in the summer) and an antique auction (held once a week, year-round). Living in a tourist area has helped to bring a high number of visitors to the home of Paul and Ruth Miller, who hand out their B&B card at the flea market.

A new bed and breakfast home in New Jersey, called Cozy Acres B&B, is just ten miles from Atlantic City's beaches and casinos. Its owner sees the potential for success because of its location. "We are in a safe, rural setting," says Cecelia Swezeny. "The best of two worlds—the excitement of the casinos and the relaxation of the country."

A home situated near a college, university, or private school can benefit from the considerable amount of traffic that always surrounds an institution of higher learning. Students come to scout the school or attend conferences, parents come to visit, alumni come back for reunions, visiting professors come to lecture—and they all need places to stay.

Take note of any short-term programs offered by schools of any type near you. People often come from all over the country to attend workshops or short sessions of intense study. One such summer program takes place at Jacob's Pillow in western Massachusetts. Aspiring professional dancers are in residence here for several weeks; friends and family coming to visit or attend their performances must seek overnight accommodations.

Do not overlook the popularity of sports, either college or professional, in your area. A contending team has a large following, and its fans will be looking for accommodations when they come to attend the games. The biggest season for Rest & Repast Bed & Breakfast Service in central Pennsylvania? "Football!" says co-owner Linda Feltman. This reservation service organization's homes near Penn State fill up for the home games, especially so in years when the team is doing well. "Everybody and their uncle wants to come to a game," says Feltman. The result is that more bed and breakfast homes are needed to accommodate all those football enthusiasts.

Remember, though, that sports are seasonal. Your home could be in great demand for several months—but only for those months, unless there is some other attraction for visitors. If you are planning to operate a full-time bed and breakfast with no other income, you'll need to have guests for more than one season in order to make a living. A nearby beach could draw guests to your home all year-round if you live in Florida, but if you're in Maine, you don't need anyone to tell you that the beach season is far too short. The same thing goes for hosts in ski country. During a snowy winter, visitors will literally tramp a path to your door, but you'll be very lonely in winters that get little snowfall, and you can count on all your guests' being long gone by spring, when the slopes have turned to mud.

If you are lucky, you already live in a home in an area that draws visitors for more than one season. If not, as long as bed and breakfast hosting is a part-time project for you, you might find that you actually prefer the seasonal nature of your B&B business. It will be easier to plan ahead from year to year.

However, if you would like to purchase a home with the intention of starting a bed and breakfast (see "Real Estate" in chapter 4), one of the most crucial points to investigate is what brings people to the area, and for how many months out of the year. Look for a place that draws visitors for three seasons. New England hosts, for example, can take advantage of the fact that people come in the summer to go to the beach, in the fall to see the foliage, and in the winter to ski.

Make the effort to find out about any major events that will take place in your area in the near or distant future, as these could turn the site where your home is located into a tourist attraction virtually overnight. Events like the World's Fair, Expo, and the Olympics have certainly done this in the past. Find out, too, about natural events for which your location might be a key vantage point. For the coming of Halley's Comet and the last total eclipse of the sun, remember how so many people were drawn out of fascination to certain parts of the world to better view these uncommon events. Being in the right place at the right time means knowing what's coming and planning for it.

Some events are thankfully more common and more frequent, so the influx of visitors is not as short-lived and unpredictable. Such annual events as the Boston Marathon, the hot-air-balloon festival in Albuquerque, New Mexico, and the Allegheny County Fair in Pennsylvania attract countless visitors from out of town each year. Is your home located near the site of activities like these, or near a fairground, a racetrack, or civic center where other kinds of activities are scheduled on a seasonal or year-round basis? Just one of these could provide the bread and butter for your bed and breakfast.

A good location also makes your home more attractive to reservation service organizations that are looking to increase the number of host homes registered with them. RSOs will be much more interested in you if the number of guests they will be able to place with you will be high.

There are some areas where RSOs can't seem to get enough hosts. Downtown Boston is a good example. What a joy it is for a tourist to leave a host home in the Back Bay or in Beacon Hill and walk along the Freedom Trail without having to hassle with public transportation or taxis. But what a task it is for RSOs covering the Boston area to find enough "downtown" hosts to meet the demand at certain times of the year.

Similarly, the manager of Pittsburgh Bed and Breakfast notes that bed and breakfast homes in the Mt. Washington section of the city would be in a highly desirable location. Mt. Washington rises above newly renovated Station Square with a breathtaking view of the river and the city's skyline. For tourists, it's perfect in every way. But again, the supply can't yet meet the demand. At the same time, there are bed and breakfast homes outside of Pittsburgh that receive few visitors because they are simply not convenient for a traveler coming to the city.

The best advice to help you determine whether your home is in a good location is this: Identify the reasons why people come to your area, and in what months of the year. Use the checklist included here as a guide. The more reasons you can find, and the more months of the year they cover, the more potential your home has to become a successful bed and breakfast.

Location checklist

Following is a list of attractions that draw visitors to any particular area. A large number of visitors from out of town can mean a large number of guests for a bed and breakfast home near any of these sites. How well located is your home for a bed and breakfast business? Use this checklist to find out.

City or town:
- ☐ Downtown area
- ☐ Retail district
- ☐ Historical district
- ☐ Business district
- ☐ Desirable neighborhood

Schools:
- ☐ College or university
- ☐ Junior college
- ☐ Technical school
- ☐ Boarding school
- ☐ Summer programs
- ☐ Religious school

Schools for the Arts:
- ☐ Dance
- ☐ Art
- ☐ Music
- ☐ Photography
- ☐ Theatre

Transportation:
- ☐ Airport
- ☐ Train station
- ☐ Bus station
- ☐ Major highway
- ☐ Local public transportation

Business:
- ☐ Major corporation
- ☐ Research facility
- ☐ Government offices

Military base:
- ☐ Army
- ☐ Navy
- ☐ Air Force
- ☐ Marines
- ☐ Coast Guard

Group residence:
- ☐ Retirement home
- ☐ Nursing home
- ☐ Hospital
- ☐ Convent/monastery
- ☐ Retreat
- ☐ Summer camp

House of worship:
- ☐ Church
- ☐ Temple
- ☐ Mosque

Beach:
- ☐ Ocean
- ☐ Pond
- ☐ River

Cultural sites:
- ☐ Theatre
- ☐ Museum
- ☐ Observatory
- ☐ Music hall
- ☐ Art gallery

Recreational sites:
- ☐ Sports arena/stadium
- ☐ Concert arena/stadium
- ☐ Convention center
- ☐ Civic center
- ☐ Racetrack
- ☐ Fairground
- ☐ Amusement park
- ☐ Carnival

Special attractions:
- ☐ Historical site
- ☐ Architectural site
- ☐ Tourist attraction
- ☐ Well-known restaurant
- ☐ Archeological site

Shopping:
- ☐ Auction
- ☐ Flea market
- ☐ Wholesale outlet
- ☐ Specialty store
- ☐ Antiques store
- ☐ Regional arts/crafts/food

Animals:
- ☐ Zoo
- ☐ Exotic animal farm
- ☐ Wildlife preserve
- ☐ Major animal hospital

Natural sites:
- ☐ Mountains
- ☐ Desert
- ☐ Nature preserve
- ☐ Wildlife sanctuary
- ☐ Park
- ☐ Glacier
- ☐ Volcano
- ☐ Hot springs
- ☐ Caves/cavern

Recreational activity:
- ☐ Swimming/sunning
- ☐ Hiking
- ☐ Climbing
- ☐ Nature walks
- ☐ Foliage walks
- ☐ Bicycling
- ☐ Boating/sailing
- ☐ Water skiing
- ☐ Fishing
- ☐ Hunting
- ☐ Golfing
- ☐ Car/motorcycle racing
- ☐ Running competition/training
- ☐ Birdwatching
- ☐ Whale watching
- ☐ Cross-country/downhill skiing
- ☐ Ice skating
- ☐ Tobogganing
- ☐ Snowmobiling
- ☐ Gambling

Comfort

Remember how you managed to get used to that banging radiator back in your first apartment? (After a while, you didn't even notice.) And those cold, cold nights every fall before the landlord turned on the heat for the winter? (It got so that a room at *normal* temperature felt "too hot.") And your roommate's white cat, which always wanted a cuddle whenever you were wearing black? (You started wearing white clothes for the first time in your life.)

We're all adaptable to an extent. If we are subjected to a minor irritation long enough, the bangs and the drafts and the cat hair don't bother us at all. We learn to live with them, even forget about them. But it takes a while, right? New annoyances can still drive us up a wall. A dog barking. A baby crying. Cigar smoke. To a large extent, comfort depends on what you're used to. As a bed and breakfast host, you will find that one of your most difficult responsibilities is providing for the comfort of a vast diversity of people who all have their own ideas about what "comfort" is really all about.

Noise

To assess how comfortable your home might seem to different people, first identify how much "noise" there is on a normal basis. Tonight, after everyone else has gone to bed, listen to your house. What do you hear? The clock ticking? The faucet dripping? The dog scratching at the door? The cat batting around its catnip mouse? The furnace kicking on? These are normal nighttime sounds to you; they make your home feel cozy. But some bed and breakfast guests might not agree. Go into the guest room, close the door, and listen for how many sounds you can still hear. If you're on the first floor, and you can still hear Grandpa snoring in his room up on the third, your guests will surely hear him, too.

There are commendably few criticisms from people about the bed and breakfast homes they have visited. Some that have been made, though, deal with the very issue of noise. A couple from Alabama loved their stay at a B&B in North Carolina—except for a shower that dripped all night long, disturbing them with its continual *thunk! thunk! thunk!* Asked what they would change if they could alter one thing about this B&B, they immediately said (you guessed it), "The dripping shower!"

And I remember all too well my unpleasant nocturnal experience at a bed and breakfast home that had a grandfather clock. Lots of people can sleep right through the bonging and chiming that come at regular intervals with this type of clock. Not me. I most unhappily greeted the night, all night, every hour on the hour, and again on the half hour. Morning couldn't come soon enough. At the time, I was convinced that my restless night was my own fault, a product of an unusual sensitivity to "normal" sounds, so I never mentioned that infernal clock to my hosts. I realize now that I should have. To this day, I have visions of countless poor, unfortunate, unsuspecting guests flopping around through endless, sleepless nights, counting the minutes (in half-hour intervals) until morning, when they can get up and check out.

The point is that there are some unnecessary noises that you *can* do something about. Get the shower fixed, even if you've gotten used to the continual dripping. (The North Carolina host later did just this, according to the Alabama couple.) If you're so fond of that grandfather clock, by all means keep it, but move it well away from the guest room, or just don't wind it on the nights you have visitors. Any kind of noise that can be eliminated should be eliminated.

For sounds that might annoy but must remain, do your best. "When I am doing dishes late at night, I turn on fans to drown out the clatter," says Donna Tanney of Gates Hill Homestead in Brookfield, New York.

There will always be the normal household sounds of conversation, the furnace or air conditioning system, the radio or television, the telephone ringing, doors opening and closing. So that these do not disturb guests after they retire for the night, any home intended for bed and breakfast should be large enough, and the walls and doors solid enough, to give everyone in it the freedom to sleep and wake at will, and to go about their activities without bothering anyone. Think about your home. Is it roomy enough to handle the presence of a few more people with sufficient quiet and privacy, or will it feel cramped, crowded, and noisy every time you have guests? Are the rooms arranged in such a way that they are somewhat insulated from one another? Do your walls and doors do a good job of blocking out the sounds from other parts of the house?

One couple visiting a bed and breakfast home felt unduly chastised for making excessive noise. Here, another guest complained that she was bothered by the couple's conversation (which they insisted was held in low tones in their own room, with the door shut). This occurred at about 10:00 P.M., which the couple considered an early enough hour to be having a conversation instead of sleeping. The other guest's sleep was disturbed by this "noise" despite the fact that the two guest rooms were

Chinguague Compound is a quiet, secluded bed and breakfast located on the banks of the Rio Grande River in San Juan Pueblo, New Mexico. Joan Blood, its owner, recalls a couple who came down from the city of Denver for several days and stayed in one of the small adobe cottages, surrounded by cottonwoods. When Joan asked the couple the first morning how they had slept the previous night, the woman hesitated and then said, "Well, I had to turn on the fan before I could get to sleep." Since the temperature that night had been down in the fifties, Joan's husband, Phil, commented, "I didn't realize it was that warm." The woman then replied, "Oh no, it wasn't that it was too warm. . . . I couldn't get used to all this quiet!"

separated by two doors and a hallway. The couple was so upset at being shushed when they were sure they were being totally considerate that they checked out a day early, vowing never to return to "the B&B with paper-thin walls."

Now whether the walls were indeed paper-thin or whether the complaining guest was just overly sensitive to noise, we don't know for sure. But you know your own home. How soundproof is it? Do you need to take measures to prevent sounds from carrying? Buying and installing soundproofing materials, such as sound-absorbing tiles or panels, can be costly. You can take lesser measures that will help to an extent. Heavy drapes and rugs (with rug pads) help to absorb the sounds within a room. And wallpaper adds an extra insulating layer that muffles sound better than bare walls covered only with paint.

Rooms that share a common wall are likely to share sounds as well. If you have a choice, do not set up your home so that you have two guest rooms side by side. (In fact, you might not want your own bedroom, or those of other household members, adjacent to a guest room.) If one room is above another, you can also expect some sounds to carry. Again, rugs with rug pads will help, but you might have to take stronger action. One host who was renovating a small apartment in her Boston townhouse to be used for bed and breakfast knew that noise would be a problem because the apartment was on the ground floor, and above it were three more floors of solid activity. Her first order of business? Calling in a contractor to complete a professional soundproofing job on the ceiling.

Unfortunately, what goes on inside your home is not your only worry. There's a whole noisy world out there that you can't do a thing about. (Ever try to tell a rooster to ignore the rising sun?) Consider whether there is some sort of recurring activity outside your home that could disturb your guests. Does loud music come from the club down the street until late at night? Do irate commuters lean on their car horns at the intersection right outside each morning? Does the dog next door get vocal at an early hour? Do church bells call the faithful to sunrise services faithfully every morning? Does the guy next door play the trumpet? Again, heavy drapes will certainly help, but they can't perform miracles. If the problem is bad, you might finally want to install those thermal windows you've been thinking about. They not only do a terrific job of insulating your home from the weather, they also help cut down on that outside noise that could affect your guests' comfort.

Children

The presence of children in a host home raises the question of noise and general disruption as well. There are travelers who have the idea (often a misconception) that their quiet and privacy will be marred by the antics of any youngsters in residence. If you have children, you will most likely lose some business because of them, regardless of how well behaved and considerate your kids might be. Some people have made up their minds in advance, and that's that. But know that for any potential guests that you lose for this reason, there are other travelers who will be attracted to your B&B for the very same reason. Parents traveling with their own kids actively seek out bed and breakfast homes where the hosts will accept them. (Who's more understanding than a host who already has a few of her own?) And some travelers who are not parents themselves simply adore children and would find it a privilege to share the company of yours.

So take heart; the fact that you have children need not crush your plans to start a bed and breakfast business. However, you do have to be concerned about how your kids behave around company. What are they like now when your friends come to visit or when strangers come to the door? It could be that they will take quite naturally to having guests in the house and go on about their business without disturbing the normal amount of privacy and quiet that guests will expect. But you know if your kids are basically unruly. If you can predict that they'll be jumping up and down on the guests' beds and throwing hot cross buns at breakfast, you might want to wait until they're older before offering bed and breakfast at your home. And if you have an infant that gets you up several times a night (and keeps you up sometimes the whole night through), you can't expect to inflict the feeding and the teething and everything else that goes with infancy on your bed and breakfast guests. You should wait at least until that stage is over.

Pets

For the amount of controversy that they can cause, pets are right up there with children. Reservation service organizations consider the presence of both in a host home carefully before deciding to include it in their listings. "Pets and small children in a host home can be a negative," says Danie Bernard, owner of an RSO in St. Pete Beach, Florida, called B&B Suncoast Accommodations. If a large number of guests are automatically going to rule out any host home that contains either, this means that the RSO won't be able to place as many guests there as in other B&B homes. Some hosts have been turned away by reservation service organizations because of this. If you are hoping to list your home with an RSO, ask the manager to be candid with you about whether the presence of your children or pets is an issue.

Why would any guest object to staying in a house guarded by old, faithful Rex? Allergies. Once you start hosting, you'll find out quickly that there are many people out there who are allergic to animals. To stay in your home would be misery for them, as hard as that might be to believe. So if you do have a dog or a cat that is allowed inside the house, note this fact on all literature that you print and in all information that you send for listing in a guidebook. And make sure that any reservation service organization that refers guests to you knows all about sweet little Hairball. It will absolutely make a difference to the comfort of some travelers looking for bed and breakfast.

Smoking

Smoking is another major issue in the bed and breakfast industry—whether you do or whether you don't, whether you allow it or whether you don't. No matter what you choose, your decision will affect your business. If you are a nonsmoker and prefer to host nonsmokers only, you have a lot of company. An informal survey shows that this is the case with most hosts. If you smoke, or there are smokers living in your household, you've got to assess the effect that this has on your home. To give yourself a more objective view, try this: Go outdoors for at least five minutes (do *not* have a cigarette while you're out there), then come back in and let your nose tell you a few things. Put it to work on the drapes, the upholstered chairs, the bedding, the rugs. Do they all smell like Sunday morning after the Saturday-night poker game? If so, you've got a problem, and it has nothing to do with the surgeon general's warning.

One manager of a reservation service organization recalls a couple who applied to her agency to become hosts. The manager found the home lovely—except for the strong odor of stale cigarette smoke that permeated everything. The two were very heavy smokers, a fact that would hinder their efforts to develop a bed and breakfast business. Fortunately, they decided soon after the manager's visit that they weren't quite ready to open a B&B (for other, personal reasons), so she was spared the necessity of turning them down as hosts. The following year they contacted her again when they felt they were "ready." The manager went back to their home to see if there had been any changes and found that they had both quit smoking. Their lovely home no longer had that disagreeable odor. They were, indeed, ready.

Madalyn Eplan, the co-owner of a reservation service organization in Georgia called Bed & Breakfast Atlanta, also had a problem with an applicant because, she says, "The cigars he smoked were too smelly!" She turned him down.

True, there are smokers who travel and who would like to enjoy the privilege of smoking while staying at bed and breakfast homes. You can always gear your B&B business to these people if yours is a smoking household. Recognize, though, that you cannot expect nonsmokers to stay there as well and be happy about it. Someone is bound to light up at the breakfast table, and before you know it, a nice breakfast could turn into an episode of "The People's Court." Some hosts have chosen to have a "limited smoking" household, in which those guests who wish to smoke may do so only in their rooms or in another designated area. This way, the comfort of the other guests, and perhaps of the hosts themselves, is not affected.

Temperature and ventilation

Other elements key to your guests' comfort are the temperature and ventilation of the bedrooms where your guests will sleep. How much, or how little, heat and ventilation there should be is a highly personal matter. One guest will need the window open a crack at night (no matter what the temperature outside may be) or he won't be able to sleep; another will need the window sealed tight in even the hottest weather or *he* can't sleep. Some abhor air conditioning; others can't live without it. Ideally, the answer is to have the heating, cooling, and ventilation all adjustable within each room so that guests have some control over the environment. Often, this is just not possible (especially with central heating or central air conditioning).

You can address individual differences among your guests by having available a portable heater, a window or ceiling fan, or an air condition-

Ellie Welch Ramsey, founder of Bed and Breakfast Brookline/Boston, tells the story of a host who was visited by a gentleman from Egypt. Accustomed to the warm, dry climate of his own country, he found the chilly, damp October weather hard to take. The host, a hardy New Englander, was, of course, quite comfortable. Not wanting to turn on the furnace at this early date, she gave her guest a stocking cap to wear around the house. The Egyptian placed it on his head and there it stayed, but he was still cold. So the host went out and bought a portable space heater and put it in his room. "Ellie, I might have spent every penny I got from this visit on the heater, but it made everybody happy," said the host.

ing unit that can be used, or not, as a guest wishes. If any of your guest rooms is a "problem room," though (sweltering in the summer or freezing in the winter when the rest of the house is just fine), more drastic action might be recommended for everyone's comfort. Here, insulation or thermal windows could be the permanent solution.

Neighborhood

Once you're confident that your home can provide the kind of comfort that your different guests will need, there's one more consideration before you're through with your checklist. This is your neighborhood. Take a stroll around the area where you live. If you're located in a rural area, fine; your guests should enjoy the outdoors as much as the indoors. But if your home is located in a city or town, ask yourself if all of your visitors will feel comfortable when they walk out the front door. Is your neighborhood "safe," with a low incidence of crime? (Or are you always looking over your shoulder?) Is it pleasant, picturesque? (Or is it somewhat run-down?) Is it integrated? (Or is it so exclusively ethnic that anyone else would feel out of place?) Some very lovely people with very lovely homes have been turned down by reservation service organizations because they are located in neighborhoods where many guests would simply not feel comfortable for various reasons. What your neighborhood is like is definitely a factor when it comes to developing your bed and breakfast business.

Atmosphere

The overall atmosphere in a home has a lot to do with whether visitors will feel comfortable. Is the host friendly and warm? Does the home look like someone cares about it? The feeling of being totally welcome when a guest walks through the front door can often override any minor problems with the heat, the ventilation, the pets, the kids, the neighborhood, the smoking, the noise. When they are inspecting the homes of people who want to become hosts, Joy Meiser and Ken Mendis of the reservation service organization called Bed and Breakfast Rhode Island let this govern their decision: "The basic criterion we use is this one simple question: Would I choose to stay there?"

Ask yourself this same question. Come in through your own front door as if you're doing it for the first time and take a look around. Is this the kind of place you would like to stay in if you were traveling? If it is, you're in business.

Cleanliness

If someone were to ring your doorbell right now, would you have to shove a few newspapers into the hall closet and kick a pair of shoes under the couch before answering the door? And would this do the trick or (be honest) would it really take a bulldozer and a half-dozen blowtorches to clean out your home before it is ready for company?

If you want to be a host, you've got to take a long, hard look at how you keep your house. Some of us might be perfectly comfortable surrounded by clutter in our homes (the lived-in look) and feel moved to wash the kitchen floor only once a year (it will only get dirty again anyway), but we cannot expect guests in our home to feel the same way. You must meet *their* standards, or you will undoubtedly be faced with refunding money to unsatisfied guests and being dropped by any reservation service organization that sends you referrals.

At this moment you might be saying to yourself, "Of course my house is clean!" But how clean is it, really? (A good test is to ask yourself if your mother or in-laws would think so.) I once knew a woman who washed her kitchen and bathroom walls every week, without fail. I thought she was obsessive; she thought this was just normal housekeeping. Personal standards do vary. Because the highest level of cleanliness is a requirement for a host home, following is a step-by-step discussion of the standards you will have to meet to make your home "guest ready."

First of all, go outside and pretend that you are seeing your home for the first time. Do you like what you see? Or do your windows need to be washed? Is the paint chipped or peeling? Are there finger marks around the doorknob? Are there papers or cans strewn around the yard or spilling over the trash barrels? Does the grass need to be cut or the hedges pruned? Does your teenager keep an old Ford in the driveway "for parts"? One reservation service organization in Pennsylvania reports that a host home was rejected not because the inside was unclean, but because the exterior was in such shabby condition that guests did not want to go inside. You want your guests' first impression to be a good one, so do whatever is necessary to make the outside of your home inviting.

Next, take a look at the bathroom that your guests will be using. Does the room need a fresh coat of paint or new wallpaper to brighten it? When was the last time you had the curtains cleaned? Does the shower curtain need to be replaced? (If the idea of running your hands over it doesn't appeal to you, it probably does.)

How much cleaning you do before and during a guest's visit depends on how much traffic the bathroom will see. If it is one that visitors will share with you or your family, or with other guests, you have to be extra conscientious to make sure that the bathroom gets clean and stays that way during a visit.

Clean the room initially by washing the floor, scrubbing the sink, wiping the mirror and any counter space, removing dirty towels or laundry or reminders of previous guests, and cleaning and disinfecting the toilet bowl, the bathtub, and the shower. All this must be done after each guest's visit to prepare the room for the next guest who comes to stay at your home. If you or other members of the household also use this bathroom, find a way to keep personal items in a certain area, in a cabinet or on separate shelves. Your family's personal items (such as shampoo, toothpaste, and razors) should be returned to their designated space after each use and not left in view.

Using at least one bathrug (two or more in a larger bathroom) will help keep the floor clean while guests are in residence. Have several sets, or more, of matching rugs so that you can change them often. It's a lot easier to throw a set of dirty rugs into the laundry hamper and replace them with clean ones than it is to repeatedly wash an exposed floor that is destined to get dirty every time someone trails water across it. The rugs will also help soak up any spillage from the shower, tub, or sink. It's not pleasant to discover that the cuffs of your trousers or hem of your bathrobe has gotten wet from being dragged through a standing puddle left after someone's shower. Make sure the rugs have a nonskid backing to avoid accidents.

While a guest is in residence, you should empty the wastebasket daily and perform touch-ups to keep the room fresh—straighten towels, sponge the sink, wipe the mirror. Keep a new sponge visible so that if a guest is so inclined to clean up after using the bathroom, he or she can take the initiative to make a few swipes at the sink or tub before leaving the room to others. If you have a long-term guest (a week or more), wash the floor and clean the sink, toilet, tub, and shower whenever necessary. And empty the clothes hamper before the dirty towels start pushing their way out.

The kitchen, too, must be immaculate. There should be no dirty dishes in the sink or stacked on counters. The floor must be washed often, and anything "turning" (or turned) in the refrigerator must be removed. Most hosts invite guests to put their own food in the refrigerator and to get ice from the freezer compartment whenever they wish. A three-week-old head of lettuce could scare them right out the front door.

Equally scary are those unwelcome creatures that sometimes decide to take up habitation in our homes, no matter how clean we are. Most of us can usually make short work of a mouse, but the more common, and more tenacious, household nuisances are those bugs—cockroaches, ants, flies, mosquitoes, fleas. If you have any kind of problem with insects, no way can you expect a guest to stay in your home and be happy about it. As with many homes located in rural areas, or in hot and humid climates, yours may be destined to get an occasional bug just passing through. (Rita Duncan, coordinator of Blue Ridge Bed and Breakfast in Virginia, says, "Show me a country home that doesn't get spiders!") Still, take precautions to ensure that some little traveler won't surprise a guest pattering to the bathroom with bare feet in the middle of the night. Find the source of the problem and fix it. Repair the broken window screen, fill the crack in the cellar door, use flea powder on the dog, hire an exterminator if you must. (*Don't*, however, supply the guest with a can of insecticide.)

Consider your living room and dining room next, along with any other common area (perhaps a library or television room) that you will be sharing with your guests. The biggest problem these rooms ever seem to present is clutter, things that should have been put away or thrown away long ago. The first place to look is the coffee table. If it holds an accumulation of newspapers that go back to the Nixon administration, it's time to clear out the clutter. From the coffee table, move to the mounds of jackets from last season and the forgotten toys. Once a room is neat, all it takes is a quick vacuuming and dusting to prepare for company.

It might not be easy to keep your home in this state of readiness. Cleaning is noted as the least favorite aspect of bed and breakfast by hosts across the country. They basically agree with Carolyn Morrow of Leftwich House in Graham, North Carolina, when she says the most difficult aspect of being a host is "keeping a clean house *all* the time."

A woman from Massachusetts noticed that among the information included in one directory of bed and breakfast homes is the length of notice that each host requires before a guest's arrival. This makes sense, of course, considering that a host needs time to prepare the home to receive guests. But the woman was intrigued by the note for the bed and breakfast home where she would be staying. "The hostess listed '15 minutes,' " she says—obviously not much notice at all. What can you do in fifteen minutes? When the guest arrived, the host explained the reason behind the extremely short notice: "Then I am excused for not putting everything in apple-pie order!"

The guest room (or rooms) should be your main concern. Guests' quarters must be spotless—vacuumed, dusted, and free of anything that is not there specifically for a guest's comfort. The president of a reservation service organization called Bed & Breakfast of Southeast Pennsylvania rejected a host because the guest room contained cartons of old shoes and soft drinks. "These had no place in a guest room," she says. But when she pointed this out to the homeowner, he said that he thought there was nothing wrong with storing these items there. He kept saying, "Well, that is cosmetic."

This "cosmetic" problem caused the RSO to refuse to list his home. Imagine how you would feel if you checked into the Ritz and someone's old shoes were in the corner of your room. A guest room in your home should be treated as if it were a room in the Ritz; remove anything that is not for guests' use exclusively. Of course, this means the closet, too. It is undeniably tempting to place some boxes of memorabilia on the shelves (what can a few hurt?) or hang up that extra coat (who will notice?), but don't do it. You do not want your guests to feel as if they are staying in a storage room.

If you would like to list your home with a reservation service organization, you can expect the RSO to inspect your home before making a decision. "If someone won't clean for me, I know they won't clean for a guest," says Lauren Simonelli, president of Greater Boston Hospitality. RSOs go to each prospective host home with a checklist for the basics, even to those places that are out in the boondocks. Bed & Breakfast Rocky Mountains, for example, covers the five states of Montana, New Mexico, Colorado, Utah, and Wyoming. "People ask us whether we really inspect all our host homes," says Kate Winters. "I've got a Honda Accord with front-wheel drive. Yes, we see them all." If you meet the standards of cleanliness, along with the other requirements, an RSO will most likely list you as one of its host homes. But know that an RSO will find out soon enough through complaints if your home falls below its standards. And that will be the end of referrals to your home.

The ultimate question here is whether meeting the high standards of cleanliness required is a big deal for you. Ask yourself if cleaning your home is going to be a major undertaking every time you expect a guest. It shouldn't be. Hosting will not be fun for you if every phone call for a reservation throws you into a panic to prepare your home.

Ask yourself, too, whether the other members of your household will do their part in keeping the house clean, or will this become a continual source of friction among you? Their willing cooperation is essential. You don't want to greet guests in a spick-and-span house full of grouchy faces.

Cleanliness checklist

Bathroom:

- ☐ Floor scrubbed
- ☐ Clean bath mat
- ☐ Clean nonskid rug
- ☐ Walls/ceiling clean and bright
- ☐ Clean shower curtain
- ☐ Tub/shower scrubbed
- ☐ Toilet cleaned, disinfected
- ☐ Sink scrubbed
- ☐ Mirrors wiped
- ☐ Clean towels
- ☐ Windows washed
- ☐ Light fixtures clean
- ☐ Cabinets wiped, polished
- ☐ Clean sponge visible
- ☐ Family items removed
- ☐ Medicine cabinet free of personal items
- ☐ Wastebasket emptied
- ☐ Paint free of chips
- ☐ No loose edges on wallpaper
- ☐ Grout between tiles free of mildew

Guest room:

- ☐ Floor clean, polished
- ☐ Windows washed
- ☐ Walls/ceiling clean and bright
- ☐ Rug vacuumed, free of stains
- ☐ Furniture polished, dusted
- ☐ Mirrors wiped
- ☐ Closet empty of family items
- ☐ Room free of storage items
- ☐ Clutter removed
- ☐ Light fixtures clean
- ☐ Curtains cleaned
- ☐ Clean bedding
- ☐ Paint/wallpaper in good repair
- ☐ Wastebasket emptied
- ☐ Under bed clean, no storage

Kitchen/dining area:

- ☐ Floor washed, polished
- ☐ Cabinets wiped, polished, dusted
- ☐ Refrigerator/stove wiped
- ☐ Counters wiped/free of clutter

- ☐ No dirty dishes
- ☐ Trash/wastebasket emptied
- ☐ No old food in refrigerator, in pantry, on shelves
- ☐ Table cleared off, wiped
- ☐ Windows washed
- ☐ Walls/ceiling clean and bright
- ☐ Light fixtures clean
- ☐ Curtains cleaned
- ☐ Rug vacuumed
- ☐ Paint/wallpaper in good repair

Common areas:
(living room, TV room, library, hallways)

- ☐ Paint/wallpaper in good repair
- ☐ Walls/ceiling clean and bright
- ☐ Rugs vacuumed
- ☐ Clutter removed
- ☐ Furniture dusted, polished
- ☐ Floors clean, polished
- ☐ Windows washed
- ☐ Curtains clean
- ☐ Light fixtures clean

House exterior:

- ☐ Windows washed
- ☐ No trash barrels visible
- ☐ No litter on grounds
- ☐ No chipped or peeling paint
- ☐ Grass cut, hedges pruned
- ☐ Leaves raked
- ☐ Snow shoveled from walk, porch
- ☐ Fingermarks removed from door

Lifestyle

Before making that final decision to open your home to guests, remember that this is your *home* we're talking about here. This is the place where you run around in your bathrobe, fight with your spouse, and have the gang over to watch "Monday Night Football." Do not make the mistake of assuming that having strangers around will not affect how you can act in your own home. It will. So think seriously about your living habits and routines before deciding to go ahead with bed and breakfast. Ask yourself whether the presence of guests will be disruptive to your household and, just as important, whether the way your household runs will be disruptive to your guests.

Consider your own daily routine. What time do you get up in the morning? Some of your guests will be early birds out of necessity (to get to appointments on time or to make travel connections) or just because they enjoy that hour of the day. Beth Kinsman of Bed & Breakfast Rochester says that she gets a lot of fishermen from Rhode Island who want to get up and going at 5:00 A.M. That's what they're used to, and they bring business to the hosts registered with her reservation service organization. If you are used to getting up later than Rhode Island fishermen do, will you be able to adjust to an earlier schedule when you have to? Or will you be cranky all day because you couldn't get enough sleep?

As a guest in a bed and breakfast home in West Hyannisport, Massachusetts, I had to be up before dawn to catch a bus that left for Boston at 6:00 A.M. This meant that my hosts had to get up when I did (around 5:00 A.M.) to prepare coffee and the oatmeal I had requested (the only food I could face at that hour). My hosts did indeed roll out of bed before the sun was up, make breakfast and keep me company while I ate (or tried to), and drive me to meet my bus. Could you do all this as graciously and cheerfully as did my hosts from House Guests Cape Cod? This is what it takes. Gloria Belknap, a host in downtown Boston, says she gets up at 5:30 A.M. whenever guests are in the house, which is most of the time.

Some hosts never get used to it. When asked what he liked least about being a bed and breakfast host, Robert Somaini of Woodruff House in Vermont did not have to think twice: "Getting up early in the morning!" One guest who enjoys staying in bed and breakfast homes says he could never take on the role of host: "Imagine having to be polite to people at that hour!" And a young man interested in becoming a host who attended a workshop conducted by bed and breakfast consultant Ellie Welch Ramsey became distressed as he realized that he couldn't stay in bed late on weekend mornings when he had guests in the house. "Saturday is my day to sleep in," he lamented.

The same consideration goes for going to sleep at night. Do you retire early? Earlier than most people? You can always make arrangements with your guests for the "last one up" to shut off the lights in the television room and ask them to please be quiet. But will this be enough? Does the sound of the television, radio, or conversation at normal levels generally prevent you from sleeping? If it does, you could be in for problems as a host. You can't expect your guests to go to sleep just because you do.

Another point to ponder is what you look like in the morning. I don't mean that dazed look that afflicts many of us for a time after rising; we're talking about your overall appearance. Can you make yourself presentable for company in the morning? Can you be dressed for the day? Your hair combed? Your face washed? Your teeth brushed?

This might sound like so much common sense, but some hosts have actually offended their guests because they simply didn't look "ready" for them when they came down for breakfast. A couple from Pennsylvania were asked if there was anything they didn't like about a bed and breakfast home they visited during their trip to the Southwest. They wrote back: "Rollers in hostess's hair at breakfast!"

Think about it. As a guest, you would come to a bed and breakfast because you wanted something special, an experience that transcended what you would find in a hotel or motel. Yes, you know that it is a private home and the hosts live there, doing what they do in their daily lives. Eating and sleeping are among their normal activities. Yet, they are supposed to want you there. They are supposed to be ready for you. So you go down to what you expect will be a treat for breakfast in a lovely setting—and your host greets you, bleary-eyed, in her housecoat and rollers. Suddenly, you feel as if you're imposing. Perhaps she would rather be in bed than fixing your breakfast and attempting polite conversation with you over a cup of coffee. The breakfast might be absolutely magnificent in itself, but somehow the magic is gone.

Now I must admit that one host did greet me at the breakfast table in her housecoat, and, to be completely honest, I couldn't have cared less. I was her only guest, it was very early, and I felt bad enough knowing I was the reason she was up to begin with. I would have felt worse if I knew she had gone to the trouble to get dressed just on my account. To this day, I hope she went back to bed after I ate breakfast and checked out.

The point is that there may be times when it seems perfectly natural, and comfortable, for you to be seen in your housecoat. (What host is going to get fully dressed just to go down the hall to the bathroom in the middle of the night?) But you must be tuned in to when it is inappropriate. When you are hosting single travelers of the opposite sex is one instance. Or when you are hosting a couple. (One is sure to bring it up later just to see if the other noticed.) And by no means give a houseful of guests something to talk about by showing up in bedroom attire at a breakfast table where there is standing room only. (We're all dressed. Why isn't she?)

What we wear throughout the day, of course, depends upon what we normally do during that time. If you work on a farm, it's not likely you'll be donning a three-piece suit to bale the hay. If you refinish furniture at home, nothing but the biggest, oldest shirts will do. Don't feel that you have to dress in a way other than what you need to just because there are guests in residence. But *do* take the time and trouble to clean up your act when all the dirty work is over. Casual clothes (tee shirts and jeans) are fine, as long as they're clean. Just be aware that there are limits to how casual a host can be. "If you are in the habit of running around in your skivvies, change your habits," says Margot

French, the proprietor of Folkstone Bed & Breakfast in Boylston, Massachusetts.

If there are other members of the household besides you, recognize that *their* lifestyle will also be affected by your bed and breakfast business. Norma and Bill Grovermann, who together operate the Prince George Inn B&B in Annapolis, Maryland, advise new hosts to "be certain that your spouse is 100 percent in support of the project and willing to do all duties if needed." Nothing breeds dissension faster than one person's bearing all the responsibilities and doing all the work.

It is interesting to discover, though, that several women who offer bed and breakfast found their husbands lukewarm about the idea at first. But after they started accepting guests, more or less on a trial basis, the husbands so enjoyed the company of the guests that they not only pitched right in and did their share of the work, but it was hard to tear them away from conversation with guests at the breakfast table.

Special consideration should go to your children. Do they have a place to play, and do their homework, that will not interfere with guests, and guests will not interfere with them? Or will you be constantly shushing them and chasing them out of the living room whenever guests are in the house? Remember, too, that they will have to be presentable for company, with clean clothes and scrubbed faces. Is this more than you (and they) can handle?

It's a good idea to have an official family meeting to discuss the idea of bed and breakfast before taking steps to open one. "It is a family business; make sure the whole family is for it," says Ken Mendis of Bed & Breakfast of Rhode Island. If not everyone can agree to at least try it (and this includes your three-year-old who is determined to keep her duckies in the guests' bathtub), then you should probably shelve the idea, at least for the time being. All the members of the household must be in complete cooperation. If they're not, it will show.

This was certainly the case when a couple from Boston stayed in a bed and breakfast home in Newfoundland that was run by a married pair. It was the husband who greeted the travelers upon arrival. "He welcomed us as though we were long-lost friends," they recall. "He showed us around the whole house and told us all about his home repairs, his B&B business, and his day job." The couple went to bed that night with the warm feeling of being totally welcome in the home. But when they got up the next morning, they found that the friendly host they had met the night before was gone for the day. In his place was his wife. Suddenly, the atmosphere was different. "She kind of begrudgingly served us breakfast," the couple remembers. The remainder of their visit was marred by how impersonal the woman continued to be toward her guests. She gave them the distinct impression that she did not want them there.

Try to evaluate objectively how everyone gets along in your household. There will always be disagreements, but are they few and far between and resolved with a minimum of broken dishware? Southern B&B Reservations Service in Baton Rouge, Louisiana, reports that it found it necessary to drop a host (one who had previously enjoyed a great deal of business) because family problems developed there that were most distressing to the guests. If your home life is stormy, don't even *consider* bed and breakfast.

Many of us are fortunate to have a happy home life and a comfortable home where guests would add to the pleasure of our daily lives. If yours is such a lifestyle, bed and breakfast hosting could very well enrich your life beyond your expectations.

The working host

Bed and breakfast is a good project for those people whose careers or other responsibilities do not take them outside of the home a great deal of the time. For this reason, many retirees welcome the opportunity to meet interesting people right in the home they at last have the time to enjoy. By offering bed and breakfast, a retiree can also bring in a supplemental income without having to go back to the rigors of even a part-time job that involves keeping strict schedules and commuting to an office.

Parents of small children, too, want and need to spend time at home. For the spouse who minds the infant or toddler, bed and breakfast hosting can instill a gratifying element of social activity into his or her life, as well as add to the family income without the necessity of leaving the home to work.

But the question comes up about the working host. Can someone who has a career and works either full-time or part-time make a go of bed and breakfast? The answer is yes.

For hosts who already have home-based businesses, bed and breakfast is a natural; it integrates easily into their daily routines. Let's take, for example, hosts who work the land for their livelihood. The owners of Lakeside Farm in Webster, South Dakota, of Sycamore Haven Farm in

Kinzers, Pennsylvania, and of Valley View Farm in Mathias, West Virginia, all successfully combine full-time work on their farms with bed and breakfast hosting. Having guests is "no trouble" says the ranch manager of Anchor Hill Lodge, a bed and breakfast in Rogersville, Missouri: "I have good ranch help and considerate guests." The only occasional problem, according to Edna Shipe of Valley View Farm, is "keeping yourself tidy the day you have dirty garden work." Some hosts have found that guests actually like to help with the chores. For many visitors from the city, farm life is a new and wonderful experience. It's a joy to pick apples and feed the animals, a refreshing change from their usual activities.

Hosts with other types of home-based businesses have also fared well with bed and breakfast. Carol Emerick of The Cottage in San Diego, California, does antique furniture restoration on a part-time basis. Because she does this at home, she is available if her guests need her for any reason.

Another host is a full-time, self-employed writer, who meets the needs of her guests this way: "I set my hours to theirs, and I hire help. I accept being 'inconvenienced' in one business as the price for having another one thrive," says Crescent Dragonwagon of Dairy Hollow House in Eureka Springs, Arkansas.

RMF Bed & Breakfast in Atlanta, Georgia, is owned by a host whose work involves word processing services. She has turned her home-based business into an attractive amenity for guests by offering to type their reports or letters.

There are other hosts who are fortunate to be in a line of work that they can relate to their bed and breakfast hosting, even though the work itself is outside the home. Pat Hunt, owner of Hunts' Hideaway in Morgan, Vermont, is an income tax and business consultant. Among her clients she now counts some area bed and breakfast hosts. To have the assistance of a professional who is experienced with bed and breakfast can be a definite advantage to a host when it comes time to prepare tax returns.

Another host works for a company that offers walking tours. Her daily contact with visitors from out of town through her job is an excellent way to publicize the bed and breakfast option available at her home. Plus, she has a call-forwarding service from her home to her office, so that telephone calls from prospective guests will not be missed. (Of course, any host involved in some sort of venture that is naturally complementary to B&B must be careful not to pressure clients of either business to use the other.)

Some working hosts are lucky enough to have flexible schedules. The owner of B&G's B&B in San Diego, California, for instance, works full-time in real estate sales. The nature of the business allows the host this leeway: "I can plan my own work hours to fit them into the schedules of my guests."

If one spouse works and the other does not, the responsibilities of bed and breakfast hosting can be shared. A host registered with Bed and Breakfast of Center City in Philadelphia is a full-time social worker. But her husband is retired. Cynthia Whited of Strawberry Castle in Penfield, New York, is a clinical microbiologist. She works full-time, but her husband does not. In both cases, the husbands' flexible schedules allow for the duties of a bed and breakfast host to be carried out easily.

Other bed and breakfast hosts work as teachers in kindergarten, elementary or high school, or college. There are also financial advisors, librarians, artists, nurses, counselors, accountants, salespersons, lawyers, economists, media specialists, interior designers, doctors, therapists, travel agents, pharmacists, realtors, and musicians. One is a full-time town manager, another a television personality, still another a minister. Reports have also come in from an electrician, a carpenter, an acupuncturist, a graphic designer, and a court reporter. Though busy, they all find ways to make bed and breakfast work for them.

As a working host, you will have to plan ahead to arrange an arrival time for each of your guests that works with your own schedule. Inform prospective guests in advance that you work and that you must agree upon an arrival time. If they tell you that they will be arriving at your door at 7:00 A.M. next Thursday, and you know that you have to leave your house by 8:00 A.M. to be at work on time, make sure that you tell them this (nicely, of course) so that they know you will not just "be there" whenever they choose to arrive. Because bed and breakfast is so new in this country, sometimes guests do not understand just how much inconvenience they can cause a host by arriving late; they must be educated.

There will be times when a guest will not be able to adjust his or her arrival time to your schedule. A Philadelphia host who works as a teacher and business consultant says, "Usually, I make arrangements to have the guests arrive when I will be home. If this is not possible, I ask someone to be here to let my guests in." This is a workable alternative, but make sure that the "someone" is a neighbor, relative, spouse, or close friend who can be trusted to greet your guests with the same warmth as you would yourself, and who will get them comfortably settled until you can return home.

A host who works part-time in retail management in Boston instructs guests that they may check in after 6:30 P.M., the time she arrives home from work. And because she works afternoons only, preparing breakfast is never a problem.

Breakfast can be a problem that has to be solved for some working hosts. A teacher in Westhampton Beach, New York, works full-time. Her solution to conflicting morning schedules is "I have someone come in to make breakfast." Another host with the responsibilities of a contract administrator found this answer to serving breakfast to her guests: "I ask if they can be seated to eat prior to my leaving if it's on a work day. If they can't eat before I leave, my husband can finish up where I leave off."

Most bed and breakfast guests are, in fact, usually flexible enough that something can be worked out to the mutual satisfaction of both the host and guest regarding breakfast. Many working hosts find that guests are just as happy waking up to a table already set, a coffee pot ready to plug in, and a breakfast that has been prepared in advance and left for them in the refrigerator or the warming oven. Some guests don't even mind making their own breakfast. (This is especially true of those who don't consider themselves "morning people" and who might be thankful for the chance to wake up a little more slowly and in private.) As long as a special arrangement for breakfast is not a surprise to guests and is not inconvenient for them, your working schedule should not be a major problem.

Departure time must also be established in advance. When guests are making a reservation with you, find out when they would prefer to check out. Then try to settle on a time that is agreeable for both of you so that you can be home if possible. Some working hosts publish in their literature definite arrival and departure periods that coincide with their own schedules. This way, they don't have to negotiate each individual guest's coming and going; guests automatically know what is expected of them.

Setting certain times for arrivals and departures has helped Lisa Hileman of Countryside in Summit Point, West Virginia, organize the

> In the big-city B&Bs, hosts generally lead a hectic life between work, play, and interpersonal relations," says Mary McAulay, partner in the reservation service organization in New York City known as Urban Ventures. "One host reported hearing a tiny voice from the bedroom about 11:00 A.M. saying, 'Please, I'm still waiting for my breakfast.' "

various aspects of her busy life better. "I run a B&B, go to college two days a week, freelance write, lecture, and take care of a husband and child," she says. "Check-in time is between 4:00 and 7:00 P.M., check-out at 11:00 A.M. This keeps our costs down and gives me and my family our private time."

What about other times of the day when guests are in residence but the host is at work? To date no one has reported this to be a major concern. One host registered with Bed and Breakfast Center City in Pennsylvania finds that her full-time work as the director of a language arts program in Philadelphia's school system does not interfere with guests' wants and needs very much at all. "Most people come to the city for recreation or business," she says. "They are not in the house to see me."

Even though bed and breakfast can go smoothly for a working host most of the time, you must be ready to turn away prospective guests, referring them elsewhere when possible, if it seems clear that your individual schedules will collide in a big way. One Kentucky host explains her schedule immediately to people who contact her for bed and breakfast—before the reservation is made. "I talk it over with them when the call comes in," says the owner of Bowling Green Bed & Breakfast. "They can then decline if they feel they'll be inconvenienced. If I cannot fit in a reservation, I say so."

This is good advice. You do not want even one guest to feel as if the bed and breakfast experience has been less than what he or she expected. Some guests will simply not be able to fit their lives into your schedule—or would be unhappy trying. Sure, a guest can get up at 6:00 A.M. to eat breakfast, but does he want to? And yes, a guest can put off arrival time until 7:00 P.M., but if she's planning to be in town at noon, why should she? Learn to recognize that scheduling conflicts like these are potential sources of dissatisfaction. Some people would be happier elsewhere, so be honest about it. They will thank you in the long run and perhaps think of you if they are ever coming to your area again. It's much better for you to take fewer guests than to run the risk of anyone's feeling neglected or inconvenienced.

And be ready to turn away guests if there will be too many all at once for you to handle. "Be careful not to overschedule," cautions a host from Graham, North Carolina. Trying to juggle your schedule for one or two guests at a time is difficult enough; for a houseful of visitors, perhaps all with different arrival and departure times, it's impossible.

Like many other working hosts across North America, you can happily integrate bed and breakfast into your life. But you must be very well organized and much more specific about what you expect from your guests and what they can expect from you. Most guests will be able to adjust their plans to fit your schedule if given enough advance notice. The main thing to remember is that you should enjoy hosting, and you want your guests to feel relaxed and comfortable about all the arrangements.

3
Getting Started

If you were living in Ireland, there would be no question about what basics you would be expected to provide for your bed and breakfast guests. The Bord Fáilte (the government-run Irish tourist board) regulates bed and breakfast operations in that country, and it has developed a precise list of requirements. There, for example, hosts must install a full-sized sink of specified dimensions with hot and cold running water in each guest bedroom in order for their bed and breakfast to be included in the board's approved accommodation list.

In the United States, no such government regulation exists. What takes its place are standards developed by reservation service organizations across the country. Hosts who list with an RSO must adhere to its guidelines; independent hosts must strive to maintain the same high standards. There is general agreement about what basics should be provided in any bed and breakfast home. What follows is a discussion of these based on information issued by Bed and Breakfast Colorado, Bed & Breakfast of Rhode Island, Pacific Bed & Breakfast, Bed & Breakfast Rocky Mountains, Folkstone Bed & Breakfast Registry, the Bed & Breakfast League, Pittsburgh Bed & Breakfast, Bed and Breakfast Associates Bay Colony Ltd., and many other RSOs throughout the United States and Canada. The combined information results in an invaluable assistance for new hosts as they start their bed and breakfast businesses.

The basics

Bedroom basics

The center of your guests' attention in the bedroom is, of course, the bed. A good bed will make all the difference in your guests' comfort.

You can economize when buying or restoring other furnishings, but the bed *must* be of the highest quality.

You've probably heard this before, but a "firm" mattress is the best kind to sleep on. There is widespread agreement about that. Now, what exactly does this mean? A hardwood floor is firm, a concrete sidewalk is firm, the ground we walk on is firm, but few people want to sleep on any of these. For a mattress, "firm" refers to how much support it gives to support a person's total body weight in the proper way, so that no stress is placed on the spine, joints, or muscles. Firmness depends to an extent on who is using the mattress. Someone who weighs 300 pounds needs more support than someone who weighs 100. The heavier person needs a mattress that is more "firm" than the lighter person.

To see if the mattress on your own bed is right for your body type, put it to this test: Lie down on your back in the center of the mattress. Try to slide your hand underneath yourself, into the space created by the curve at the small of your back. Is there no room for it because the mattress pushes up to fill the space completely? If so, the mattress is too soft for you. Or is there plenty of room for your hand, and maybe some to spare? Then the mattress is too hard, too much like that concrete sidewalk. If, however, the mattress rises gently to fill the hollow of your back but still allows you to slide your hand between, you've got a winner. It's just firm enough, giving where it should (head, shoulders, hips) and supporting where it should (primarily the source of discomfort for many people—the back).

Now check this: How far are your feet from the end of the mattress? There should be at least six inches to spare beyond your feet, as well as a few inches above the head. If there is ample room to accommodate your height, congratulations. Your mattress is the right size.

You might be thinking that this information is terrific if you're looking for the best mattress for yourself. What about your guests? You've got to be ready for anyone, of any size, to walk through your door—the ones who look like Sumo wrestlers, as well as the ones who could make their living riding horses at the racetrack. To evaluate a mattress that you already have in your guest room, or to guide your choice if you are buying a new one, first look at its size. A normal twin-sized mattress is seventy-five inches in length, which will accommodate a six-foot-tall person with only three inches to spare. Not good if the Lakers or the Celtics are coming over. An extra-long twin mattress is an option. This comes in eighty to eighty-four inches, giving that same six-footer eight to twelve inches of extra length.

Typically, a double (full) mattress is either seventy-five or eighty inches long, a queen-sized mattress eighty inches long, and a king-sized one eighty or eighty-four inches long. (Some manufacturers might make their mattresses in sizes other than these. Inquire before you buy.) If you do intend to buy a new bed (mattress and base) for your bed and breakfast business, it's best to acquire one that has sufficient length to make both your pint-sized *and* your giant-sized visitors happy. If you aren't buying a new bed, measure what you've got so that you know if there will be a potential problem making your statuesque visitors sufficiently comfortable. If so, one of the questions you should add to your list for "screening" visitors is: "Are you over six feet tall?" Then let the guest decide what's best for his comfort; it's better for someone to go elsewhere than to stay at your bed and breakfast and not be able to get a good night's rest.

Now we come to how "firm" the mattress should be for your guests, all of them. This is a tough one. There is no one answer because your bed and breakfast is going to get all body types. Fortunately, any mattress has a range of weight that it is designed to accommodate. The best advice is to settle on a mattress geared for a "normal" range of weight. Ask the dealer a lot of questions about this and try the bed yourself, using the test for firmness I've already provided. You might want to take a friend or two (of different body types) with you to the showroom to help you try out the stock. (Take friends who do not get embarrassed easily. You'll all have to do your thinking lying down.) See if all of you can agree on one mattress. Take your time before choosing; this is probably the most important purchase you will make.

If you are furnishing a guest room with twin beds, consider purchasing two slightly different mattresses, each designed to give a different amount of support. Then you can point out to your guests which bed is "firmer" than the other and let them decide which they would prefer.

Ordinarily, a mattress should last about ten years. With a bed and breakfast business, though, you can't realistically expect your mattresses to last that long. However, there are some things you can do to prolong their life as much as possible. First, make sure that there is a comfortable chair in the room to discourage guests from sitting on the edges of the bed. Nothing wears down a mattress quicker than constant sitting on its edge. Air the mattress each day by pulling back the bed covers (for at least twenty minutes) so that moisture is not trapped beneath the covers. (Also, make sure that you remove the wrapper from a new mattress before use to avoid trapping moisture inside.) A mattress pad and cover will protect it from stains, but wash these often, stripping the bed completely to air it out. A mattress should be turned around (and over) every once in a while (every three months is good) so that it doesn't tend to "settle" in certain spots.

Your next concern should be the base on which the mattress will lie. A bad bed base can completely counteract the positive effects a good mattress is designed to provide. Most bases are of the type that is filled with springs to support the mattress. This is fine as long as the springs are in good shape and do not cause the mattress to sag anywhere. For those who want their beds to be as "firm" as possible, there are bases on the market that are essentially just wooden platforms. Some people with complaints of a bad back prefer a more solid base.

What about other kinds of beds—hide-a-beds, sofa beds, waterbeds, hanging beds? Can these be used to accommodate bed and breakfast guests? Yes and no. Yes, in some situations if the bed is of high quality; no, if the bed does not offer the comfort that a guest is entitled to expect.

"Once I had a hide-a-bed that I had to make for myself, and it was *not* comfortable," says a woman from California who included this note in her evaluation of a bed and breakfast home she had visited on the West Coast. There are folding beds that slide one under the other (for a twin-bed or bunk-bed arrangement), or that disappear into a wall. These are great space savers (and sure solve the problem of making the bed in the morning). They can indeed be used to accommodate guests—but only if they are well made and comfortable, and you don't expect the guest to find it, make it, unmake it, and hide it again.

A sofa bed or a cot is *not* acceptable unless there are unusual circumstances. A cot is terrific, for example, whenever parents prefer that their child share their room, or whenever three or four economy-minded friends would rather share the cost of bunking in one room instead of two. And a sofa bed can come to the rescue whenever a group of friends really wants to be together in the same bed and breakfast home and they explicitly state that a sofa bed would be fine as a way to accommodate everybody. As a general rule, though, a cot or sofa bed should not be substituted for a "real" bed in a guest room.

A waterbed can be a great adventure for people who have never experienced its ebb and flow with their nocturnal activities. You can make it as "firm" as you (or they) wish by just adding more water, and the accompanying heating pad ensures a cozy welcome for skiiers or anyone who is visiting your area in the colder months. A waterbed is considered an amenity that could be used to attract people to your B&B.

A hanging bed, too, with its slight swinging sensation, can be a unique experience for guests. This is a platform suspended from the ceiling with a mattress placed atop it. Like a hide-a-bed, it can disappear into the ceiling if you wish by use of a pulley system. It should be installed only by a good carpenter or builder. Where the bed will be placed in the bedroom depends upon the location in the ceiling of the structural beams that will be able to support the weight of the bed, and your guest, safely and securely.

Now that you've decided upon the perfect bed, you will need to dress it in upper and lower sheets and matching pillowcases. (If color coordinated with the room, these can make the bed especially attractive.) Always wash new sheets before using them. Buy good-quality sheets and avoid totally synthetic fabrics, as they tend to trap moisture more than cotton or cotton blends, or the more expensive linen. Change the sheets after a guest checks out and before the next one arrives to use the same bed; if a guest is staying a while, change the sheets at least every three days—every two days in hot, humid climates. It's a good idea to keep extra sheets and pillowcases right in the guest room, so that if a guest needs a change before you have planned to do it, the guest can do it himself.

The life of your sheets depends in part on how clean you can manage to keep them. Never outfit a guest's bed in sheets that are stained in any way. Attack a new stain as soon as you can before it sets (you'll see them all—coffee, tea, juice, soft drinks, wine, chocolate, perfume, lipstick, mascara, blood, ink). Then at least you have a fighting chance to prolong the life of your sheets, but expect that you will have to replace them more often than you do for those on your own bed. As a bed and breakfast host, you'll soon find yourself waiting with keen anticipation for each annual January white sale.

Every bed should be supplied with two pillows per guest, and it's a good idea to put one or two extras in the closet for those who crave more than two to get them through the night. The ultimate in luxury is a pillow filled with goose down, but as you probably know, these are also the most expensive type available, with duck down a close second. A down-and-feather mixture is sometimes a good economic compromise that does not sacrifice that soft, light quality. Keep in mind, though, that pillows containing a polyester fill or latex foam are sometimes a better choice for people who suffer from allergies. You might want to keep such a non-allergenic pillow on hand if you do decide to outfit your guests' beds with the more luxurious down or feather pillows.

A good pillow can last as long as ten years, a so-so pillow two or less. (Enclose your pillows in both a slip cover and in a pillowcase for their protection.) To tell if your pillows are "dead," put them to this test: stretch one arm straight in front of you and balance the pillow on top of it. If the pillow droops, really *droops* (not just a gentle curve downward on each side), it's time for it to go to its final resting place.

Some people believe that adding certain herbs to a pillow makes for a better night's sleep. Marjoram, for example, is said to induce sleep. Mixed with lavender and thyme, it is purported to be the answer to stress and headaches. Cloves and cinnamon supposedly clear the head. Certainly, these items will imbue the pillow with a pleasant scent regardless of the effectiveness, or lack thereof, or their reputed medicinal properties. If you would like to try out this idea, it's best to enclose the herbs of your choice in a small cloth packet and place it inside the pillow cover instead of opening the pillow and mixing the herbs with the stuffing. (Use only about a teaspoonful, as you don't want to overwhelm your guests with the scent.) Then if you decide that the magic just isn't working for your bed and breakfast business, the packet can be easily removed and the pillow returned to its former odorless state with a little airing and fluffing.

A guest's bed should be equipped with at least one blanket, even in very warm weather (some people will be cold no matter what the temperature is), and extras should be stored right in the guest room so that your visitors can help themselves if they want an additional cover for the night. A quilt or electric blanket is a wonderful amenity in colder months. If you do supply an electric blanket, always inquire of your guests whether they understand how to use it. If they haven't used one before, you might have to explain its special features—how to set the temperature, whether or not the ends of the blanket can be tucked in, and the fact that other blankets should not be piled high on top of it while it is heating.

Wash or dry clean your blankets periodically (before they look like they need it), and air them out frequently to keep them in good shape. The first thing to go is usually the binding along the edges. You can buy binding separately and give older blankets a fresh look by sewing the new over the old. Once the blankets develop worn spots or holes or become stained, however, they can no longer be used on a guest's bed.

If you furnish a quilt for your guests, this can take the place of a bedspread. A quilt used in conjunction with matching sheets, and perhaps dust ruffles to hide the base of the bed, can create a pleasing, total look for the bed. (A wall hanging of the same quilted material, or a color-coordinated roll blind or canopy, can easily extend that look to the rest of the room.) If you choose to place a bedspread on the bed, there are a number of attractive possibilities made of chenille, lace, or yarn that has been crocheted or knitted. To help keep a bedspread clean and in good repair, consider providing the "amenity" of turning down your guests' beds at night, removing the spread to a safer place such as the shelf in the closet or the top of the cedar chest at the foot of the bed. And again, the presence of a chair in the room will help to discourage guests from lounging on the bed (and the spread).

Getting out of bed should be as pleasant as getting into it. Your guests' feet come into contact with waking reality before any other part of their body—so make that first step as inviting as possible by providing some kind of covering on the floor next to the bed. If you prefer not to furnish the guest room with a room-sized carpet (perhaps to show off your beautifully maintained hardwood floors), at least place a good-sized scatter rug (with a nonskid backing) next to each side of the bed.

Other than the bed, there are a few pieces of furniture that you will need in each guest room as well. A comfortable chair has been mentioned several times already as an enticement away from the expensive mattress that was not designed to support a person's weight except in a prone position. If there is an alternative to the bed—a big, comfy armchair, a rocking chair, or a straight-back chair with a padded seat—it will not only help lengthen the life of your mattress, but it will also preserve the good condition of the bedspread. And, too, having a chair in the room is most considerate of your guests who might want to write letters or read without having to resort to the only other place to do either of these—the bed.

A suitcase rack is also a practical addition to a guest room. Guess where the suitcase goes if there's no designated place to put it? Right—on the bed. Again, think of the mattress and the spread, and then either buy a rack designed expressly for this purpose or put together your own improvised version—an old trunk, perhaps, or a low, flat table. Be careful about positioning it in the room so that the edge of an open suitcase will not rub against your favorite painting or scrape against the wall.

You can help discourage your guests from continual foraging in their suitcases (which, in turn, cuts down on the rubs and scrapes) by supplying ample clothes hangers in the closet. For each guest, plan on at least six, more if a guest will be staying longer than two or three days, or if the weather is chilly and there are more layers that need to be dealt with. Scented, padded hangers are an especially nice touch for finer garments. It's a good idea to include special hangers for trousers or skirts as well. Install a few hooks on the bedroom door or the inside of the closet door so that guests can use these for their robes or nightgowns.

The closet should be completely empty of any items outside of those that guests have brought with them and the extra blankets, pillows, and sheets that are intended for their use. In addition to this space to temporarily store their clothes, guests should also have access to at least two drawers each in a bureau. Line the drawers with paper and change the lining often. It's a nice touch to place a packet of sachet or herbs or some cedar blocks in each drawer.

People have lots of things that they like near them at night—eyeglasses, a book they want to finish, a glass of water, their false teeth. To hold these kinds of personal items, there should be a night table next to the bed. If the guest room has a double, queen-sized, or king-sized bed, you'll need two—one for each side. On the table, place a box of facial tissues, an alarm clock (one that runs quietly), and a radio if you have an extra. If you allow smoking, it's best to place the ashtray elsewhere in the room so as to discourage smoking in bed.

It's a good idea to have another small table in the room besides the night table, as that can get cluttered quickly. You'll need to provide several glasses per guest for water and other beverages, plus a pitcher of water (which is optional but a nice touch), a basket of goodies to eat in case your guest wants a snack, maybe some of your business cards or stationery, a vase of flowers, and perhaps a phone extension. The top of the bureau can hold some of these items, and a writing desk is also an option, but a separate table can be arranged to hold these items in a more attractive way.

There should always be a reading lamp near the bed, as many people do like to read before going to sleep. This can be placed on the night table or above the bed. If your guest room has a double, queen-sized, or king-sized bed, you'll need the two reading lamps, one on each side of the bed. And too, that comfortable chair that you hope your guests will be using needs a good source of light.

Your guests will be preparing to meet the outside world from the confines of their room, so provide a large mirror to help their efforts. A full-length mirror is best, but any large mirror (positioned so that it can accommodate the widest range in heights) is fine. A hand mirror is a considerate addition to the items on top of the bureau.

Place a wastebasket in a convenient location in each guest room. Lining the baskets will protect their surfaces from the more messy discarded items, such as banana peels and old cigarette butts. Some surfaces (like wicker) are harder to clean than others, and some (like metal) will discolor. The lining will make your job easier and the life of your baskets longer. Still, resorting to that durable plastic bag from Stop 'n' Save somehow breaks the tone you've tried so hard to establish. Old newspapers, too, don't give quite the right impression, and neither do plain brown paper bags. Some hosts have found this solution: They stock quantities of tissue paper (the kind used for wrapping gifts), either in white or in a color that coordinates with the décor of the room, and arrange a few sheets inside the wastebasket. These make an attractive accent in the room and, at the same time, provide some protection for the basket's inside surface. While a guest is in residence, empty the wastebasket each day, clean the inside if necessary, and line it with new tissue paper.

The furnishings in your guest room do not have to be new, but they do have to be in good repair. "Old" furniture sometimes looks drab, and maybe you should consider a new upholstery job on that faded chair, a new finish on that night table, or a new shade on that lamp to get the room "guest ready." If any piece of furniture detracts from the charm of the room, it will be noticed—so take care of it.

The overall comfort of a room depends, in large part, on adequate heat in the cooler months and adequate ventilation or a cooling system in warmer months. If there is a problem with too much, or too little, heat or air conditioning in any of your guest rooms, you have to take steps to alleviate the problem. (See "Comfort" in chapter 2.)

All windows in the guests' bedrooms must be screened in good weather, have storm windows in cool weather, and have some sort of window covering for privacy—even if the nearest possible Peeping Tom is the neighbor's cow that sometimes wanders out of the pasture and into your yard. "Don't laugh," say Linda Feltman and Brent Peters, co-owners of a reservation service organization in Pennsylvania called Rest & Repast. "Many of our hosts live in woods, and so shades are not necessary, but guests don't know that!" Anyone used to living in a more densely populated area is accustomed to guarding personal privacy more carefully. Draw curtains or window blinds (venetian or the roller type) will help assuage the habitual fears of city dwellers traveling to more rural areas. If your bed and breakfast home is in a more urban area, you should have not only curtains or window blinds on bedroom windows, but window locks as well.

A privacy lock for the bedroom is also recommended. Some people just don't sleep well in a strange place (no matter how nice it is) knowing that someone can just walk in through the door at any time. A hook-and-eye type of lock is fine. One final note about the door: Make sure that you have for each guest room a proper door that is solid and closes into a frame. An accordion door might be serviceable for your own purposes, but it gives a less private feeling to a room and should be avoided when it comes to outfitting a guest room with the basics.

So now you've got it all—the bed and the "firm" mattress, a comfortable chair, a rug, the sheets and pillows, the blankets, the reading light. Are you ready for guests? There's one sure way to find out—try it out yourself. Spend a night in the guest room. Read in bed, write a few letters you've been putting off for a while, have a glass of wine, eat a snack. Then go to sleep. There's no better test than to see how you like your own hospitality. Sweet dreams.

Bedroom basics checklist

- ☐ Reading lamp
- ☐ Night table(s) next to bed
- ☐ Suitcase rack
- ☐ Comfortable chair
- ☐ Bureau with at least two drawers
- ☐ Wastebasket
- ☐ Closet free of personal items
- ☐ Six hangers per guest in closet
- ☐ Hooks to hang robes
- ☐ Large mirror/hand mirror
- ☐ Rug next to bed
- ☐ Drying rack (if bathroom is shared)
- ☐ Window covering (blinds/draw curtains)
- ☐ Privacy lock on door
- ☐ Window screens in warm weather
- ☐ Storm windows in cold weather
- ☐ Window locks (if on first floor)
- ☐ Box of facial tissue
- ☐ Alarm clock
- ☐ Ashtray (if smoking is allowed)
- ☐ Two glasses (for water/other beverages)
- ☐ Ventilation (fan/air conditioning)
- ☐ Heat in cold months
- ☐ Firm mattress in good condition
- ☐ Bed base with good support
- ☐ Mattress pad
- ☐ Mattress cover
- ☐ Two clean sheets (upper/lower)
- ☐ Two pillows
- ☐ Slip covers on pillows
- ☐ Pillowcases
- ☐ Clean, fluffy blanket on bed
- ☐ Bedspread or quilt
- ☐ Extra sheets and pillowcases available
- ☐ Easy access to extra blankets
- ☐ Extra pillows available

Bathroom basics

For the bathroom that your guests will be using, your initial concern should be whether or not the current plumbing and fixtures are in good working order and can handle the increased demand on them that bed and breakfast hosting will cause. A host who has only one or two guests every once in a while should encounter no problem. However, if you've got big plans to fill the five extra rooms in your home every night of the week, you might have to do some renovations.

Each guest bathroom must have an adequate supply of hot and cold running water. Does your hot water tank have the capacity to produce all the hot water you'll be needing when you open the doors to your bed and breakfast? (If you will be able to accommodate eight people, that means a potential of eight hot showers in a row, plus your own, plus those of any other household members.) If yours can't, here are your options: Buy a new, larger tank; install an auxiliary tank or individual water-heating unit; take fewer guests per night; or schedule your own showers around those of your guests.

Consider, too, whether your present sewage system can handle greater use. More than one host reports having to finance a completely new sewage treatment system before being able to open for business. Be advised that all sanitary facilities must meet the regulations in force where you live and that water must be from an approved source.

A bed and breakfast home need not provide a private bath for each guest room. There are many flourishing B&B homes in which bathrooms are shared among guests, or with the host and other household members. Guests generally understand that they are staying in a private home and are not uncomfortable at all about this arrangement. One gentleman visiting a bed and breakfast farm in South Dakota had a "half-bath" (without tub or shower) adjoining his room. For a shower, "I had the use of the family's improvised shower facility in the basement, off the family rec room," he says. "I used it during my stay." No problem.

One couple staying at a bed and breakfast home in Nova Scotia were accommodated in the one guest room that happened to have an adjoining bathroom. Although the place did have another bathroom for guests to use, that one had no shower. Only the bathroom that was accessible through the couple's bedroom contained a shower. "We were pre-warned and asked if we minded the traffic through our room," the couple reports. "We often had folks who wanted a shower tiptoeing through our room in the early morning." An inconvenience, yes, but the couple looks back on their visit there as one of the most enjoyable vacations they've ever taken. For some, sharing a bathroom is just not an issue.

Others are more private people and would truly be happier with a bathroom to themselves, no matter what you do to make their stay comfortable. A New Jersey woman wrote a rave review of the bed and breakfast home she visited in Rhode Island—how helpful, nice, friendly, and generous the host was; how "terrific" breakfast was; and how she would absolutely love to stay there again. Yet, when asked if she would like to change anything about this wonderful place, her comment was "private bath."

A Pennsylvania couple had a similar reaction to a bed and breakfast ranch in Arizona. They loved it. They even had a private bath, but they had to go downstairs to use it. This was an inconvenience that they noted in their report in spite of their answer to whether or not they would want to stay at the ranch again: "Definitely!" The truth is that some people will never be completely happy about the bathroom arrangements (too small; too distant from the bedroom; it's upstairs; it's downstairs; it's shared), but a good measure of hospitality can often outweigh someone's idea that a private bathroom adjoining the guest room is the ultimate in comfort.

This is true, however, only when the inconvenience is indeed minor. With a shared bath, people have different schedules and can usually work things out. But one woman stayed in a bed and breakfast home in the White Mountains of New Hampshire where the sole bathroom had to accommodate eight people. And it could be reached only by going through the kitchen to the back of the house. She was uncomfortable, for good reason, and so will your guests be if your home does not offer a proportionate number of bathrooms for the number of guests it accommodates. Four people sharing one bathroom is plenty; more can manage, but the risk of a traffic jam at the bathroom door is greater.

For the privacy of your guests (especially where there is a shared bathroom), make sure that there is some sort of lock on the door (hook-and-eye type is fine), a door or curtain on the shower stall, and blinds or draw curtains on windows. For the safety of your guests, any rugs placed in the bathroom should have a nonskid backing, and there should be a nonskid bath mat or strips in the tub. A grip rail for the tub and the shower is also recommended. (A towel rack cannot substitute for this; it isn't made to support the full weight of a person needing to steady himself getting in or out of the tub or shower.)

For the comfort of your guests, the bathroom should have ventilation, either an extractor fan or a window that can be opened. The addition of some live plants or a vase of flowers here can also help to make the room more pleasant. Keep a new sponge and cleaning supplies handy, along with air freshener or deodorizer so that guests who wish to do so can freshen up the room a bit after use. (Burning a match is a simple but effective way to deodorize a bathroom; a small box of matches left out for guests is a considerate touch.) There should be a wastebasket in the room—emptied on a daily basis.

A box of facial tissues should be put in both the guest room and the bathroom. Many of us have discovered that the "generic" brands of tissue are often just as soft and serviceable as the name brands. It makes economic sense to supply these for your guests, but the austere packaging might give the impression that you are cutting corners instead of seeking the best for your guests' comfort. Still, if the idea of spending one-half more for a brand name just because the tissues are packaged in attractive boxes doesn't set well with you, consider the purchase of a few decorative tissue box holders (they come in wicker, ceramic, plastic, and fabric). If you use these, you need never advertise what brand you're using.

Where the economy brands do not seem to contain the quality of the more well-known products is in toilet tissue. For this item, you're probably better off watching for sales on the brand you favor and stocking up. There should always be a roll of tissue on the holder in the bathroom, along with a second roll (and a second box of facial tissues as well) located on a shelf or in another convenient spot in the room. It's common to think that the dyed and perfumed toilet tissue would be preferred by guests as an "amenity," but keep in mind that some people are sensitive to these things and would be happier with a good brand of soft, plain white, unscented tissue that will not trigger allergies. (The spare roll can be of this type.)

Each guest should be given a bath towel, a hand towel, and a washcloth, preferably a matching set. It's not a bad idea to include a medium-sized towel as well, as some people like the luxury of this extra to dry their hair after washing it. The towels must be clean (no stains) and in good repair (no holes, tears, frayed edges, or worn spots), preferably thick and fluffy, and of high-quality material. Change them often—at least every other day, every day if possible. For a guest, there's nothing worse than coming back to the bed and breakfast to clean up for a night on the town after a long day of sightseeing and finding used towels still damp and dirty from the morning's post-jogging shower. Some hosts show guests where the stacks of clean towels are stored and invite them to help themselves to fresh ones as needed. If you prefer this method, also explain to guests where they should deposit their used ones. For this, you might want to place a small clothes hamper or laundry bag in the bathroom (also a good idea for those sandy beach towels that guests bring back to the house after swimming and sunning).

If there will be more than one person using a bathroom, the best way to help guests keep their towels separate is to give everyone a complete towel set in a different color. This works especially well when the colors of the towels are coordinated with the colors of the guest rooms (blue for "The Blue Room," yellow for "The Sunshine Room," and so forth). Some hosts put a towel set for each guest inside a large basket and place it inside the bedroom. Guests can also use this basket to transport their own toilet articles back and forth to the shared bath. (Do make some shelf space available in the bathroom for those guests who wish to leave their own toothpaste, toothbrush, shampoo, etc., there.)

If a bathroom is shared, placing a drying rack in each guest room will allow guests to bring their own towels back into their room and spread them out there to dry. (A drying rack will also save your bedposts and chair backs from discoloration as a result of guests' resorting to the most convenient makeshift rack for their wet towels.) Do this only if the moisture will not damage your floors or floor covering. In the bathroom, install enough towel racks so that guests can hang up their towels while bathing and leave them there to dry afterwards. (Heated towel rails connected to the hot water system are a nice touch in colder climates. They not only give your guests warm, comfy towels after their bath or shower, but they also facilitate the drying of the towels.) And make sure that there are a few hooks in the bathroom where guests can hang their robes.

Include a small, individually wrapped bar of soap in each guest's "bathroom basket" if the bathroom is to be shared, or place some liquid soap at the sink. If guests have a private bath, a new bar of soap at the sink is also an option (but sometimes a more expensive one, as bars used by one guest really shouldn't be left for the next one who checks in). If you do choose to stock bar soap instead of liquid soap, make sure that you have soap dishes on hand; either place one in the guest's basket along with the soap and towels, or set out a few in the bathroom. Supply some liquid soap at the tub or shower. And a bowl or basket of small, wrapped scented soaps and some packets of bubble bath set out in the bathroom are a nice touch. (Sample sizes of toilet items are usually available at discount drugstores.)

Each guest will need a water glass. These may be placed in the bathroom or, if the bathroom is shared among three or more people, on a small tray in each guest room. Disposable paper cups are fine and probably the most sanitary solution. Some hosts have installed a cup dispenser in the bathroom; other hosts feel that this device detracts from the décor of the room. Remember that you will also be providing a glass for each guest to use for soft drinks or wine. Either keep the water glass clearly separate from the other—by placing it in the bathroom or on its own tray with a water pitcher—or set out several glasses for each guest in his or her own room. Change or wash the glasses every day.

If you decide that renovations are necessary in order to accommodate your guests, consider the following alterations. If there is not already a good light source by the mirror, have a qualified electrician install one. (It must have a pull-cord switch for safety, and a guard so that no one can touch the "live" part of the unit.) And if your bathroom does not already have an electrical outlet where guests can plug in a shaver, curling iron, or hair dryer, you might want to have this added as well. (Note that there are building codes that govern the use of electricity in bathrooms. Such an outlet should be positioned high and at least five feet from the tub, and it should be fitted with a waterproof plastic cover plate. Ask your electrician if any other regulations apply.) You might decide that it's best to pass on the bathroom outlet as a safety measure; as long as there's an outlet in the guest's bedroom that can be used for a hair dryer, this should be fine. Placing a supply of disposable razors and a can of shaving cream in the bathroom should satisfy anyone who finds that he cannot use his electric razor there.

You might think that you need to add an entire second bathroom to meet your guests' needs. Before you go ahead and do this, be advised that there are alternatives. One is to remodel the existing bathroom (if it's large enough) so that the bathing and showering area is partitioned off for privacy. This allows others who share the bathroom to come and go while someone else is using the bathing facilities. Remember, too, that showering usually requires less water than does a nice soak in the bath tub. If you need to conserve your hot water supply, you might want to establish a "showers only" policy. (One other advantage to this is that showers are usually quicker than baths—which means that the shared bathroom will be tied up for less time.)

Now that the tradition of bed and breakfast has crossed the Atlantic, hosts in this country can better appreciate the experiences of our fellow hosts across the way. During its years of operation, a bed and breakfast home in Dublin, Ireland, offered only showers (no baths) so as to use the hot-water supply more efficiently. "This arrangement—of showers only—never gave us any problems . . . that is, until two Englishmen stayed with us who wanted to have a bath together," says Patrick Boland, former proprietor of the Linden Lodge. "We would not have agreed to it anyway, because one of them was carrying a very dangerous-looking toy submarine already armed with two dangerous-looking toy torpedoes that, had they struck the other fellow amidships, would certainly have caused damage."

Another possibility is adding a sink with hot and cold running water in one or more of your guest rooms. This would relieve the demand on the main bathroom when all guests want to do is wash their face and hands or brush their teeth. Individual units (electric or gas) for heating the water can be installed right under the sink so that there is no extra demand on your central water-heating unit. You should consider this alternative only if the plumbing in your home can be extended easily into a guest room. (If a guest room shares a wall with the bathroom, for example, or is positioned directly above the kitchen, additions to pipes can be made more easily than if a plumber has to burrow through a couple of walls to install the sink.)

These alternatives to financing a new hot water tank and building a second bathroom could be less costly, but in the words of a plumbing supply dealer, "nothing's cheap." It's best to give some thought to different alternatives, get estimates on all of them, and then decide what's best for your situation. Because new pipes and electrical cables may have to be laid to provide adequate bathroom facilities for your guests, be warned that walls, ceilings, and floors could suffer some damage in the process. So make no other major renovations anywhere in the house (such as laying down new linoleum in the kitchen or repapering the walls in the guest rooms) before taking care of this priority.

Bathroom basics checklist

- ☐ One bath towel per guest
- ☐ One hand towel per guest
- ☐ One washcloth per guest
- ☐ Nonskid bath mat in tub

- ☐ Wastebasket
- ☐ Nonskid rug on floor
- ☐ Curtain or door on shower
- ☐ Window covering (blinds/draw curtains)
- ☐ Privacy lock on door
- ☐ Plenty of hot water
- ☐ Separate towel racks for each guest
- ☐ Drying rack for towels/hand washables
- ☐ Plumbing/fixtures in good working order
- ☐ Extra bath mats and rugs (if bath is shared)
- ☐ Sewage system adequate
- ☐ Well-lighted mirror at sink
- ☐ Shelf space for toilet articles
- ☐ Box of facial tissue (plus one extra box)
- ☐ Roll of toilet tissue (plus one extra roll)
- ☐ Water glass for each guest
- ☐ Hooks for robes
- ☐ Liquid soap in tub/shower
- ☐ Liquid or unused bar soap at sink
- ☐ Soap dishes if needed
- ☐ Air freshener
- ☐ Fresh sponge and cleaning supplies
- ☐ Ventilation (fan/window that opens)

The amenities

Rita Duncan, director of a reservation service organization in Virginia called Blue Ridge Bed & Breakfast, has this to say about the hosts who list with her agency: "I fully trust their good taste and graciousness." As long as the requirements of cleanliness and a good, hearty breakfast are met, "the rest is left to the hosts' discretion," she says.

What Rita is referring to here are the amenities, extras that hosts provide to make their guests comfortable. Just what these might be is a highly individual matter, depending on a host's own interests, hobbies, like and dislikes, and location. From the amenities you decide to offer, your bed and breakfast home will take on its own character and make the B&B experience exactly what it's supposed to be for your guests—special. No two bed and breakfast homes are alike. And this is a large part of the attraction.

The discussion of amenities that follows shows what different hosts throughout North America do to add that extra-special character to their bed and breakfast homes. You should look at them as food for thought. How do they spark your own imagination?

An "amenity" is anything extra that goes beyond the basics. A host is not obligated to provide more than a clean, comfortable accommodation, but the finer touches will make the bed and breakfast experience special for the people who stay with you. The basics are what guests expect; the amenities are what they remember.

There are some amenities that are easy to provide and cost little or nothing, but that make quite an impression. A couple visiting the 3B's Bed and Breakfast in Spring Valley, Ohio, report that they came back to their room in the evening to find that their host had "turned back our bed while were out—nice touch!"

A woman staying at Shir-Will Farms in Bloomfield, Ontario, was delighted to find a single rose in a vase on her bedside table. Fresh flowers, or a few plants, always add a special something to a guest room.

Gloria Belknap, owner of The Terrace Townehouse in Boston, invites guests to place their shoes outside the door of their room when they retire. In the morning the shoes will be right where they left them—polished and shined.

A host is expected to furnish breakfast for guests. Nothing more than this is actually necessary, but it's very thoughtful to offer drinks, and sometimes food, at other times as well. People arriving at your home at night might be hungry after traveling, but because of the late hour they might be unable to go out to a restaurant. A bedtime snack to help latecomers get through the night is an amenity offered regularly at Leftwich House in Graham, North Carolina; The Shaw House in Georgetown, South Carolina; and many other bed and breakfast homes. A couple who list their home with House Guests Cape Cod are known to bring out a platter of homemade peanut butter cookies in the evenings. Be Our Guest in Plymouth, Massachusetts, suggests to hosts listed with that agency that they make popcorn as a snack or offer apples in season.

The manager of a reservation service organization in South Carolina called Historic Charleston Bed & Breakfast recommends to its hosts that they place a "goody basket" containing fruit and candy in each guest room so that visitors can help themselves.

At the Brinley Victorian Inn in Newport, Rhode Island, guests will find mints on their pillows. A national RSO based in the state of Washington takes this idea one step further. Bed and Breakfast Service (BABS) sends a supply of gold labels to each of its hosts so that they can affix them to paper doilies. These are then placed on guests' pillows with a chocolate "kiss" that is wrapped in foil. The labels say, "A Kiss to Build A Dream On"—a touch that is "very popular with guests," say BABS's owners.

Boston host Gloria Belknap makes a hit with her visitors by offering an "afternoon tea" at which she serves her own special homemade scones, hot from the oven. Some guests enjoy this amenity so much that they ask if they may invite friends over to join them for the occasion.

Phil and Joan Blood, owners of Chinguague Compound in San Juan Pueblo, New Mexico, are more informal about providing extra food for guests. "In season, we encourage guests to go out and pick fresh fruit from the trees."

Some guests will bring their own snacks and drinks. Linda and David Nichols, owners of Hidden Brooks Bed & Breakfast in New Hampshire, allow guests the use of their refrigerator to store cold drinks and any food they might have brought with them. Ellie Welch Ramsey, also a Boston host, offers to put any food that guests are carrying in their own cooler in her refrigerator when they arrive, then fills the cooler with ice when the guests are ready to check out.

A host should always make sure that there is ice available for guests to use with drinks they have bought themselves. A reservation service organization called the Bed and Breakfast League recommends placement of a full ice bucket, along with several glasses, in each guest room. Some hosts prefer to simply let guests know that they are welcome to get ice from the freezer compartment of the refrigerator whenever they wish.

Providing complimentary drinks is a nice touch. Greater Boston Hospitality encourages hosts listed with this reservation service organization to place a few cans of soft drinks or mineral water in an ice bucket for each guest room. (You might want to ask guests what they prefer and then supply the drinks of their choice.) The Prince George Inn B&B in Annapolis, Maryland, stocks a refrigerator with complimentary soft drinks and wine. A glass of sherry or other nightcap before bed is an amenity usually welcomed by guests. For newlyweds, hosts listed with the Bed & Breakfast Society of Houston will supply a complimentary bottle of champagne.

Some hosts extend kitchen privileges to those who ask for it, especially guests who are staying longer than two or three days and would like to make their own meals rather than eating out all the time. Others invite guests to join the family for lunch or dinner (usually with an adjustment to the final bill). Still others have found that the best solution is to prepare meals together. A woman from Pittsburgh who was staying in her first bed and breakfast home ate all of her meals with her hosts.

"We discovered that we were all into vegetarian cooking, and we tried a new recipe or two," says Lauren Schneider, recalling her week-long visit with a young Canadian couple. They relied upon fresh vegetables from the garden, split the cost of beer, and "shared things like cooking and washing dishes," she says. A few guests have even been known to surprise their hosts by cooking up a special dinner for everyone to enjoy.

If a guest is celebrating a special event, take the opportunity to acknowledge it in some way. Lisa Hileman, owner of Countryside in Summit Point, West Virginia, says, "We make birthday cakes, give birthday gifts, anniversary gifts, wedding gifts—all at no extra charge." If it seems appropriate, a remembrance of a special occasion—a card, a small gift, or a cake if you want to take the time to bake it—is a wonderful personal touch that your guests will never forget.

Transportation is another amenity that is often needed, and always appreciated, by travelers. Some of your guests will be coming to the area by means of bus, train, or plane. Without their own car, they must rely upon taxis or other public transportation to get to and from your home. Pickup at airports and bus and train stations is offered by a number of hosts as a courtesy to their guests. If providing this service is convenient for you (sometimes hosts can't arrange to do this because of work or family responsibilities), it's a good amenity to offer. One guest writes that she was met at the airport by her host, which was an hour's drive from the bed and breakfast home. The drive itself turned out to be one of the highlights that she remembers the most about her trip: "We spent about three hours driving along the shore and stopping at various small museums," she says. Some hosts will give their guests tours of the area if they wish; others have negotiated agreements with local car-rental companies to provide their guests with discounts on rentals.

A supply of reading material is a good idea. Travelers often look for a relaxing diversion before they retire for the night, want to read up on the area they're visiting, or just want to keep up with the news of the day while they're away from home. At Corner House in Rhinebeck, New York, there is a bookcase full of books in each room, along with magazines and brochures of local attractions and interests. Catherine Hatala, a host registered with Bed and Breakfast Center City in Philadelphia, subscribes to a variety of current periodicals (the *New York Times*, *The New Yorker*, *Prevention*, *Reader's Digest*, *U.S. News & World Report*) to satisfy the different reading tastes of her guests. A morning paper is always available for guests at The Shaw House in Georgetown, South

Carolina. (Subscribing to a local paper, as well as any magazine devoted to your city, state, or area, is also recommended. Note that these subscriptions are tax deductible; see chapter 9.)

Some magazines (such as *Working Woman*) will offer you or your guests discounted subscriptions: If you find that you host a large number of people who fall into one or two main categories (female business executives, fishermen, birdwatchers, musicians), contact the offices of any magazines directed to these special audiences and inquire about any amenity program currently offered to hotels and discuss such an arrangement for your bed and breakfast.

Some hosts offer additional diversions for their guests' enjoyment. At Gates Hill Homestead in Brookfield, New York, guests will find a card table and some decks of cards waiting for them. Be Our Guest suggests to its hosts that they put up a dartboard game in the yard or the family room. There's a piano at Leftwich House in Graham, North Carolina, and at Woodruff House in Barre, Vermont. (For guests who prefer the more meditative diversions, there are also rockers on the porches of both of these establishments.) Gull House in Avalon, California, offers visitors the use of a stereo. In each guest house on the Chinguague Compound in New Mexico, there is a television set.

Depending on the area where you live, other amenities might come to mind. One couple from New Mexico were pleasantly surprised that their host in Bodega Bay, California, had thought of a way to help them enjoy the scenery even more. "There was a large telescope so we could look over the bay," they recall. Some hosts registered with Christian Hospitality Bed & Breakfast lend guests a fishing pole if they want to try their luck. Other hosts offer the use of binoculars for birdwatching, golf clubs, volleyball and net, tennis racquets, sleds, toboggans, surfboards, water skis or snow skis, canoes, bicycles, and weights and exercise equipment.

There are some hosts who even allow guests the use of their personal memberships in social or athletic clubs, museums, and libraries. The owner of Singleton House in Arkansas invites visitors to join her on Sunday mornings for a jaunt with the local hiking club. Cozy Acres B&B in New Jersey provides beach badges during the summer; Spindrift Bed & Breakfast in Oregon offers rain gear for the beach to those who can't resist a walk on the sand, despite the weather. At High Tide in Orleans, Massachusetts, guests are supplied with beach umbrellas and towels. Visitors to the state of Maine have a chance to go sailing with one of the hosts listed with Bed & Breakfast of Maine, or lobstering with a host listed with Bed & Breakfast Down East.

Daily activities that seem quite ordinary to you could, in fact, be quite exciting to someone from a different environment. Watching cows being milked is greatly enjoyed by guests at Sycamore Haven Farm in Kinzers, Pennsylvania. Take stock of your own situation. Do you live in an area where you could offer horseback riding, hay rides, hiking, jogging? These special features can attract visitors to your bed and breakfast.

Do you have a special skill that you could accord guests as an amenity? The owner of RMF Bed & Breakfast in Atlanta, Georgia, offers to type reports and letters for guests, and to make translations from Spanish and French. Bed and Breakfast USA in Croton-on-Hudson, New York, lists some hosts who offer their services as interpreters. "I board cats," says Elaine Samuels, owner of Ivy Chimney in Syracuse. Among the amenities she extends to her guests is, "a cat to sleep with if desired."

"We believe in your own uniqueness," says Kate Winters as she offers advice to the hosts registered with her reservation service organization, called Bed & Breakfast Rocky Mountains. Take a close look at your own skills and lifestyle and how you can draw from these to make your guests' visit special. As Kate says, "Be creative."

There are more common amenities that will enhance the overall comfort of your guests. The climate will dictate some of these extras—suntan lotion or sunscreen for beachgoers; insect repellent in humid areas; umbrellas for rainy days. Shop around for a supply of small sample-size containers of hand cream, shaving cream, shampoo, hair conditioner, and toothpaste. Other items that guests appreciate are disposable razors, bath salts, scented soaps, toothbrushes, cotton swabs, and disposable shower caps. Some hosts place a pin cushion with needles and thread in every guest room and make available a hair dryer, curling iron, make-up mirror, iron, and ironing board.

Guests will find robes at The Beach House in Huron, Ohio. At Marjon Bed & Breakfast Inn in Leaburg, Oregon, they may help themselves to a pair of multi-colored "soxlets" from a large wooden bowl in the living room to wear around the house.

You can expect that guests will have their own individual needs beyond the things that you have thought to provide for their comfort. "Bandages, rags for cleaning bicycles, safety pins—you name it and I've been asked for it," says Ellen Madison, owner of Woody Hill Guest House in Rhode Island. At times Lona and George Smith, owners of Summerwood in New York, have loaned sweaters, boots, and scarves to guests who came unprepared for the local weather.

The subject of laundry is bound to come up. If you wish, permit guests to use your washer and dryer, or run a load of laundry for them. (Most hosts add on an extra fee for this privilege.) Or you might want to provide some liquid laundry soap and a drying rack, or clothes line and clothes pins, for hand washables.

As many guests will be unfamiliar with the area, you can do them a favor by helping to arrange their entertainment. If visitors are coming for the specific purpose of attending a play, concert, museum opening, or festival, offer to reserve tickets for them through your local connections. Strawberry Castle Bed & Breakfast in New York will arrange horse-and-buggy rides for its guests. Dairy Hollow House in Arkansas will set up guided fishing trips (and then cook the catch for the guests' dinner!). If guests decide to take a side trip, it's a nice gesture to store their unneeded luggage for them. Consider what attracts people to your area and think of ways you can be helpful to your guests as they explore it.

Some amenities should be given freely, as part of the hospitality provided by your bed and breakfast at no extra charge. Most of these are obvious—turning down the bed at night, flowers in the guest rooms, mints on the pillows, a complimentary glass of wine in the evening, a bedtime snack.

Other extras cost a host time and money—traveling a great distance to pick up someone at the airport, spending half a day sailing, doing laundry, baking cakes. The following section, "Pricing Your Bed and Breakfast," will help you determine how to cost your rooms, taking amenities into consideration. In preparation, look at the list of possible amenities that appears in this chapter. Check off the ones that you can, and want to, offer your guests. Remember that you need not try to do more than what is possible for you. Just a few extra touches here and there are enough to let your guests know that they are special to you. The personal touch is what they're looking for, and they'll be sure to find it with the opportunity to visit with you in your home. According to Robert Somaini, owner of Woodruff House in Vermont, this is the greatest amenity that any guest can receive: "a chance to meet an eccentric native—me!"

Amenities checklist

- ☐ Packets of sachet/potpourri in dresser drawers
- ☐ Turn back bed covers
- ☐ Shine shoes
- ☐ Flowers/plants in guest room
- ☐ Bedtime snack
- ☐ Fruit bowl/"goody basket" in room
- ☐ Mints/candies on pillow
- ☐ Afternoon tea
- ☐ Complimentary soft drinks/tea/coffee/mineral water
- ☐ Complimentary wine/beer/liqueur
- ☐ Ice bucket in room
- ☐ Complimentary champagne for newlyweds/anniversary couples
- ☐ Kitchen privileges
- ☐ Lunch/dinner with host
- ☐ Cards/gifts/cakes for special occasions
- ☐ Pickup at airport/bus or train station
- ☐ Tours of area
- ☐ Car-rental discounts
- ☐ Reading material
- ☐ Magazine subscription discounts
- ☐ Games
- ☐ Piano/other musical instruments
- ☐ Stereo
- ☐ Television/VCR
- ☐ Computer/word processor
- ☐ Sauna
- ☐ Radio
- ☐ Hot tub/jacuzzi
- ☐ Swimming pool/pond
- ☐ Suntan lotion/sunscreen
- ☐ Insect repellent
- ☐ Hand cream
- ☐ Shaving cream
- ☐ Shampoo
- ☐ Hair conditioner
- ☐ Toothpaste
- ☐ Toothbrushes
- ☐ Disposable razors
- ☐ Bath salts
- ☐ Scented soaps/bubble bath
- ☐ Cotton swabs
- ☐ Disposable shower caps
- ☐ Small packets of common cold/hay fever remedies in medicine cabinet
- ☐ Pin cushion with needles/thread/safety pins
- ☐ Hair dryer
- ☐ Curling iron
- ☐ Make-up mirror
- ☐ Iron and ironing board
- ☐ Laundry privileges/service
- ☐ Arrange tickets to events
- ☐ Store luggage
- ☐ Beach badges
- ☐ Beach umbrellas/towels
- ☐ Sunglasses/straw hats
- ☐ Umbrellas/slickers
- ☐ Earmuffs/hand warmers
- ☐ Robes
- ☐ Slippers/socks
- ☐ Sports/recreational equipment:
  - ☐ Telescope

- ☐ Fishing poles
- ☐ Binoculars
- ☐ Golf clubs
- ☐ Volleyball and net
- ☐ Tennis/badminton racquets
- ☐ Sleds/toboggans
- ☐ Surfboards
- ☐ Water skis
- ☐ Snow skis
- ☐ Canoe/boat
- ☐ Bicycles
- ☐ Weights/exercise equipment
- ☐ Use of membership in clubs/museums/libraries/gym
- ☐ Sailing/boating excursion
- ☐ Fishing/lobstering excursion
- ☐ Horseback riding
- ☐ Hay rides
- ☐ Hiking/jogging trails
- ☐ Typing/secretarial services
- ☐ Foreign-language translation; interpreter services
- ☐ Farm animals
- ☐ Note paper/envelopes and pen

Pricing your bed and breakfast

How much should you charge your guests? "There is no strict answer to this question other than to say, 'Be sensible,' " says Peg Tierney, manager of a reservation service organization called Bed & Breakfast of Maine. Being sensible means not charging too much or too little. Following are guidelines that will help you price your bed and breakfast. (If you list your B&B with a reservation service organization, the price is usually reached by compromise between the individual host and the agency.)

First, try to categorize your rooms according to the following classifications based on double occupancy. (A single room should be priced at 10 to 20 percent less than a double.)

Modest: Rooms are clean and comfortable, with no frills. ($30–$40)

Average: Rooms are pleasant. There are a few amenities. ($40–$60)

Above Average: Rooms are tastefully furnished. Some amenities are included. ($60–$80)

Luxury: Extraordinary accommodations in a good location. Outstanding aesthetic features. Some amenities are included. ($80–$130)

Whether your bed and breakfast rooms should be at the low end or the high end of the suggested price range in your category depends in part on the amenities that you make available to your guests. It is best to adjust the price of the room to include the cost of providing the amenities that will be enjoyed by the majority of your guests. True, some guests will not watch the television in their bedroom, and some won't care to ride the bicycle you provide. But for those who do, you can make them feel a lot more comfortable by making these amenities part of the whole package deal. (Charging a separate fee for each typical amenity could make your guests feel as if they're on the meter every time they make a move to enjoy what your B&B has to offer.)

Following is a list of typical amenities that should be included in the overall room price. (Also check the section "Amenities" in this chapter.) For each of the items listed here, add $.50 to $3 to the lowest base price given in your category. So if you chose "Average" as the classification for your bed and breakfast, your base price would be $40. To this amount, you would add $3 if your home is right near the beach, and $1 if you have a small deck where guests may sit. This makes your total price $44. (Any room that has a private bath can be adjusted in price for an additional $10.)

King- or queen-sized bed
Waterbed
Scenic view
Spa/hot tub/sauna
Near beach
Swimming pool or pond
Fireplace
Horseback riding
Telephone in room
Tennis court
Ice skating/skiing nearby
Hiking/nature walks
Shopping and restaurants nearby
Guest refrigerator
Sitting room

If your bed and breakfast offers extras that are above and beyond the typical amenities, you should charge for these separately. Some hosts arrange and conduct tours, hay rides, horse and buggy rides, and sleigh rides for an additional fee. Some hosts allow guests to use the washer and dryer for their personal laundry. Others offer to babysit for guests' children. And still others rent out sports equipment (skates, skis). Then there are those hosts who offer to put their own special skills to work for guests (such as typing, word processing, foreign language translation). All of these are services that go beyond what a guest normally expects in a bed and breakfast situation. Because many of your guests will not want babysitting services or word processing, these types of unusual amenities should not be included in the room price.

For your overall room price, there are times when the rate should be adjusted: a third adult staying in the same room on a cot or sleeping bag (usually $10 extra); a child under twelve years of age staying in the same room with parents ($5 to $10 extra); a pet ($5 extra). If your bed and breakfast is located in a resort area, your off-season rates should be lowered 20 to 25 percent. And hosts usually add a surcharge ($10) for a guest who is staying one night only.

Now you should have an approximate amount calculated for your guest rooms. The next thing you should do is compare your prices with those of area hotels and motels. "We suggest to hosts that local budget-motel prices are a good starting point to determine rates," says Gary Winget, owner of Bed & Breakfast Registry in Minnesota. A survey of hosts and reservation service organizations throughout North America shows that an overwhelming majority of B&B accommodations cost less than the hotels and motels near them. So if you find that the estimated prices you have just come up with exceed what commercial establishments near you are charging, you are probably asking too much and need to rework your prices.

It's also wise to take a look at what other bed and breakfast hosts in your location charge and compare your estimated prices with the national average. If your prices are more the exception than the rule, you should have very good reasons to justify them. Before guests make reservations at a bed and breakfast, they usually shop around to see what's available for the best price. That is only good sense. If your prices seem too high, or even too low, you can expect that they will wonder why. And you'd better have some good answers.

Coming up with the right price is never an easy task because it depends on such a variety of factors. Some new hosts tend to price their rooms too low. "My bit of advice to new hosts is to make your fee high enough to cover the service you give," says an experienced host from West Virginia. "I did not. I started too low and gave so much. Our house is one of West Virginia's grand old houses, and my guests walk on my oriental rugs and use my best china, crystal, and silver. I serve a good, big home-cooked breakfast. Not only do they have my house, but 225 acres to wander over with my ducks, cats, dogs, and cows to feed, my garden to enjoy. They can also fish in my two ponds." After a time, she adjusted her prices to better reflect the quality of accommodation her guests were receiving.

Peg Tierney offers new hosts this advice for pricing their rooms: "Don't charge so much as to shut yourself out of any business. But don't charge so little that you are giving away your time and effort." After all the calculations are done, this is the best test of your prices.

4
Getting Connected

Reservation service organizations

"Join an RSO." This advice comes from a host registered with Bed & Breakfast Center City, a reservation service organization in Philadelphia. "I could not have started without it," she says.

It's good advice. For new hosts, getting connected with a local or national reservation service organization has enormous advantages. RSO personnel have the experience, know-how, and resources to help new hosts set up and run their bed and breakfast homes. Most local RSOs do practically all of the nitty-gritty work that an individual host would have to do if he or she were to go it alone. As the owner of Cherry Valley Ventures, an RSO in LaFayette, New York, puts it: The reservation service organization takes care of "everything that is necessary except hosting the guest."

The primary function of a reservation service organization is just what the name indicates—it's an agency that makes reservations for guests in bed and breakfast homes. A host pays a membership fee (usually), plus a commission to the RSO for each guest referred through the service. Some RSOs represent hosts in a particular city or town exclusively; some are statewide; others are regional, covering a certain area of a state or several neighboring states; and a few are national. There are even some with contacts in other countries. As a new host, you will find that one of your biggest problems will be getting guests to come to your home. If an RSO does no more than solve this problem for you, it's still worth the amount that you pay the agency, especially in the early stages when your bed and breakfast is essentially unknown. Beyond the very valuable service of connecting guests with your B&B, an RSO generally offers other kinds of assistance that is helpful to both new and experienced hosts.

"We handle all the bothersome details," says the manager of Folkstone Bed & Breakfast, an RSO located in Boylston, Massachusetts. These include confirmations and deposits, plus local, regional, and national advertising. "Descriptions and directions and requirements are forwarded to guests without troubling the hosts," says the manager of Covered Bridge Bed and Breakfast in West Cornwall, Connecticut. "Hosts don't have to do the telephone and administrative work of arranging reservations," says the manager of Bed & Breakfast in Marblehead and the North Shore, an RSO in Massachusetts. "We do all the paperwork for them and supply them with receipts, booklets, pamphlets, etcetera," says the manager of Bed & Breakfast Center City in Philadelphia. "Hosts have the advantage of our careful screening and ability to match guests with hosts," say the managers of Bed & Breakfast of Tidewater, Virginia. The manager of Bed & Breakfast Rochester cites anonymity as a major advantage to hosts who wish to protect their privacy; RSOs will give out a host's home address and telephone number only when a reservation is confirmed. The list goes on. A good reservation service organization can make the life of a host much, much easier.

So if an RSO is the answer to your prayers, you might be wondering why some hosts choose to stay independent. They give different reasons. "We believe that guests should have direct access to B&Bs, as they do in Europe," say a couple of independent hosts from New England. They'd like to see the day when B&B hosts can just put a sign in the window, as you often see in Europe, so that guests can stop at whatever B&B strikes their fancy. Some hosts have the time, the desire, and the know-how to do all the work themselves; they enjoy being totally self-reliant. Some hosts are located in areas where no local reservation service organization yet exists. (When asked if she lists with an RSO, one very successful independent host in a rural area said, "What's an RSO?") And some hosts are reluctant to list with an RSO because their prices are so low already that once they deduct the percentage that goes to the RSO for a commission for placing each guest and then deduct their expenses, there's just not much left.

So yes, a host can survive, even thrive, without ever connecting with an RSO. The question is: What's best for you? Are you willing and able to answer all the inquiries you will be receiving by telephone and through the mail (including those that do not result in reservations), to print and distribute your own brochures, to do your own advertising, to handle the screening of guests yourself, to send out confirmations? Some hosts just don't have the time, energy, and skill to take care of all these details, and some honestly do not enjoy these aspects of bed and breakfast, although they love the actual hosting. Consider your own situation, your likes and dislikes, your skills. Do you want and need some help? If so, take the time to contact the national reservation service organizations for more information, and investigate local RSOs to see what they could do for you. Consult the listing of reservation service organizations in the appendix to locate those near you. The RSOs that have indicated an interest in increasing their number of hosts are noted. Be aware that an RSO in your area might not be looking for new hosts in your particular location. This is due mainly to the law of supply and demand. If there are not enough hosts in a certain location to meet the demand from prospective guests for lodging there, then the RSO manager will look for more hosts. But if there are too many hosts, and not many guests, then the referrals from the RSO will be spread among them. For this reason, some RSO managers try to maintain an optimum number of hosts to make the referral system work to the hosts' advantage.

There could be more than one RSO in your area. Check them all out according to the guidelines given in the following section. Talk with the manager, get the literature, ask a lot of questions about how the RSO operates, and then make the decision that's best for your bed and breakfast.

What assistance does the RSO offer new hosts?

Someone who is just starting out as a host needs advice about how to do it. The manager of a local RSO will usually come to your home to see if it has the right kind of set-up for accommodating guests, and he or she will talk to you about bed and breakfast hosting. If you pass the initial inspection and interview to the RSO's satisfaction, and your home is located in an area where it will attract guests, then the RSO will be interested in listing your home. What you need to know is what kind of help you can expect from the RSO to get ready for that first guest. At the very least, the RSO will provide you with a listing of the standards you are expected to meet and the guidelines you are expected to follow. Some RSOs, however, provide more than this.

"We offer one-on-one training, a beginner's manual on hosting, and Monday-through-Friday office hours for new hosts to call with questions," says Arline Kardasis, co-owner of Bed and Breakfast Associates Bay Colony, an RSO in Boston. Ken Mendis of Bed & Breakfast of Rhode Island says, "For a small fee we teach a course on how to start your own B&B business. We also provide free information on guests' expectations, income potential, decorating ideas, and breakfasts needs." Irmgard Castleberry, manager of Pacific Bed & Breakfast in the state of Washington, offers "an initial two- to three-hour session for training, then ongoing help and assistance, including copies of books on hosting." A number of RSOs, in fact, have developed their own booklets or host packets on how to be a host. These are given out to their new hosts, for example, by Bed & Breakfast Rocky Mountains, Kingston Area Bed & Breakfast in Ontario, Rest & Repast in Pennsylvania, Bed & Breakfast International in California, and Carolyn's Bed & Breakfast Homes in San Diego.

The manager of Bed & Breakfast Center City likes to give new hosts a good example. "First, I show them my B&B," she says, then she spends time with them discussing how to turn their own home into what a B&B should be. If you wish, an RSO manager will usually give suggestions for making your guest rooms more comfortable and attractive and will offer opinions about decorating, both minor and extensive. "I have just signed on a couple who have just poured their foundation, and we worked out their B&B from blueprints!" says the manager of Orleans Bed & Breakfast Associates in Massachusetts.

To help new hosts get ready to handle different types of situations that they can expect to encounter with their guests, Orleans Bed & Breakfast Associates and The Bed & Breakfast Society of Houston both arrange role-plays so that hosts can practice typical scenarios. Then when it's time for the real thing, they're ready. Ellie Welch Ramsey, founder of Bed and Breakfast Brookline/Boston, has even been asked by a new host to be at her home when she greeted her very first guest. "She was nervous about it," she says. Having a representative of the RSO with her made the first time easier.

New hosts also need to be apprised of the local regulations governing zoning and fire and safety guidelines, as well as tax and insurance information. A reservation service organization has already had to investigate these, so the agency can give you the guidance you need to have in order to operate a bed and breakfast home in your community.

What kind of ongoing assistance does the RSO provide?

There are some responsibilities that automatically go along with the RSO's job of making reservations for guests at its bed and breakfast homes. These include answering telephone and mail inquiries, screening and matching guests with hosts (see "Screening Your Guests" in Chapter 6), mailing out confirmations to guests who make reservations, and promoting bed and breakfast through the distribution of brochures and advertising.

You should expect these services, done well, from any reservation service organization that you choose to join. It's not unusual, though, for an RSO manager to go above and beyond the call of duty. The Bed & Breakfast Society of Houston, for example, sends regular newsletters and reprints of helpful information to its hosts. Bed & Breakfast Rochester helps hosts with recordkeeping and tax preparation and supplies year-end cumulative records of reservations. Nutmeg Bed & Breakfast in Connecticut offers "listening, guidance, and sympathy" to hosts who need to talk about a problem. And the owner of Blue Ridge Bed & Breakfast in Virginia says that she's even helped a host clean at the last minute to get ready for a guest!

The "extras" that a host will receive from an RSO really depend upon the person who is running it, determined by that person's strengths and total time commitment to RSO activities. Where these extra benefits are concerned, there can be wide differences among RSOs. So do not expect them, but feel lucky if you find that your RSO manager is the kind of person who can, and will, go beyond the basics needed for your bed and breakfast business.

How does the RSO publicize its services to potential guests?

For an individual host, one of the main advantages of joining a reservation service organization is that the agency takes the responsibility for drumming up business. While the individual host remains comfortably anonymous, the RSO reaches out to the public in search of potential guests, doing all of the work and bearing all of the expense.

If you are considering joining an RSO, take a look at the available bed and breakfast guidebooks to see if the RSO is listed in them, with the correct address and telephone number. Many people looking for a bed and breakfast use guidebooks as a source of information. An RSO manager has to be conscientious about supplying the authors with all the necessary up-to-date information for each new edition. (Otherwise, an RSO could be listed with an out-of-date address or phone number, or not included at all.) A new RSO, especially, has to make sure that the information gets into the right hands at the right time. If your area RSO is listed in a selection of guidebooks, you can be assured that prospective guests will be able to find and contact the RSO easily—and your bed and breakfast, in turn, will benefit.

Check the Yellow Pages of your phone book under the section headed "Bed and Breakfast" to see if the reservation service organization is listed there. Inclusion makes the RSO readily accessible to people seeking a bed and breakfast. (Be aware, though, that some RSOs choose not to list themselves in the Yellow Pages because they want to discourage calls from last-minute travelers who arrive in town and go to the nearest phone booth with change in their hand. It is difficult to screen people who do not make advance reservations, so this is done for your safety.)

The literature that the reservation service organization prints and distributes will be representing your bed and breakfast home, so examine it closely. Does the RSO have a brochure that is attractive and professional? Is the artwork appealing, well executed, and appropriate? Is the information easy to read and to understand? Are the name, address, and telephone number of the RSO printed clearly, with office hours included? Does the brochure explain how to make a reservation?

Find out where the RSO distributes its brochures beyond mailing them out to people who inquire directly about bed and breakfast accommodations. Bed & Breakfast of Tidewater, Virginia, for example, supplies brochures to all Welcome Centers run by the state of Virginia. Southern Comfort Bed & Breakfast in Baton Rouge, Louisiana, makes special rack cards to be placed in the literature display racks located at all the state Visitors Information Centers. Bed & Breakfast Atlanta reaches out to local institutions, businesses, and special-events coordinators.

Ask the RSO manager where the agency places advertisements to let travelers know that bed and breakfast accommodations are available in the area. Bed & Breakfast Down East, for example, advertises in magazines and travel guides that focus on the state of Maine, such as *Yankee Travel Guide to New England* and *Down East* magazine. Five Pennsylvania RSOs advertise jointly in such publications of national interest as *Better Homes & Gardens*, the *Christian Science Monitor*, the *New York Times*, and *Country Magazine*. The managers of one of these RSOs, called Rest & Repast, have found it worthwhile to advertise in publications directed to Penn State University alumni and parents because so many of its host homes are located near Penn State. Such specific advertising that targets the travelers who come to your area frequently can be very effective.

A lot of great publicity comes not from paid advertisements but from articles written about bed and breakfast. Does the RSO make it a point to get in touch with writers for local and national publications to try to interest them in doing a story about bed and breakfast? "Say yes if we ask you to give a travel writer a free night," Cherry Valley Ventures in LaFayette, New York, tells its hosts. Outreach to the press should be part of the promotion plan undertaken by any RSO.

It makes sense that the publicity done by your reservation service organization will affect the number of guests that your bed and breakfast will receive. If the RSO's overall promotion and publicity are good, a host who decides to list with the RSO will be at a definite advantage.

Is the RSO affiliated with any organizations?

Just as an individual host can benefit from joining together with other hosts, so can an RSO increase its effectiveness by affiliating with appropriate organizations. If you are considering joining an RSO, investigate what affiliations the RSO has that could benefit your bed and breakfast.

There are two organizations that are just for RSOs. One is a non-profit trade association, open to all RSOs, called Bed & Breakfast Reservation Services World-Wide (Post Office Box 14797, Department 174, Baton Rouge, Louisiana 70898). An RSO that belongs to this association is part of an important network that works together to establish and maintain high standards of cleanliness, safety, and comfort for each of its host homes. Participating members issue a Gold Medallion certificate for display by their hosts as a quality-control guarantee to the traveling public. Members also work together to solve problems that arise as the bed and breakfast industry continues to grow, and to promote the concept of bed and breakfast by education and advertising. Hosts listed with member RSOs can acquire liability insurance coverage through the association.

The other association is called Bed & Breakfast, The National Network (Post Office Box 4616, Springfield, Massachusetts 01101). This organization has criteria that members must meet to enforce high standards within the bed and breakfast industry. Like the other RSO association, The National Network is made up of members who work together to promote bed and breakfast, to maintain high standards, and to deal with problems as they arise. The main difference between the two organizations is that The National Network selects one RSO per geographical area as its representative. Hosts listed with The National Network RSOs can purchase liability insurance coverage through the organization.

Membership in the American Bed & Breakfast Association is open not only to reservation service organizations, but to individual hosts and to guests as well (16 Village Green, Suite 203, Crofton, Maryland 21114). Members of this organization receive regular newsletters from ABBA to keep them up to date on the latest developments in the bed and breakfast industry, and they are welcome to attend conferences called to discuss trends and problems. (Please note that a description of ABBA appears in "National Bed and Breakfast Groups" in this chapter.)

In addition to bed and breakfast groups, membership in the local or state tourist bureau can be extremely beneficial to a reservation service organization and the hosts it represents. Through literature and referrals, tourist bureaus will promote bed and breakfast as a way to encourage tourism in their jurisdictions. And very often, the bureau will provide maps, calendars, and sightseeing brochures free of charge or at a low cost to its members. "We are an active member of the Worcester County Convention & Visitors Bureau, and it has sent us the major portion of our business," says the owner of Folkstone Bed & Breakfast, an RSO in Boylston, Massachusetts. "It is the best investment I could have made. They provide me with all the information about the area, which I distribute to my host homes. Tourism is booming in this part of our state, and my host homes are reaping the benefits."

The chamber of commerce is also an important affiliation for a local RSO. A number of chambers are cooperating with local RSO managers to help new hosts set up their bed and breakfast homes. An RSO that becomes a member of the chamber of commerce can establish important ties in the community where the bed and breakfast homes operate.

From more guests to free maps, a new host can directly benefit from joining an RSO that is well integrated into the community and in touch with the national bed and breakfast scene. Finding out what affiliations an RSO has will tell you about the resources that agency is in a position to offer its hosts. The more an RSO networks, the better off you'll be.

Does the RSO encourage communication among its hosts?

Remember that once you join a reservation service organization, you become part of a network of bed and breakfast homes, usually sight unseen. Yet, every one of these hosts who belong to the same RSO as you do automatically affects your bed and breakfast business. It's important for you to be confident that all of your "brothers and sisters" are as conscientious about hosting as you are, working hard to keep up the standards of comfort, cleanliness, and congeniality set by the RSO. You have a reputation to maintain.

In recognition of this, more and more RSO managers are making an effort to give their hosts the opportunity to meet one another and to establish a support network among them. Some arrange "house tours," where hosts can visit one another's homes not only to get acquainted but also to compare notes and share ideas about hosting. Some RSOs organize annual get-togethers that are part business and part social. Cherry Valley Ventures in LaFayette, New York, gives awards at these events: An "Honored Host" award goes to the members who hosted one hundred nights during the previous year. The "Preferred Host Award" goes to the member who received the highest percentage of compliments from guests' letters and evaluations.

By encouraging communication among its hosts, an RSO can play an important role in developing the kind of personal commitment among them that will work to the benefit of all the members. This is the kind of RSO a new host should look for.

Does the RSO keep in touch with former guests?

Many hosts report that a large percentage of the guests who stay with them are repeat customers. Some say that up to *one-half* of their guests have visited before! This means that once your bed and breakfast has established itself, it could be largely dependent upon people who have already enjoyed your hospitality. But be warned: Your guests cannot be trusted to remember your name or your B&B's name, let alone your address and telephone number. And if they have trouble finding you again, they could end up somewhere else instead of at your B&B. To refresh their memories every once in a while, either you or your RSO has to keep in touch with former guests. (See "Memories" in chapter 7.)

Find out if the RSO has any method for communicating with former guests on a regular basis. Folkstone Bed & Breakfast in Massachusetts, for example, sends an updated host-home directory to former guests. B&B Suncoast Accommodations in St. Pete Beach, Florida, sends pictures, cards, and brochures to people who have made reservations with that RSO in the past. Greater Boston Hospitality sends a thank-you letter that also explains its "Frequent Guest Program," whereby a guest who books a total of twenty-one nights with that RSO is eligible for two free nights for two people at one of its host homes. Bed & Breakfast of Rhode Island provides a discount coupon to returning guests.

Leatherstocking Bed & Breakfast in central New York sends out notes on holidays and lets former guests know in advance about special seasonal attractions in the area. Rest & Repast in Pennsylvania places a large number of football fans in host homes near Penn State University. Many come back each year because the RSO has a follow-up plan. "Football guests who have booked at least two seasons and two games each year get a letter in December telling them that they have priority booking until March 1 for next year's football season," says Linda Feltman, co-owner of Rest & Repast. The owner of Bed & Breakfast of Southeast Pennsylvania also ties her notes in with the special interests of former guests. "If I know someone is interested in, for example, the Bach Choir, I will send information about the next time they are performing in the area," she says.

Some RSOs do not keep in touch with former guests because the cost of postage for mailings to so many people is prohibitive, or it is just too enormous a task. "As of right now, we have 10,000 names of former guests but have not been able to keep in touch with them since our time is so limited," reports one west coast RSO. This is understandable. Some RSOs rely upon their hosts to maintain communications with former guests. It is, nonetheless, an added bonus for a host to list with a reservation service organization that can, and does, follow up on guests who have made reservations through that agency sometime in the past.

What obligations does an RSO have to its hosts?

Beyond the assistance that an RSO provides to its hosts, there are a number of professional courtesies that the RSO manager should extend to the hosts as part of a good business relationship. These are outlined here by Ellen Madison, a host who grew up in a home that accommodated tourists and who is now the operator of her own bed and breakfast home in Westerly, Rhode Island, called Woody Hill Guest House.

Accessibility is at the top of the list. "RSOs should be available to their hosts as much as possible," says Ellen, "particularly in the evenings and on weekends when the need for an immediate clarification or a referral is probably the greatest. If nothing else, an answering machine should be in use and calls returned as quickly as possible."

She goes on to say that RSOs should get back to hosts as soon as possible in the event of cancellations or deposits that never arrive. If the host is not notified of a change in plans, he or she will go ahead and make all the necessary preparations for a guest's arrival—cleaning the house, clearing the schedule, and buying food. For an RSO to let the host know at the last minute that no one is coming doesn't mean much when you've got a refrigerator full of honeydew melon. Now you've either got to eat it or let it go to waste. ("And honeydew melon for a week is very boring," Ellen says.)

Ellen advises RSOs to be aware of their hosts' financial situations when determining their rates. "They should be aware of the costs to a host for operating a B&B, which will be different depending on all sorts of conditions—whether the host is single or married, whether he or she is trying to earn a living by operating a B&B, how much investment the host had to make initially." Room rates that are too low might not cover a host's costs; and a commission that is too high might take away the possibility of making a profit. And, too, if payment in full is made directly to the RSO, prompt remittance to the host is in order.

It is only fair to mention that there have been a few (and thankfully only a few) complaints about certain reservation service organizations because they did not pay the host promptly, they did not remit the total amount due, or the check issued by the RSO manager bounced. One of these RSOs is now out of business, and, fortunately, there are guidelines set by both the national RSO associations that their members are expected to follow. As a host, you should insist upon the professional treatment due to you by your reservation service organization and report any problems to the associations that the RSO is affiliated with. On the whole, RSOs operate efficiently and to the benefit of the hosts they represent. We can expect that they will stay that way if people involved in the bed and breakfast industry continue to safeguard the high standards that have been set.

What obligations does a host have to his or her RSO?

Just as you can expect professional courtesies from your RSO, so should the RSO be able to expect certain courtesies from you as one of its hosts, beyond your responsibility to maintain the standards set by the RSO for comfort, cleanliness, and congeniality.

Again, accessibility is very important. You must either be reachable by phone during the RSO's business hours or have an answering machine and respond to your messages promptly. Remember that most RSOs will check with a host first before confirming a reservation. This means that a prospective guest is usually waiting to hear by a return phone call whether the bed and breakfast home he or she wants is available. If a definite answer is too long in coming, there's nothing to stop the person from making a few more calls to other places to try to confirm a reservation.

If you list with an RSO, the agency will expect your bed and breakfast to be available for guests unless there is an emergency situation or if you are scheduled to be out of town for a vacation or another reason. "If a host is almost never in, or turns down a request to take guests too often (we keep records), we tend to call hosts who are reachable and who will take guests even though it may be an inconvenience," says the owner of Kingston Area Bed & Breakfast in Ontario. "If their personal life is not to be interfered with—such as on long holidays, or when personal guests or family members are home (the list goes on)—I ask the hosts if there is any point in continuing to offer B&B on a whenever-it-suits-me basis." If you really want to be a host, you can't take your responsibility lightly. An RSO may drop you in favor of hosts who are more reliable.

Being organized is almost as important as being accessible. "Keep a good calendar," advises Arline Kardasis, co-owner of Bed & Breakfast Associates Bay Colony, an RSO in Boston. If you've booked guests, you've got to remember that they're coming, and you've got to be careful not to double-book your rooms! If you're disorganized, get organized fast or you're in for problems, and so is your RSO.

One of the major concerns of many RSO managers is the fact that some of their hosts try to go around the agency when former guests want to stay at their homes again. Sometimes a guest will contact the host directly because he or she happens to have the name and address handy and feels like an old friend. The host, in turn, tries to keep the arrangement a secret from the RSO so that he or she can avoid paying the commission. This is unprofessional behavior that undercuts the very structure within the bed and breakfast industry that allows individual hosts a measure of the privacy and protection they want and need. So if a former guest contacts you directly, do the right thing: Contact the RSO that originally processed the reservation and route the guest through the procedure that you and the RSO have agreed upon.

Does the RSO require a host contract?

You can expect that any RSO that you wish to list your bed and breakfast home with will ask you to sign a host contract that outlines certain obligations on your part and explains the services that the RSO will provide to you.

The content of the agreement varies from RSO to RSO. Some stipulate that a host must list with that agency exclusively, ruling out referrals from any other agency. Other RSOs have no such stipulation, and hosts are free to list with more than one RSO if they wish and to do as much independent business as they feel like. The ones that require an exclusive arrangement have their reasons. According to Jean Brown, the director of an RSO in San Francisco called Bed & Breakfast International, one of the main reasons is that the RSO needs to be almost certain that a room is available before taking the time, the trouble, and the expense to describe it to a potential guest, interesting the person in one particular bed and breakfast, only to find that the reservation is refused by the host. Then it's back to square one—more time, more trouble, more expense. For this reason, RSOs generally prefer that a host list with them exclusively even if the host contract does not require it.

Other items that a host contract usually covers are the membership fee and the commission to be paid to the RSO, the procedure for handling reservations and confirmations, deposit and cancellation policies, and the duration of the agreement and renewal and termination procedures—as well as any other items that might be desired by the RSO, such as insurance requirements for individual hosts or the right of the RSO to make periodic inspections of its host homes.

What fee is paid to the RSO for its services?

You can't get something for nothing, of course. If you wish to take advantage of the services that a reservation service organization will provide for your bed and breakfast, you must support the effort. Most RSOs have a payment structure that involves, first, a membership fee, and second, a commission for each guest that the agency places with a host. Fees vary. Some RSOs have no membership fee at all; others charge between \$25 and \$100, with the average somewhere around \$75. The commission is usually between 20 and 35 percent of a guest's total bill.

Fees collected by a reservation service organization from its hosts go to pay for advertising costs; telephone expenses; printing and copying literature; postage; any city, county, or state licenses that might be necessary; professional fees for membership in tourist bureaus, the chamber of commerce, and bed and breakfast organizations; and, of course, the time the manager spends on the work. There are long hours. "My phone rings until 11:00 at night," says Mary Chapman, manager of Orleans Bed & Breakfast Associates in Massachusetts. Her experience is not unusual, if one is to judge from reports from RSO managers throughout North America.

And more than one RSO manager has pointed out the low profit margin from their activities on behalf of hosts. This is because of the relatively low fees charged hosts and the high expenses that the RSO has. Be aware that many RSO managers are also bed and breakfast hosts who established RSOs in their areas because they saw a need for it. "My B&B room supports my RSO business or I'd be out of business," says the owner of a Florida RSO. So before you balk at paying a membership fee and commissions to an RSO, consider how much it would cost you otherwise if you were to take care of all the advertising, mailing, printing, and telephone bills yourself. In the vast majority of cases, the fee structure is quite a bargain for what your bed and breakfast will receive in return.

Special-focus B&B groups

One way to attract larger numbers of guests to your bed and breakfast is to reach out to people who share your special interests. Already a number of reservation service organizations and specialized programs have been established for the purpose of providing bed and breakfast accommodations to people who have a common interest. Some are national organizations; others are regional. Some advertise widely; some publicize exclusively among their own memberships. Listed in this section are some of the bed and breakfast organizations that have a special focus. If you believe that your background, interests, or affiliations qualify you for listing your bed and breakfast with any of these, write or call for more information.

After checking this list, it's a good idea to set out on your own trail of discovery for others. Check with any social or professional group to which you belong to learn if it might already have a bed and breakfast program for its members. (If not, you could take the initiative to organize one.)

It is important to note that B&B groups of this type generally operate according to the true bed and breakfast spirit—in which money is not of the utmost importance. You can expect that any fee that you receive as a result of affiliating with a special-focus bed and breakfast organization will be minimal. The value for you lies in the good will that you will have the opportunity to establish among a number of people, as well as the good word that will spread about your bed and breakfast as a result.

Hosts who are, or were, teachers, or who have some other type of connection with the teaching field, should investigate the following organizations, which coordinate bed and breakfast for people involved in this profession:

Educators Inn
Post Office Box 603
Lynnfield, Massachusetts 01940
(617) 334-6144

Educators' Vacation Alternatives
317 Piedmont Road
Santa Barbara, California 93105
(805) 687-2947

Teacher's Co-Op Travel Club
Post Office Box 729
Windsor, California 95492
(no phone)

University Bed & Breakfast
12 Churchill Street
Brookline, Massachusetts 02146
(617) 738-1424

Boston Bed & Breakfast
16 Ballard Street
Newton Center, Massachusetts 02159
(617) 332-4199

If your bed and breakfast home is located in an area that draws visitors who love winter sports, contact:

B&B Ski America & Canada
Post Office Box 5246
Incline Village, Nevada 89450
(702) 831-5350

Skiers Bed & Breakfast
Bed & Breakfast Rocky Mountains
P.O. Box 804
Colorado Springs, Colorado 80901
(719) 630-3433

Hosts who have homes that are listed on the National Historic Register or that have other historical significance should find out about listing their landmark homes with this organization:

American Historic Homes
Post Office Box 336
Dana Point, California 92629
(714) 496-7050

Active, retired, or reserve military personnel can get involved in hosting other members of the military and their families. The RSO listed below coordinates host homes in Virginia, Maryland, Florida, and Washington, D.C.

Commissioned Host & Toast
Post Office Box 2177
Springfield, Virginia 22152
(703) 678-5858

A bed and breakfast agency for gays (nongays are welcome) is:

Bay Hosts
1155 Bosworth Street
San Francisco, California 94131
(415) 337-9632

Hosts who are fifty years of age or older may join a membership club that provides bed and breakfast accommodations for this age group:

The Evergreen B&B Club
c/o American Bed & Breakfast Association
16 Village Green, Suite 203
Crofton, Maryland 21114
(301) 261–0180

The organization listed below is also a membership organization devoted to sharing travel advice. Among the services it offers its members is the opportunity to participate in a bed and breakfast program. Please note that it is not a money-making enterprise for participants, but rather a benefit of T.I.E. membership.

T.I.E. Bed & Breakfast Exchange
Traveler's Information Exchange
356 Boylston Street
Boston, Massachusetts 02116
(617) 536–5651

Some bed and breakfast groups were founded in the spirit of brotherhood and sisterhood. Of these, two serve the Christian community, one is a network of the Reformed Church in America (RCA Bed & Breakfast), one was started within the Unitarian Church but is open to anyone who considers himself or herself a humanist (Homecomings), and one is a worldwide organization that is nonprofit and interfaith (Servas).

Christian Hospitality Bed & Breakfast
636 Union Street
Duxbury, Massachusetts 02332
(617) 834–8528

Christian Bed & Breakfast
Post Office Box 388
San Juan Capistrano, California 92693
(714) 496–7050

RCA Bed & Breakfast Publications
3975 Cascade Road, S.E.
Grand Rapids, Michigan 49506
(no phone)

Homecomings
Post Office Box 1545
New Milford, Connecticut 06776
(no phone)

Servas
U.S. Servas Committee
11 John Street, Room 406
New York, New York 10038
(212) 267–0252

Some alumni organizations affiliated with different colleges or universities, or national sororities and fraternities, arrange bed and breakfast programs among their members. Check with any affiliations you might have in these areas to see if there are bed and breakfast programs in existence. And some members of the League of Women Voters will act as hosts for members of this organization; call your local chapter to obtain more information.

National bed and breakfast groups

New hosts can benefit considerably by connecting with one or more of the national bed and breakfast groups that are in existence. All enjoy high visibility, drawing consistent attention from the media. The guidebooks and directories published by these organizations are marketed to prospective guests to help them find the kind of bed and breakfast accommodations they are seeking. As a member, your host home would be included in these well-known publications, enabling you to easily reach thousands of potential guests. In addition, you can expect to receive updates on developments in the bed and breakfast industry that could affect you. The four national bed and breakfast groups are listed here.

The American Bed & Breakfast Association

The American Bed & Breakfast Association serves as a clearinghouse for information on bed and breakfast in North America. Its purpose is to promote and extend the concept of bed and breakfast by providing an efficient source of information needed by prospective guests and by coordinating communications among those engaged in bed and breakfast activities. Members are listed in the national directory and regional guidebooks. Members also receive a newsletter, are eligible to participate in selected joint advertising, and may order bed and breakfast–related books at a discount. Memberships are available to guests and reservation service organizations, as well as to individual hosts. For information and a membership application, contact:

The American Bed & Breakfast Association
16 Village Green, Suite 203
Crofton, Maryland 21114
(301) 261–0180

The National Bed & Breakfast Association

The National Bed & Breakfast Association is a network of privately owned bed and breakfast homes and small family-run and/or -operated inns spanning the United States, Canada, Bermuda, Puerto Rico, and U.S. Virgin Islands. "We give free referrals to any traveler who calls or writes us to any of our listed members," says President Phyllis Featherston. Members are listed in the organization's guidebook, *The Bed & Breakfast Guide for the U.S. and Canada*. For information and a membership application, contact:

The National Bed & Breakfast Association
Post Office Box 332
Norwalk, Connecticut 06852
(203) 847-6196

Tourist House Association of America

As a member of the Tourist House Association of America, you have the opportunity to list and describe your bed and breakfast home in the book published yearly by this organization, *Bed & Breakfast U.S.A.* According to the director, Betty Rundback, "Your bed and breakfast listing will also be available, through our auspices, to the United States Department of Travel (a division of the U.S. Chamber of Commerce), which maintains offices in principal cities throughout the world. As a result of their using *Bed & Breakfast U.S.A.* as a reference to our accommodations, you can expect to receive reservations on an international scale." The organization also publishes a newsletter that serves as an idea exchange among members and offers group liability insurance. (See "Insurance" in Chapter 9.) For information and a membership application, contact:

Tourist House Association of America
R.D. 2, Box 355A
Greentown, Pennsylvania 18426
(717) 857-0856

Inn Reference

Inn Reference is not an association in the same sense as the other organizations described above. Rather, it functions as a referral service for guests seeking accommodations anywhere in the U.S. It works like this: A guest calls the Inn Reference 800 number, an Inn Reference staff member consults the computer listing for the desired location, the referral is made, and the guest takes it from there. (Inn Reference does not make reservations for the guest.) For an annual fee, you can list your bed and breakfast home with this service. Contact:

Inn Reference
211 Woodward Avenue
Sausalito, California 94965
(800) 442-8844
In California (415) 332-7147

Regional bed and breakfast groups

More and more bed and breakfast hosts and innkeepers are joining together to form regional associations for mutual benefit and support, to set guidelines for bed and breakfast operations, to share ideas and solve problems, to act as a lobbying force when necessary, and to increase community awareness of bed and breakfast. Some groups participate in group buying to purchase items at bulk rates (such as paper towels, soap, and sheets), as well as in group advertising in newspapers and magazines. Some will provide a speaker, slides, or materials for a workshop.

Listed here are some of the regional organizations that have been established. If one exists in your area, find out its criteria for membership, how it operates, and its possible benefits to you as a host. Some regional groups restrict membership to those hosts whose bed and breakfast operations qualify as full-time commercial "businesses"; others welcome membership from both owners of small commercial inns, as well as hosts who use only one or two rooms in their private homes for bed and breakfast. A few limit their membership to bed and breakfast homes that share a unique characteristic, such as historic homes.

California

Association of Bed & Breakfast Innkeepers of San Francisco
737 Buena Vista West
San Francisco, California 94117
(415) 861-3008

Bed & Breakfast Association of Napa Valley
Post Office Box 5059
Napa, California 94581
(707) 257-7757

Bed & Breakfast Innkeepers Guild of Santa Barbara
Post Office Box 20246
Santa Barbara, California 93120
(no phone)

Bed & Breakfast Innkeepers of Northern California
2030 Union Street
Suite 310
San Francisco, California 94123
(415) 563–INNS

Bed & Breakfast Innkeepers of Southern California
Post Office Box 15385
Los Angeles, California 90015–0385
(no phone)

Bed & Breakfast Inns of Amador County
215 Court Street
Jackson, California 95642
(209) 223–0416

Bed & Breakfast Inns of Humboldt County
Post Office Box 40
Ferndale, California 95536
(707) 786–4000

Bed & Breakfast Inns of Gold Country
Post Office Box 462
Sonora, California 95370
(916) 626–6136

Bed and Breakfast Innkeepers of Santa Cruz County
Post Office Box 464
Santa Cruz, California 95061–0464
(408) 425–1818

Historic Country Inns of the Mother Lode
Post Office Box 1849
Placerville, California 95667
(916) 626–5840

The Inns of Point Reyes
Post Office Box 145
Inverness, California 94937
(415) 663–1420

Inns of the Central Sierra
Post Office Box 462
Sonora, California 95370
(209) 533–3445

Mendocino Coast Innkeepers Association
Post Office Box 128
Westport, California 95488
(707) 964–2931

Monterey Peninsula Bed & Breakfast Association
598 Laine Street
Monterey, California 93940
(408) 372–4777

Sacramento Innkeepers Association
2209 Capitol Avenue
Sacramento, California 95816
(916) 441–3214

Wine Country Inns of Sonoma County
Post Office Box 51
Geyserville, California 95441
(707) 433-INNS

Connecticut

Bed and Breakfast Inns of Connecticut
c/o Fowler House
Post Office Box 432
Moodus, Connecticut 06469
(203) 873-8906

Maine

Maine Innkeepers Association
142 Free Street LL
Portland, Maine 04101
(no phone)

Massachusetts

Hampshire Hills B&B Association
Box 307
Williamsburg, Massachusetts 01096
(no phone)

Association of Massachusetts Bed & Breakfast Reservation Services
P.O. Box 1312
Orleans, Massachusetts 02653
(508) 255-3824

New Hampshire

Traditional Bed & Breakfast Association of New Hampshire
Post Office Box 6104
Lakeport, New Hampshire 03246
(no phone)

New Jersey

Bed & Breakfast Association of the Delaware River Valley
(see Pennsylvania)

New York

Finger Lakes Bed & Breakfast Association
c/o Sherry Roseman
Rose Inn
Post Office Box 6576
Ithaca, New York 14851
(607) 533-4202

Bed & Breakfast Association of Western New York and Northwestern Pennsylvania
Post Office Box 1059
Sinclairville, New York 14782
(no phone)

Pennsylvania

Bed & Breakfast Association of the Delaware River Valley
c/o Bucks County Tourist Commission
125 Swamp Road
Doylestown, Pennsylvania 18901
(215) 345-4552

Bed & Breakfast Association of Western New York and Northwestern Pennsylvania
(see New York)

Rhode Island

Guest House Association of Newport
Post Office Box 981
Newport, Rhode Island 02840
(401) 846-5444

Washington
Washington Bed & Breakfast Guild
2442 NW Market Street, #355
Seattle, Washington 98107
(no phone)

Leavenworth Country Inns & Recreation Association
Post Office Box 417
Leavenworth, Washington 98826
(800) 57APPLE

Seattle Bed & Breakfast Association
c/o Kate McDill
Chambered Nautilus B&B
5005 22nd Avenue NE
Seattle, Washington 98105
(206) 522-2536

Whidbey Island Bed & Breakfast Association
Post Office Box 259
Langley, Washington 98260
(206) 678-3115

Canada
London and Area Bed & Breakfast Association
c/o Serena Warren
720 Headley Drive
London, Ontario N6H 3V6
(519) 471-6228

The Helping Hands network

"I had a lot of trouble getting started. It was hard to get information, and there was no one to talk to," says one host about her experience in trying to set up a bed and breakfast home. This is not uncommon. There are resources out there, but you have to know where to look. Once you connect with a reservation service organization, you can rely upon the RSO for information and guidance. But maybe there is no RSO in your area. Or maybe you're just beginning to begin to think about the idea of hosting. Where can you turn if you just want to ask a simple question? What if you want someone's honest opinion about the advantages of getting involved with a reservation service organization? What if you want to find out if joining a tourist bureau or chamber of commerce has paid off in guests for anyone else before you go ahead and do it? What if you want to quietly investigate local rules and regulations concerning home-based businesses and don't know how to go about it? One of your best sources of information is another host, someone who has already done what you're about to do. But you don't know any. You feel as if you're out there all alone. Take heart: As of now, you're not.

The need that new hosts feel to talk to someone experienced with bed and breakfast was the inspiration for Helping Hands. This is an informal network of hosts across the United States who are willing to answer questions from new hosts and give advice, based on their personal experience, on setting up and operating a bed and breakfast home. In addition, they constitute a nationwide publicity network to help spread the word to guests about others' bed and breakfast accommodations. (See chapter 5, "Publicizing Your Bed and Breakfast.")

When the research for this book was being conducted, the call went out for hosts who wanted to get involved in the new Helping Hands network. The result: More than sixty individual hosts in more than twenty-five states came forward (and the list continues to grow). They represent a good cross-section of people who are part of the bed and breakfast industry in this country. There are hosts who run their bed and breakfast homes independently, without the assistance of a reservation service organization; there are hosts who accept guests through an RSO only; there are hosts who do both; there are even a few hosts who themselves run reservation service organizations. Helping Hands are located in cities, towns, suburbs, and the country. The accommodations they offer range from luxurious to economical. And each bed and breakfast home reflects each host's own unique style. Together, Helping Hands represent a rich resource for a new host.

Of the Helping Hands listed in the special section appearing in the appendix, the most fruitful contacts for you to make are those who live in your own state or region, or whose situation seems similar to your own. People who live in the same geographical area that you do will be familiar with the regulations that could affect your bed and breakfast operation and will be able to advise you about problems unique to your particular state or community. Someone who lives in the same type of environment that you do (urban, rural, suburban) can give you insight into the kinds of problems that you might face as a host in the middle of a big city, on a farm, or in a rigid community setting. Much of the advice and observations in this book comes from the hosts listed in Helping Hands. Reading what they have to say on different aspects of hosting should provide you with a good introduction to the hosts who participate in the Helping Hands network and the bed and breakfast homes that they run. When you are looking through the Helping Hands listing, please note that some hosts are involved in the publicity network only. (Contact these individuals only if you wish to trade a supply of your B&B literature with them.) Those hosts willing to answer your questions are indicated in the listing.

If you would like to get in touch with Helping Hands participants, please bear in mind that they are most likely receiving more than just the inquiry from you. Do not expect them to give you a lengthy course in how to be a bed and breakfast host; rather, they are there to help you with specific problems or questions, giving information and advice that you can't get anywhere else. You may either write or call the host you would like to contact, but if you do call, out of courtesy always ask if you are calling at a convenient time. If you are not, call back at a time the host suggests. Then try to restrict the call to questions that you have preferably written down in advance, and keep the call as brief as possible. This might not be easy (you might find that both of you have a lot in common), but remember that the host is a busy person. Helping Hands are volunteers providing a new and valuable resource for new hosts, but in their debut on the bed and breakfast scene there are only sixty-three of them and thousands of people who are thinking about becoming hosts. That's a lot of questions. (It would be a terrible thing if hosts found that being part of Helping Hands was so demanding that they all decided to remove themselves from the list!) One answer to this potential problem is to expand the number of Helping Hands who are available to answer questions from new hosts. The invitation is open. Any hosts who would like to be included in the revised listing of Helping Hands should send their name, address, telephone number, and a brochure or business card for their bed and breakfast to Helping Hands, in care of *How to Open and Operate a Bed and Breakfast Home*, The Globe Pequot Press, 138 West Main Street, Chester, Connecticut 06412.

Resources

Whether you are just beginning to think about offering bed and breakfast or are already an experienced host, it is always worth your while to check out the resources that are available so that you can become as informed as possible about what's happening within the bed and breakfast industry.

Newsletters

To keep abreast of new ideas and developments that could affect you, get onto the mailing list for one or more newsletters directed toward owners of bed and breakfast homes, small inns, or both. Although there is a distinction between the two, often some of the information can be useful to owners of both types of accommodations. Listed here is a selection of these newsletters. Remember, too, that the national bed and breakfast organizations publish newsletters for their membership. (See "National Bed and Breakfast Groups" in this chapter.) In addition, some of the larger reservation service organizations (such as Bed & Breakfast Rocky Mountains) also issue newsletters to keep their members updated.

The Complete Guide's Gazette
Lanier Publishing International, Ltd.
375 40th Street
Oakland, California 94609
(no phone)

Inn Review
111 East Court Street
Post Office Box 1789
Kankakee, Illinois 60901
(815) 939–3509

Innkeeping
1333 Bath Street
Santa Barbara, California 93101
(805) 965–0707

Innsider Magazine
821 Wanda
Ferndale, Michigan 48220
(313) 541–6623

Country Inns/Bed & Breakfast Magazine
Post Office Box 182
South Orange, New Jersey 07079–0182
(201) 762–7090/7175

America's Bed & Breakfast Report
Post Office Box 3730
Ridgewood, New York 11386
(718) 436–4719

Innquest
Oates & Hyde
Post Office Box 1162
Brattleboro, Vermont 05301
(802) 254–5931

Yellow Brick Road
2445 Northcreek Lane
Fullerton, California 92631
(no phone)

Real estate

If you intend to purchase property for the purpose of offering bed and breakfast, examine the classified ads in existing newsletters and magazines devoted to inns and bed and breakfast establishments. Understand that local real estate agents may or may not have a sense of what your needs are, so if you choose to enlist the help of an agent to locate property, be sure to make your own checklist, putting zoning regulations and location as top priorities. After locating real estate that you think has potential, it can't hurt to engage the services of a bed and breakfast consultant to help you evaluate its pros and cons. (See list of consultants below.) If you wish to purchase commercial property to open an inn as a business, you may contact Oates & Hyde (P.O. Box 1162, Brattleboro, Vermont 05301, 802–254–5931), a consulting firm working exclusively in the country-inn field. In addition to offering seminars and consultations and publishing the newsletter *Innquest*, the firm helps aspiring innkeepers locate and purchase commercial property.

Consultants and workshops

For new hosts, or people thinking about hosting someday, attending an introductory workshop can be a valuable experience. Here, you can become more acquainted with what is happening with bed and breakfast on a local level, meet others with the same interests, and get your specific questions answered face to face by someone knowledgeable about bed and breakfast. Check your local adult education center for current offerings as well as listings of evening classes or weekend seminars held at nearby colleges and junior colleges (especially those that work with the Small Business Administration to foster local businesses). In some areas, the chamber of commerce helps to organize workshops to inspire interest in hosting. But your best bet is to check with the manager of any reservation service organization in your area. Often it is the manager who is conducting workshops locally, so he or she can let you know when and where the next one will be held. And of course, the manager will be happy to help a new host get started by visiting the home and making suggestions, assuming that the host plans to list with the RSO. Some RSOs charge a small fee for this service; others do not. Some bed and breakfast consultants operate independently and are not affiliated with a particular reservation service organization. Of these, some prefer to work with hosts within their own geographic area; others are willing to travel or will arrange private consultations by mail or phone. (If you decide that your best alternative is to hire a consultant to come to you from out of town, or even out of state, consider first assembling a small group of people who are interested in hosting to attend the workshop in order to cover the costs of the consultant's time and travel expenses.) Following is a selection of individuals who offer workshops and/or private consultations on a regular basis.

Michelle Souza
Nutmeg Bed & Breakfast
P.O. Box 1117
West Hartford, Connecticut 06107
(203) 236-6698
(workshops)

Anne Diamond
Bed and Breakfast Brookline/ Boston
Box 732
Brookline, Massachusetts 02146
(617) 277-2292 or 884-7748
(workshops)

Joy Meiser
Bed & Breakfast of Rhode Island, Inc.
38 Bellevue Avenue, Suite E
P.O. Box 3291
Newport, Rhode Island 02840
(401) 246-0142
(workshops; consultations; purchases)

Janet Turley
1797 House of Amacord
Charlemont Road
Buckland, Massachusetts 01338
(413) 625-2975
(consultations; arranged by mail and phone)

Carol Emerick and Barbara Brandt
The Cottage
P.O. Box 3292
San Diego, California 92103
(619) 299-1564 or 6850
(workshops)

Kate Winters
Bed & Breakfast Rocky Mountains
P.O. Box 804
Colorado Springs, Colorado 80901
(719) 630-3433
(workshops)

Rick Madden
P.O. Box 20596
Denver, Colorado 80220
(303) 333-3356
(workshops; nationwide consultations in person or by phone)

Helena Champion
Bed & Breakfast Marblehead & North Shore
54 Amherst Road
Beverly, Massachusetts 01915
(508) 921-1336
(workshops)

Jody Weaver
Hanson House Bed & Breakfast
1526 Palm Avenue S.W.
Seattle, Washington 98116
(206) 937-4157
(workshops; consultations)

Aster Mould
Bed & Breakfast Adventures
Suite 132, 103 Godwin Avenue
Midland Park, New Jersey 07432
(201) 444-7409
(consultations)

Ruth Judkins and Betty Cox
Eye Openers Bed & Breakfast Reservations
P.O. Box 694
Altadena, California 91001
(818) 797-2055 or (213) 684-4428
(workshops)

Barbara Notarius
Bed & Breakfast U.S.A., Ltd.
P.O. Box 606
Croton-on-Hudson, New York 10520
(914) 271-6228
(nationwide consultations/ workshops; monthly workshops in New York City)

Margaret Lobenstine
The Wildwood Inn
121 Church Street
Ware, Massachusetts 01082
(413) 967-7798
(consultations; workshops; apprenticeships)

Pat Hardy
Inn Transition
1333 Bath Street
Santa Barbara, California 93101
(805) 966-0589
(workshops; consultations)

Carl Glassman
The Wedgewood Inn
111 West Bridge Street
New Hope, Pennsylvania 18938
(215) 862-2570
(workshops; consultations; apprenticeships)

Maureen Vesey
All Seasons Bed & Breakfast Agency
Box 5511HT, Station B
Victoria, B.C., Canada V8R 6S4
(604) 595-2337
(workshops; consultations)

Tom and Phyllis Lupher
Bed & Breakfast of Idaho
109 West Idaho Street
Boise, Idaho 83702
(208) 342-8066 or 336-5174
(workshops)

5
Publicizing Your Bed and Breakfast

You may have the loveliest bed and breakfast in the world, but if you wait until someone "discovers" it, you could be waiting a long, long time. Hosts who choose to list their bed and breakfast homes with a reservation service organization can expect that the RSO will do the outreach needed to bring guests to their homes. (Be aware, though, that no RSO can guarantee guests as a result of its efforts.) You can do some extra PR yourself if you wish to host more guests than the number you receive through your RSO, or you can choose to list with several RSOs (provided that you don't have an exclusive contract with one of them) as a way to attract more guests. But if you choose to be independent and not list with any RSO at all, you've got to go out there and get those guests yourself.

Understand that doing all of your own publicity means several things. One is that the anonymity that hosts listed with a reservation service organization enjoy is not possible for you. An RSO protects the names, addresses, and phone numbers of its hosts; there's no reason to use such specific information in its advertisements, brochures, or press relations because the RSO uses its own. An independent host, on the other hand, has no choice but to use this information on his or her literature. (The guests do have to have a way to get in touch with the host to make a reservation.) So before you start an all-out campaign to have guests beating a path to your door, be aware that they might do just that. You must be ready to take on all the phone calls (day and night), to handle all the mail, and to even deal with occasional visitors who arrive on your doorstep after seeing your address listed in a guidebook.

As a way of retaining some privacy (you want to have a home life, too), some hosts rent a post office box and use that for an address, instead of printing their street address in their literature and in guidebooks. This discourages walk-ins. Still, your bed and breakfast will be in the public eye, so make sure that you know where your B&B stands in terms of local zoning ordinances, health and safety regulations, fire codes, and insurance coverage. (See chapter 9, "The Business of B&B.") It's not a bad idea to consult an attorney about your responsibilities in these areas before you start publicizing your bed and breakfast. When you've satisfied these conditions as best you can, you're ready to go public.

Creating your literature

Your literature represents your bed and breakfast. Prospective guests will see your brochures, your business cards, and your stationery long before they ever set eyes on you and your bed and breakfast home. The decision to visit—or not—will be made on the basis of the literature they see. How well it's done, or how poorly, will have a direct effect on your business. The literature does not have to be expensive, but it must entice visitors to your bed and breakfast home, and it must give all of the information necessary for prospective guests to follow through on reservations. Literature that is attractive and functional is essential for the success of your bed and breakfast business.

Your B&B brochure

The brochure is the most important piece of literature that you need. You will be sending it out in response to requests for more information, leaving it in strategic places to generate interest in your bed and breakfast, giving it to anyone who will make referrals to you, and mailing it to Helping Hands across North America to give to their guests. Everything about it—the content, the colors, the paper stock, the artwork, the typography—should work together to create an appealing image for your bed and breakfast.

Your B&B's image

First, consider the sort of image you want to create. How would you describe the ambience of your bed and breakfast? What is special about it? What is appealing about it? Does it have a distinctive architectural style? What colors predominate in the guest rooms, or perhaps in the whole house? What type of furnishings do you have? Are you located in the country, the city, the suburbs?

Taking all of these things into consideration, what would you say is the most salient feature of your bed and breakfast? Is it the fact that your home is listed in the Historic Register; that it is surrounded by apple orchards; that you are a purple freak, and all of your rooms are decorated in shades thereof? You can use the prominent feature of your bed and breakfast to build an image for your brochure.

Choosing colors and paper

The colors you choose for your brochure can add to or detract from that image. Certain colors carry certain connotations. If you want to emphasize a nature theme because your home is located in the country, then of course green is a good choice as a color, either for the ink or the paper stock. Other earth colors could work well, too. The use of warm brown, burnt orange, or deep red can evoke an image of the beauty of autumn in the country—which will be to your advantage if you're located in an area to which tourists come in droves to enjoy the fall foliage. If your B&B is in the heart of ski country, you might want to use white and blue ("cold" colors) as a way to suggest winter. If your guest rooms are decorated in a particular color, or there is a predominant color in your home, then that color is a natural one to use in your brochure.

Be aware that the cost of a brochure goes up if you want to use that all-important color to create your bed and breakfast's image. Colored ink costs more than black ink. Colored paper stock costs more than white paper stock. Other cost factors are the weight of the paper and its surface. The thicker (or "heavier") the paper, the more it costs, but this is a necessary expense. Brochures are generally printed on heavier paper stock so that they will hold up well. A brochure printed on paper that is as flimsy as typing paper (20-pound paper) will wrinkle and rip far too easily. You need something more hardy to withstand all the handling, mailing, and even storage. Having your brochures printed on 60-pound paper will be worth the investment. The cost goes up if you want paper that has been specially coated (for a slick and shiny look) or that has a special texture. Smooth but uncoated paper is less expensive.

Cutting costs

You should always ask for prices before ordering. Sometimes you can reach a compromise with a printer to get closer to what you really want without paying full price for it. For example, the printer might be willing to use colored ink on your brochure at no extra charge if another client has ordered colored ink for another job. If the ink will already be on the printing press (so the printer doesn't have to clean the press and change the ink just for you), then there is no set-up cost involved. True, you might be asked to accept a color other than the one you had in mind, but the savings could be worth the compromise on your part. Also, sometimes a printer will have in stock a lot of paper that he'd like to sell, so he might be willing to discount it to you because he knows that it's to his advantage. This usually occurs with specialty papers (the coated and the textured and the unusual colors that are not ordered by large numbers of people), the kind that cost more than plainer papers, so you could pick up quite a bargain. It can't hurt to ask. So what if the off-white you wanted turns out to be an elegant eggshell color? No big deal if you can save a significant amount of money and maybe even make your brochure look better than you thought your budget would allow.

Naming your B&B

The image of your bed and breakfast that you want to present to prospective guests can be captured well by choosing a name for your B&B. Printed right on the front of the brochure, a good name will leave no question in a prospective guest's mind what the main feature of your B&B is. (Naming your B&B will also help former guests find you again when they are planning a return trip to your area or want to recommend your B&B to friends. See "Memories" in chapter 7.) Are you trying to entice visitors to your B&B on the basis of your location in the country? Peeping Cow Inn sure does a good job of it. Do you have animals, rather exotic ones at that? Camel Lot is not only a B&B but also a breeding farm for unusual animals. Do you offer a refuge from the hustle and bustle of city life? Hunt's Hideaway sounds good.

Using artwork effectively

While you're thinking of a name, imagine the type of logo that could go with it. A logo is a small, uncomplicated illustration that acts as a symbol, in this case, of your bed and breakfast. (Sometimes thinking up a logo first can help you with the name.) The two do not necessarily have to echo each other, but it helps. Countryside, a bed and breakfast located in Summit Point, West Virginia, uses a drawing of an apple tree, its branches laden with enormous apples. "We use the apple tree logo because we are surrounded by apple orchards," says owner Lisa

Hileman. Meadow Spring Farm in Kennett Square, Pennsylvania, uses a cow standing next to a farm house. Mayflower Bed and Breakfast in Belmont, Massachusetts, uses a logo of the *Mayflower* itself. Longswamp Bed and Breakfast in Mertztown, Pennsylvania, uses cattails. The Wild Rose of York, located in York, Maine, uses a wild rose.

Tying in your logo with your location, as the owners of the Wild Rose of York do, can be effective. The logo for Bed and Breakfast Pocono Northeast, located in Bear Creek, Pennsylvania, shows three little bears contentedly asleep in a bed, a quilt pulled up to their fuzzy chins. The House of Snee, located on Ocean Road in Narragansett, Rhode Island, uses an anchor partially submerged in water. Anchor Hill Lodge in Rogersville, Missouri, also uses (guess what?) an anchor. Mrs. K's Bed & Breakfast is in Kennett Square, Pennsylvania's "mushroom capital." Her logo? A mushroom.

Many hosts also like to use an illustration of their home on their brochure in addition to, or instead of, the logo. "People like to see what they're getting," says Boston host Susan Naimark, a graphic designer who has produced some literature for bed and breakfast homes. An illustration showing your B&B to best advantage can give prospective guests a good idea of what to expect. The likeness must be a good rendering, clean and precise. It should also emphasize something about your B&B that is visually appealing. A drawing done from any old angle is not nearly as impressive as one that focuses on an interesting feature of the house. The brochure used by Betsy's Bed and Breakfast in Baltimore, Maryland, for example, uses a lovely illustration of the home on the cover. The drawing exaggerates the height of her three-story townhouse (built in 1871). A lamppost of the same period and a flag streaming from an upper window saying "Betsy's Bed & Breakfast" give a prospective guest a very clear image of what this place is like. Inside the brochure, guests find out through a short description what it's like inside the house.

Another bed and breakfast that uses an illustration of the house well is Spindrift Bed & Breakfast in Bandon, Oregon, which is located right next to the beach. The drawing shows a very peaceful, pleasant home right next to the waves and the sand. Exactly what beach lovers want to see.

Locating illustrations

So if you do want to use an illustration of your home in the brochure, and a logo as well, what's the best way to go about getting the artwork you need without spending your life's savings? Know that you can't just cut out a drawing that you like from a magazine or newspaper or book and start using it on your literature. Most artwork that has already been prepared and used has been copyrighted; you can't use it unless you obtain permission from the owner. But the good news is that there are some copyright-free illustrations available to anyone who wishes to use them. It's possible that you can find something ready-made that is right for your purposes. These are printed in books, and the king of free art is Dover Publications, which prints a whole line of books containing different types of artwork that you can cut out and use. These include monograms, floral designs, food and drink illustrations, Art Nouveau and Art Deco graphics and borders, and designs from different countries. There's even a book containing ready-to-use teddy bear illustrations. Using something from one of these books (if it fits into your image you're trying to create) is probably the least expensive way to obtain your artwork. Most of these books sell for $3 to $4 each, plus a postage and handling charge. (For a catalogue, write to Dover Publications, 11 East 2nd Street, Mineola, New York 11501.) Be aware that these illustrations may not come in the exact size that you want (a lot of them are printed bigger than your needs will require). So if you do locate an illustration that would be perfect as your logo, you will probably have to take it to a printer or copy center to have a reduction (or an enlargement) made for your brochure.

One other inexpensive way to obtain artwork is to have a talented friend or relative help you out. And sometimes, art students are more than happy to create a custom-made logo for clients for a small fee because they know that the resulting literature can be used to enhance their portfolios. So don't hesitate to contact the art department of a local school or college.

For hosts who do want to have a professional artist design and render their artwork (and perhaps even the whole brochure) the way you want it, the best advice is to shop around for the right person to do it. "Insist on seeing sample work," says Susan Naimark. Even if the artist has not produced anything similar to what you have in mind, you can still get a sense of that artist's style by looking at other work he or she has done. Then talk price and get a figure in advance for the work you want done. Be warned that some artists will want to charge you an arm and a leg; others will ask for so little that you'll wonder how they make a living. It's a good idea to get several bids if you're talking about the design and production of the whole brochure.

One very good way to locate an artist to do the job you want is to look at the literature that other hosts use. If you see something that you really like, get in touch with the host and ask if you can get a referral to the artist, even if that person lives in another part of the country. Is there a problem doing literature long distance? Not really. It's nice to be able to get together, face to face, as the project progresses, but it's not absolutely necessary. Let the artist know exactly what you want through letters and telephone conservations. Supply photographs of your home or your own sketches if you wish. From these, the artist can sketch out ideas for you to look at and send them through the mail. The copy of the final paste-up can be handled the same way. The process can work if you've contracted the services of an artist you know you want.

Doing it yourself

The graphic designer can also provide you with knowledgeable advice about the colors, paper, type styles, and layout that would be most effective for your brochure. Still, no host has to rely on a graphic designer to produce a brochure, especially if economizing is an issue. You can design a brochure yourself, typing the contents neatly on a sheet of paper, pasting a copy of an illustration where you want it, and then getting it copied. If you wish, you can have the contents typeset for a more professional look, and you can paste this up yourself (but only if you've got a good eye and can use a ruler well). The owner of a print shop is often willing to help clients with suggestions for layout and even arrange for the typesetting and paste-up to be done according to your design at a reasonable cost.

If you want to do as much as you can yourself, without the help of a professional graphic designer, there are a few basics you should keep in mind for the best results. The main rule is to keep everything simple, clear, neat, and clean. Your brochure should not look cluttered. Use headings for the different pieces of information you include so that readers don't have to hunt for anything. If you're telling people how to make a reservation, put a title on it that says "How to make a reservation." And it's best to stick to one typeface for the body copy if you do decide to have everything typeset (instead of typing it yourself). For the headlines, you can either use the same typeface (except larger, in bold), or you can choose a different face altogether. But don't use more than two typefaces in your brochure or it will take on a confused appearance. If you're a whiz at using a word processor, you might want to think about using your skills to produce the copy you need for your brochure right in your home or office. Be sure that the grammar, spelling, and punctuation are correct. (If the King's English has always given you trouble, ask a knowledgeable friend to double-check your copy.)

The content

The look of your brochure is, of course, very important, and you should do whatever is necessary to produce one that is as attractive as possible within your budget. However, the content of your brochure can't be emphasized enough.

This might sound obvious, but don't forget to include the name and address of your bed and breakfast, and your telephone number! Sometimes hosts get so wrapped up in the other aspects of designing their brochure that they forget to include the most important information. And remember that most of your calls will be coming from people outside your locality, so make sure that you include your area code. One Michigan bed and breakfast printed literature without this detail. Yes, it's a little thing. But it's an inconvenience for the guest to have to call Information. So make sure that you put *all* the necessary contact information in the brochure—and this includes the ZIP code, too!

Somewhere in your brochure, you should explain how to make a reservation. If you have certain "office hours" when you will be available to answer your telephone, write them down in the brochure. "After 6:00 P.M. evenings, and weekends" reads one brochure. Right away, a guest knows that calling during the day might not result in a connection. Maybe you prefer that people call you only during certain hours. Say so. Many hosts also include a reservation form on one part of the brochure so that guests can mail it back to make a reservation. If you wish to accept reservations through the mail, then take a look at the screening checklist provided in chapter 6 for a listing of the information you should obtain on your reservation form.

In your brochure it's wise to give a brief description of what bed and breakfast is (not everyone who sees the brochure will know) and to explain *why* a guest should come to *your* bed and breakfast home. Are you near the beach? Are you right downtown? Do you offer a romantic hide-away? Is there great hiking nearby? If there's something especially attractive about your bed and breakfast, mention this in your brochure. Some hosts who are terrific cooks like to lure guests to their homes by describing the goodies that will be theirs to enjoy. If you serve a mean blueberry blintz, it can't hurt to mention this fact in your brochure.

There are other helpful items that can be included in the brochure if you wish. For example, Gwen's Guest Home in Ottawa, Ontario, prints a street map on the inside of her brochure, with the B&B clearly marked. The back of the brochure contains a listing of useful telephone numbers that a visitor might have occasion to use—everything from a dentist and a barber to an optician, dry cleaners, a florist, as well as emergency numbers. The brochure even includes a place for guests to make their own notes. Now there's a useful brochure!

As you begin to work on your own ideas for your brochure, collect some from other bed and breakfast hosts to spark your imagination. Translating the uniqueness of your bed and breakfast home into a piece of literature is no easy task, but sometimes seeing how other hosts have approached the job can help you to do your own even better.

Your B&B stationery

You might decide to make your brochure a self-mailer so that you don't need an envelope every time you need to mail a copy to anyone. (In your brochure design, you'll have to set aside a portion of space for the return address, the address of the person you're mailing the piece to, and the stamp.) Still, it's unlikely that you'll be able to exist without ever using paper and envelopes. You will want to write notes to guests on different occasions. This raises the question of whether or not you should have your own special bed and breakfast stationery, in addition to your brochure, designed and printed.

It's nice to have your stationery custom-made, with the name and address of your B&B and your logo imprinted on the envelopes, note paper, and perhaps even business cards and postcards. If your budget can handle it, by all means have a designer work with you to create stationery that complements the image you've worked on for the brochure, coordinating colors and style. But if you've got to economize (as most hosts do until their businesses get rolling), there are ways to keep costs down.

The best way to minimize your expenses for stationery is to purchase plain paper and envelopes (preferably during sales) and use either a custom-made rubber stamp or stickers to imprint your bed and breakfast's name and address on them.

A rubber stamp involves the least investment, and one can usually be ordered through copy centers or print shops. The cost starts at around $10 and goes up the larger the size of the stamp, or if you wish to include some sort of design with the address. You might want to consider having just your logo made into a separate stamp so that you can repeat the image more than once on the paper you're using for letterhead. Using different-colored inks can produce very attractive results, though inexpensive.

The alternative to rubber stamps is to purchase a quantity of address stickers. These will probably cost you more than a stamp and an inkpad, but keep your eye out for bargains, such as those occasional advertisements in newspaper inserts that offer 1000 address labels for as little as $1. The $1 buys very, very plain stickers (black ink on white labels) that require moistening. They might be plain, but they sure get the job done with little capital investment on your part. The price rises if you want colored ink, colored paper, or special type styles, but not by so much that it is prohibitive. You can usually still order 1000 address labels through these mail-order offers for no more than $12, no matter what color or style you choose.

If you like the idea of stickers but want to see samples or want more of a choice in what you're getting, check with print shops or copy centers in your area to see what they offer. Prices are competitive, but the selection increases. Stickers come in a variety of shapes and sizes—ovals, circles, squares, rectangles. You can get them in gold or silver, with just about any ink color you can imagine. You can have your logo printed on them with your name and address if you wish. The more elaborate the sticker design, the more they cost. A roll of 1000 stickers can cost $40, $50, or more depending on the size, shape, ink, paper stock, and length of the message imprinted. Still, this is only five or six cents per sticker. If you find that the price of stickers is near enough to the printing costs of customized stationery, you still might want to go with the stickers because of their versatility.

Self-stick labels work well not only on envelopes and note paper—they're also great to label other items as well. You can affix them to wrapped soaps that you put in the guest bathrooms. You can wrap some cookies in plastic wrap and place a sticker on the wrapping—a nice addition to a complimentary snack tray for your guests in the evening. Place them on the covers of magazines that are left out as reading material for guests. Place them on the covers of guidebooks that you lend to your guests but don't want to lose—the label is a good reminder of ownership. And you should place the labels on any brochures that you give to your guests about area sightseeing. If you like to give your guests a gift when they leave your bed and breakfast, put the sticker on the small jar of rhubarb jam you made yourself, the section of honeycomb from your own beehive, or the recipe card that goes with those muffins for the road.

When you're first starting out, any unnecessary expenditure is unwise. For a time, you might want to use just plain stationery on which you type your B&B's name and address whenever you need to send a letter. The important thing, of course, is to communicate with your guests. Once your B&B is regularly accommodating a good number of guests, it's time to think more seriously about upholding, through improvements in the look of your stationery, that image that you worked so hard to create in your brochure.

Distributing your literature

Once you've gone to the trouble and expense to have a brochure designed, it's not going to do you any good at all if the copies you ordered sit in the closet. You have to make sure that the brochures get into the right hands. Of course, anyone who writes or calls to inquire about your bed and breakfast should be sent a brochure to give them more information. But these people have already found you through other means; you also want your literature to lead others to your B&B. Your brochure is an important promotional item.

One effective method of distribution to potential guests is using the Helping Hands network. This special listing, available only in this book, includes sixty-three individual hosts in twenty-six states who are willing either to answer questions from new hosts or to make brochures advertising the bed and breakfast homes of other Helping Hands available to their guests—or both. Almost all of the hosts listed in Helping Hands participate in the publicity aspect of the network, which can be valuable to a new host as a way to spread the word. Someone staying in a B&B in California, for example, could very well be planning a trip to Utah, Georgia, or Rhode Island. So if your brochure is available from that Helping Hand in California—and you happen to live in Utah, Georgia, or Rhode Island—you're one step closer to a reservation. (It's also nice to have a personal reference for a guest from another B&B owner.)

If you wish to take advantage of the Helping Hands publicity network, send notification of your interest and information about your bed and breakfast in care of this book's publisher. You will be included in the next Helping Hands listing that is printed, but you need not wait until that happens before you can get involved. Feel free to send a small number of your brochures (no more than twenty) to any, or all, of the Helping Hands who are keyed as willing to make other hosts' brochures available to their guests. (Check the appropriate key in the appendix.) With the supply of literature, include a note explaining that you are joining the Helping Hands network. Then be ready to extend the same courtesy to all the bed and breakfast hosts that you contact.

For local distribution of your literature, there are different avenues you can explore. Sometimes the tourist bureaus of chambers of commerce will make available to the public copies or brochures for those bed and breakfast homes that are members of their organizations. If you join either of these organizations, inquire if this is a practice. In addition, take brochures to area hospitals, senior-citizen homes, real estate agents, churches and other houses of worship, and colleges (especially alumni offices and offices that deal with new students or parents). All of these places come into frequent contact with people visiting from out of town for various reasons—to see a patient at a hospital, to spend some time with a relative who lives at a residence for senior citizens, to check up on a son or daughter at college, to look for a house, to attend a wedding. And contact the directors of local performing arts centers that bring in talent from out of town. More than one performer who is "on the road" has preferred the quiet, homey charm of a bed and breakfast to a hotel. (One host reports the pleasure of providing accommodations for Cloris Leachman, who is well known for her role on Mary Tyler Moore's television show. Another talks of hosting Mary Travers of Peter, Paul and Mary.)

Keep your eyes open for other possibilities in your neighborhood for distribution of your literature. One very successful bed and breakfast owner gives out her brochures at an area flea market. Some hosts even leave a few brochures with the clerks at nearby hotels in the event of an overflow situation. One host reports that he takes literature to bridal shops and stores that rent tuxedos; obviously the clientele will know people coming to town for the big event, and they'll need places to stay. Another host who doesn't mind making last-minute arrangements leaves brochures at gas stations to help out people who are stranded because of car trouble.

Keep in mind, though, that you should be selective about where you leave your literature. You want to attract guests who fit the model of a "bed and breakfast person," and ideally, you should have enough advance notice of a reservation to check out references. It's not a good idea, for example, to leave a stack of brochures on the bar at the local joint. The last thing you want is a guest who has had one too many stumbling to your front door in the middle of the night.

If there is a local tour company that offers walking tours or bus tours of your area, try to establish a working relationship with the owner or tour operators. Sometimes tour companies will make information about lodging available to their clients. You might also want to talk to the owner about arranging package deals for clients—that include bed and breakfast lodging. It's no coincidence that some tour operators became bed and breakfast hosts when they discovered that one activity so naturally complemented the other.

Another possible avenue to explore is any car-rental company in your area. The more well-known chains offer discounts to members of certain groups; a local representative might be very interested in talking with you about providing discounts to your guests if your bed and breakfast regularly accommodates visitors who are interested in renting cars. So find out if you can offer discounted car rentals to your guests as an amenity, and, at the same time, see if the company will make your brochures available in its literature display rack. (You might also want to check out possibilities with any local office connected to a national moving company. The people who come and go in your area are bound to need the services of either one of you at one time or another. Perhaps your bed and breakfast and the moving company could cooperate in filling the needs of these people.)

Some hosts undertake more innovative measures to publicize their bed and breakfast homes. One host has found an approach that has been quite effective for her business. She puts on her Victorian red-and-white pin-striped maid's costume with its ruffled apron that's embroidered with the name of her B&B and walks downtown with a basket full of brochures. "Those who are interested come to me and ask for a brochure. It's loads of fun."

No, you don't have to follow her example in order to be successful. But don't close your mind to new ideas for distributing your literature. Maybe you can think of your own unique method of spreading the word that would be a good addition to the suggestions made here.

How to use your community resources

If you join your local reservation service organization, you can rely upon the RSO's memberships with the local tourist bureaus and the chamber of commerce as a way to take advantage of these organizations' resources. But if you're going it alone, with no affiliation with an RSO, you're going to have to seriously consider taking out a membership in these organizations yourself.

Your local tourist bureaus can be an enormous help to you if you are a member. They publish current information directed to visitors, including listings of recommended lodging. Because local tourist bureaus generally operate on a membership system, these listings tend to be restricted to those hotels, motels, and bed and breakfast homes or RSOs that are members. So if you're not a member, you will most likely not appear in any of their publications. The lesson is that it's worth the price to join because the tourist bureau is the first place that people contact for information to help them plan a visit to the area. So check membership guidelines and fee requirements for local tourist bureaus. (Consult the appendix for the tourist bureaus in your area.)

In addition, tourist bureaus publish a variety of information that they make available to their members in bulk for free or at a low cost. You want to be able to orient your guests to the area as best you can, so having copies of sightseeing brochures, calendars of events, and maps will help you give your guests a better introduction to the community. (See "Orientation" in chapter 7.)

Every state's Department of Commerce also has an interest in meeting the needs of visitors to the state. So in addition to contacting your local or regional tourist boards, get in touch with this state agency as well. Some now print and distribute their own guides to bed and breakfast in their own states. (The Department of Commerce in Massachusetts, for example, publishes a guide booklet to the state's bed and breakfast facilities that it makes available free as a service to vacationers.)

Membership in the chamber of commerce can also be helpful to an independent bed and breakfast owner. Chambers are concerned with developing tourism in their areas and work to promote their members. It's not uncommon for someone planning to visit the area to contact the local chamber of commerce to ask for specific referrals to bed and breakfast homes. Your membership will put you in the right place at the right time.

Because your relationship with the tourist bureaus and the chamber of commerce is so important, why not invite the staff to visit your bed and breakfast? Inviting the director or president of each organization for one of your gourmet breakfasts and a tour of your B&B is a great idea—but so is asking the receptionist, the secretary, and/or the administrative assistant. These are the people who end up answering most of the inquiries from the public; they are the ones who will be responding to questions about bed and breakfast and making referrals. It's to your benefit to get to know them personally, if you can, and to familiarize them with your bed and breakfast. You might even want to offer a free weekend stay to some of the staff to introduce them to your B&B.

How to get listed in B&B guidebooks

Guidebooks are an important source of information for people as they make their travel plans. To have your bed and breakfast described in even one guidebook will benefit your business because thousands upon thousands of people will see it. So how do you go about getting this terrific publicity? Your job is to bring your bed and breakfast to the attention of the people who are writing the books and make them want to include you.

First, you've got to identify which books you would like to have your bed and breakfast included in. There are now a number of guidebooks on the market that are devoted exclusively to bed and breakfast; become familiar with all of the ones that would be appropriate for your bed and breakfast's location and features. (A listing of some of the books that focus on bed and breakfast is included here for your convenience.) Make a list of the ones you want to be mentioned in.

Look at the preface or introduction of each book to see if the author explains how she or he selects the bed and breakfast homes for inclusion. Note that some bed and breakfast organizations publish their own guidebooks to publicize their members. These include *Bed & Breakfast U.S.A.*, produced by the Tourist House Association of America, the *Treasury of Bed & Breakfast* series by the American Bed & Breakfast Association, and *The Bed & Breakfast Guide for the U.S. and Canada* by the National Bed & Breakfast Association. To be added to the next edition of any of these books, you must be a member of the organization, so it makes sense to join if you qualify. (There are descriptions of each organization in the section "National Bed and Breakfast Groups" in Chapter 4.) Write for membership information and an application.

Other guidebooks are not associated with any B&B group. They are researched independently by the author, and the author makes the decision about which bed and breakfast homes to include (or not). Some of the books are general guides, but most have a special angle. Some are regional guides; some focus only on luxury bed and breakfast homes; some are cookbooks; and others publish information about reservation service organizations only. You will find that a selection of these books will be appropriate to your bed and breakfast, and others will not. A book devoted to RSOs, for example, will not list your individual B&B, so there's no point in trying to get information to the author for an upcoming edition. And if you live on the east coast, you can't expect that a guide to west coast bed and breakfast homes will be likely to mention your B&B. (On the other hand, *Bed & Breakfast in New England* or *Bed & Breakfast in the Mid-Atlantic States* very well might.) So ferret out the ones for which your B&B might qualify.

Now you've got to convince the authors that the omission of your bed and breakfast in the next edition of their books would be a great loss indeed. Writers look for something special about any B&B that they include in their books. Maybe you make baked apple pancakes according to a recipe that has been handed down for five generations in your family, and no one else knows the secret ingredient except the last of the line (you). Now you want to share the secret with the world, via a bed and breakfast cookbook. Now that might interest an author. Is your bed and breakfast home an architectural oddity? Was it remodeled into a B&B from a lighthouse or a barn? Was it designed by a well-known architect? Does it have historical significance—part of the underground railroad during the Civil War, for instance? Details like these will interest a reader in coming to your B&B, so therefore an author will be interested in you.

Write a letter to the author explaining the feature of your B&B that you think makes it special. (Sometimes the author will give an address for reader correspondence within the book. If not, write in care of the publisher.) In the letter, offer to answer the author's questions by telephone (inform the author that you would be more than happy to accept a collect call) and extend an invitation to visit your B&B on a *gratis* basis. Be aware that authors must research many, many bed and breakfast homes—which can involve a lot of time and expense—so these courtesies will be appreciated. With the letter, send a brochure, a copy of a newspaper or magazine article that mentions your B&B (if one is available), and a photograph that makes a good impression of your home (this is optional).

Don't overlook guidebooks that are not devoted to bed and breakfast exclusively but rather describe your city, state, or region in a more general way for tourists. A book such as *Daytrips, Getaway Weekends, and Vacations in the Mid-Atlantic States* makes recommendations for bed and breakfast lodging. So take a look at the guidebooks written about your area. If you see that an author recommends lodging for tourists, it can't hurt to send the writer information about your bed and breakfast.

One final thing to keep in mind when trying to get listed in guidebooks is that writers write, and once they've finished one project, they start on the next. Maybe you've noticed that a particular author has several books out about bed and breakfast but has not produced a work about your region. An educated guess is that he or she will get around to it soon enough. It's a good idea to send information about your bed and breakfast to selected authors who have written a series of books and articles about bed and breakfast and travel in general, in the hope that the material will eventually be used.

Bed and breakfast booklist

Following is a selection of books that focus exclusively on bed and breakfast accommodations or that feature bed and breakfast homes as part of the text.

Bed and Breakfast in New England
Bed and Breakfast in the Mid-Atlantic States
by Bernice Chesler

Bed and Breakfast in the Caribbean
Bed and Breakfast in California
by Kathy Strong

Recommended Country Inns: Mid-Atlantic States and Chesapeake Region
by Brenda Boelts Chapin

Recommended Country Inns: South
by Sara Pitzer

Recommended Country Inns: Midwest
by Bob Puhala

Recommended Country Inns: Rocky Mountain Region
by Doris Kennedy

Recommended Country Inns: Arizona, New Mexico, and Texas
by Eleanor Morris

Recommended Country Inns: West Coast
by Julianne Belote

Daytrips, Getaway Weekends, and Vacations in New England
Daytrips, Getaway Weekends, and Vacations in the Mid-Atlantic States
by Patricia and Robert Foulke

Guide to Nantucket
Guide to Martha's Vineyard
by Polly Burroughs

Guide to Cape Cod
by Frederick Pratson

The American Bed & Breakfast Cookbook
by The Bed Post Writers Group

The Bed and Breakfast Traveler: Touring the West Coast
by Lewis Green

The Globe Pequot Press
138 West Main Street
Chester, Connecticut 06412

* * *

Bed & Breakfast America (The Great American Guest House Book)
by John Thaxton

Country Inns, Lodges, & Historic Hotels of the South
Country Inns, Lodges, & Historic Hotels of the Middle Atlantic States
Country Inns, Lodges, & Historic Hotels of the New England States
Country Inns, Lodges, & Historic Hotels of California, Oregon, and Washington
Country Inns, Lodges, & Historic Hotels of the Midwest & the Rockies
by Jean Lindgren and Anthony Hitchcock

Burt Franklin & Co., Inc.
235 East 44th Street
New York, New York 10017

* * *

Bed & Breakfast American Style
by Norman Simpson

Harper & Row Publishers, Inc.
10 East 53rd Street
New York, New York 10022

* * *

Bed & Breakfast Cookbook
by Pamela Lanier

Running Press
125 South 22nd Street
Philadelphia, Pennsylvania 19103

* * *

The Bed & Breakfast Guide for the U.S. and Canada
by Phyllis Featherston & Barbara Ostler

The National Bed & Breakfast Association
P.O. Box 332
Norwalk, Connecticut 06852

* * *

Bed & Breakfast Homes Directory—West Coast
by Diane Knight

Knighttime Publications
P.O. Box 1597
Freedom, California 95019

* * *

A Treasury of Bed & Breakfast: North America
A Treasury of Bed & Breakfast: Northeast
A Treasury of Bed & Breakfast: Mid-Atlantic and Southwest
A Treasury of Bed & Breakfast: Central
A Treasury of Bed & Breakfast: West

The American Bed & Breakfast Association
16 Village Green, Suite 203
Crofton, Maryland 21114

* * *

Bed & Breakfast in Michigan and Surrounding Areas
by Norma Buzan and Bert Howell

Bed & Breakfast North America
by Norma Buzan

Betsy Ross Publications
3057 Betsy Ross Drive
Bloomfield Hills, Michigan 48013

* * *

Bed & Breakfast Northwest
by Myrna Oakley

Bed & Breakfast: California
by Linda Kay Bristow

Bed and Breakfast: Colorado and the Rocky Mountain West
by Buddy Mays

Chronicle Books
One Hallidie Plaza, Suite 806
San Francisco, California 94102

* * *

Bed & Breakfast U.S.A.
by Betty Rundback & Nancy Kramer

Tourist House Association of America
R.D. 2, Box 355A
Greentown, Pennsylvania 18426

* * *

Inn World Directory/Catalog
by Norman Strasma

Inn Review
P.O. Box 1789
Kankakee, Illinois 60901

* * *

The Complete Guide to Bed & Breakfasts, Inns & Guesthouses in the United States and Canada
by Pamela Lanier

John Muir Publications
P.O. Box 613
Santa Fe, New Mexico 87504

* * *

Wake Up to Missouri
edited by Deb Woodson

Missouri Division of Tourism
Dept. MT88
P.O. Box 1055
Jefferson City, Missouri 65102

* * *

Bed & Breakfast and Unique Inns of Virginia
Crystal Springs Publishing
P.O. Box 8814
Roanoke, Virginia 24014

* * *

Fodor's Bed & Breakfast Guide
by Mary Winget

Fodor's Travel Guides
2 Park Avenue
New York, New York 10016

* * *

Bed and Breakfast Goes Hawaiian
by Al Davis and Evelyn Warner

Bed & Breakfast Hawaii
P.O. Box 449
Kapaa, Hawaii 96746

* * *

Texas Bed & Breakfast
by Ann Ruff, Gail Drago, and Marjie Mugno

Texas Monthly Press
P.O. Box 1569
Austin, Texas 78767

* * *

The Canadian Bed and Breakfast Guide
by Gerda Pantel

Fitzhenry & Whiteside
195 Allstate Parkway
Markham, Ontario L34 4T8

* * *

Best Places to Stay in the Pacific Northwest
by Marilyn McFarlane

Best Places to Stay in Hawaii
by Bill Jamison and Cheryl Alters Jamison

Best Places to Stay in New England
by Christina Tree and Bruce Shaw

Best Places to Stay in the Southwest
by Gail Rickey

Best Places to Stay in America's Cities
edited by Kenneth Hale-Wehmann

The Harvard Common Press
535 Albany Street
Boston, Massachusetts 02118

* * *

Official Guide to American Historic Bed & Breakfast Inns and Guesthouses

Association of American Historic Inns
P.O. Box 336
Dana Point, California 92629

* * *

Myrna Oakley's Bed & Breakfast Northwest
by Myrna Oakley

Solstice Press
North Country Book Express
P.O. Box 9223
Moscow, Idaho 83843

* * *

Frommer's Bed & Breakfast North America
by Hal Gieseking

Bed & Breakfast Guide: East Coast
by Roberta Garner

Bed & Breakfast Guide: West Coast
by Courtia Worth and Terry Berger

Prentice Hall Books
1 Gulf & Western Plaza
New York, New York 10023

* * *

The Complete Guide to American Bed and Breakfast
by Rik and Nancy Barnes

Pelican Publishing
P.O. Box 189
Gretna, Louisiana 70053

* * *

The Canadian Bed and Breakfast Book
by Patricia Wilson

William Street Press
53 William Street
Stratford, Ontario N5A 4X9

* * *

Bed and Breakfast Inns of New England
by Deborah Patton

Yankee Books
Depot Square
Peterborough, New Hampshire 03458

* * *

Bed and Breakfast in the Deep South
by Sarah-Margaret Brown and Ruth Bruns

Variety House
P.O. Box 8128
New Orleans, Louisiana 70182

* * *

The Bed & Breakfast Directory
by Barbara Notarius

John Wiley & Sons
605 Third Avenue
New York, New York 10158

* * *

Affordable Bed and Breakfasts for $40 or Less for Two People
by Loris Bree

Marlor Press
4304 Brigadoon Drive
St. Paul, Minnesota 55126

How to get press coverage

Ironically, one of the best kinds of publicity you can get for your bed and breakfast is free. Articles written about your bed and breakfast in local, regional, or even national newspapers and magazines cost you virtually nothing, but the benefits continue long after the articles have been written. Once you've been operating a bed and breakfast for a while, it might happen that writers will come to you looking for a story, but don't sit too long by the telephone waiting for the calls to come in. If you want an article written about your bed and breakfast, *you* convince a writer that readers would like to hear about it, that it's "news."

To get the process under way, the first thing you must do is identify those newspapers and magazines that would be likely to do a story on your bed and breakfast. Your hometown newspaper is a good bet because your B&B is local news; if you live in a large city, it'll be harder to get an article into print because there's a lot more competition for the available space. Still, it's not impossible. The larger newspapers have major sections on lifestyle, business, food—all of which could have good reason to include an article about bed and breakfast. Magazines devoted to your city, state, or region are also good possibilities when it comes to a story about an area bed and breakfast.

Keep in mind that an article in a local paper will not really pay off for you in terms of guests. (After all, why should people who live where you do stay in a B&B in their own community?) It's true that local people have friends, relatives, and business acquaintances who might be interested in your services at some point, but the real advantage of local coverage is that you can use the article to generate more articles that could attract considerably more visitors to your bed and breakfast. To get national press coverage, it helps if you've got a reprint of a local article to spark some interest. Somehow, the fact that your B&B has already been written about shows that someone thinks it's news (one point in your favor), and it also lends a certain "legitimacy" to your operation (another point in your favor). That reprint of a local article could open a few doors, so it's best to work on obtaining local coverage before you contact national publications.

When it comes to national publications, you're going to have to pick and choose carefully to try to tie in a certain aspect of your bed and breakfast with the focus of a particular publication. Is your B&B used as a base by people who come to the area for birdwatching, skiing, sunning, sailing, hiking, rock climbing, spelunking, or other special interests? It's a good bet that whenever a number of people follow a particular interest, there's a magazine devoted to it somewhere. If you don't already know what it's called and what it looks like, find out. (The reference librarian at your public library can help you locate guides to periodical literature, which will tell you what you need to know.) Then get a copy of the magazine. Subscribe. Become familiar with the types of articles it includes and the different writers who work for it.

For whatever publication that you're targeting, get to know the writers through their work. Identify one who would be likely to cover the subject according to the angle you're thinking about. This is the person you'll want to direct a press release to.

Quite simply, the press release will explain "the story." Writing one is no big deal if you know what you want to say. First, you'll need a title that impresses upon the recipient of the press release the significance of the story. "Historic Home Opens Its Doors to Bed and Breakfast Guests" should interest a writer who deals with historical subjects. "A Bed & Breakfast for Birdwatchers" should interest someone who writes about birds and animals for a nature magazine. Tailor yours to the publication and the writer.

In the first paragraph of your press release, explain the meaning behind the title by answering, briefly, the questions of "who?" "what?" "where?" and "when?" This is the place to give the name of your bed and breakfast, what its special feature is that makes it news, its location, and some indication whether this is a new or continuing development.

In the second paragraph, give some details on how the B&B came about, quote someone who has enjoyed your hospitality and/or is an expert on the special feature you're discussing (skiing, architecture, sailing), or just discuss the special feature a little more specifically. In the last paragraph, give your name, the address, and the telephone number of your bed and breakfast as a contact for further information. And that's it. You've written a press release. Check the spelling, grammar, and punctuation and type it double-spaced. It's ready to mail.

Along with the press release, include a covering letter directed to the individual writer. Invite the writer to call you (collect if the call will be long distance) if he or she has any questions, and to spend a few days at your bed and breakfast on a *gratis* basis. In addition, include a brochure for your B&B, plus a good photograph of your home if you have one. (Do not ask for it to be returned.) And if you have a reprint of any article written about your B&B, send it along as well.

Don't get discouraged if nothing happens right away. Information that you send out might not result in a story for months and months. And sometimes a writer will take you up on that free visit, but no story is published until quite some time later. Recognize that it's all part of the process. For now, the important thing is that you get that process under way.

Advertising your bed and breakfast

While you're doing your best to get some free publicity, you might find it necessary to buy space in newspapers or magazines to advertise your bed and breakfast. (At the very least, buy a listing in the Yellow Pages under "Bed and Breakfast.")

If you haven't discovered this already, you soon will: Advertising is not cheap. If you think that a full-page ad in the *New York Times* is just what you need to bring those guests to your door, you'd better be prepared to mortgage your home and take out a loan. Fortunately, there are ways to beat the typically high cost of paid advertising.

One solution is to participate in joint advertising with other bed and breakfast homes. If you belong to a national or regional bed and breakfast association, find out about joint advertising opportunities through those organizations. Together with other bed and breakfast hosts, you can purchase an ad that's large enough to be noticed, but you pay only a percentage of the total cost. You might also want to talk to other independent bed and breakfast operators in your area to see if they would be interested in purchasing an ad with you in a national or regional newspaper or magazine. Ads in local papers can pay off in guests, too. There are always area residents who will be needing accommodations for out-of-town friends, relatives, or business associates. Ad rates in small, community papers are usually quite reasonable, and the more times you run the same ad, the better deal you get on the cost. Remember the "law of frequency" when deciding upon an advertising schedule. You can't run an ad just once and expect the inquiries to come pouring in. A smaller ad run a number of times is more effective than a large ad run just once.

You should try to get an article written about your bed and breakfast in any type of specialty magazine that is of interest to visitors to your area, but one way to be sure to reach aficionados is to buy an ad in that specialty magazine. For example, the owners of Fireacre Farm in central New York started their bed and breakfast business by hosting rockhounds who came to the area on mineral-collecting trips. The best way to let rockhounds know about Firecare Farm? Advertise in mineral collectors' magazines.

One type of advertising that is inexpensive but often overlooked is the placement of an ad inside a program for a particular event taking place in your area. Does your area host events for which a number of people come from out of town? Chamber-music concerts, art shows, dance performances, flower shows, state fairs, plays, sports competitions—all of these have programs that are provided to the people who attend. And most of them print advertisements from local businesses as a way to fund the events. Buying an ad in a program is not expensive, and it reaches the people who will most likely be returning to your area for similar events in the future. In addition, there's no greater public relations for your bed and breakfast than to support a community event by means of your advertising.

Creative marketing for off-season business

Inevitably, every host faces empty rooms during the off-season. So what can you do to fill those rooms? First survey your own lifestyle and identify your talents. Do you have a degree from a culinary school? Try offering a "culinary arts" weekend where you introduce guests to the secrets of making exotic desserts. Do you have expertise in quiltmaking, knitting, embroidering, or woodworking? Offer a package deal where registrants can learn a craft as they enjoy your hospitality. And don't be too quick to discount your talents as nonmarketable! Come March and early April, I can easily envision scores of feet beating a path to the door of any accountant host who offers a weekend of tax consultations!

If your B&B is large enough to accommodate a group, and has meeting space, go after businesses that might use your B&B for weekend retreats or weekday seminars. If cost effective, hire someone to offer a special fun weekend. Some larger B&Bs hire community actors to present a "Murder Mystery Weekend" complete with murder victim, suspects, detectives, and witnesses. The guests all play a part and everyone has a great time. Another idea for the slow season was launched by Bed & Breakfast of Rhode Island—a weekend of ballroom dance instruction. Guests stay in any of four participating B&B inns and enjoy dancing in the ballroom of a small Newport mansion.

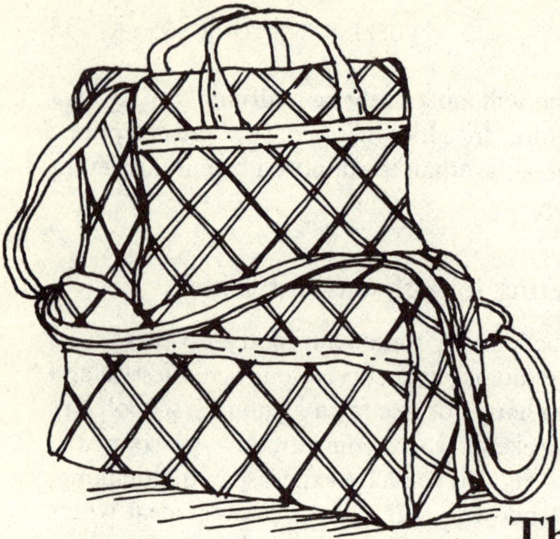

6
The Perfect Guest

There are two main reasons to screen prospective guests before opening your home to any of them. One is to make sure that your bed and breakfast can meet their requirements; the other is to make sure that they can meet yours. Bed and breakfast is not for everyone, and the screening process is as much an education as anything else. A number of people seek out bed and breakfast accommodations without really understanding what it's all about. Some people honestly would not enjoy staying in a bed and breakfast, and the screening process can help them discover this.

Screening your guests

If you choose to operate your bed and breakfast home independently, then the screening responsibility falls to you and you alone. If you list your home with a reservation service organization, the RSO will take care of screening for you. (See "Reservation Service Organizations" in chapter 4.) Either way, you should be knowledgeable about the process so that you can make it work to your best advantage. Following is the procedure that you will need to follow if you plan to do the screening yourself.

Meeting your guests' needs

To ensure that your bed and breakfast can meet the needs of your prospective guests, you have to find out what kind of accommodations they are looking for, exactly. This information can be obtained by having them fill out a reservation request form (some independent hosts print such a form on their brochure), or the information can be taken over the telephone. More than one host has noted the importance of a telephone conversation as a way to get a "feel" for the prospective guest. For this reason, many hosts will make a reservation by telephone only, or they follow up a written reservation request with a phone call.

A screening checklist is provided here as a guide for the kind of information you need to obtain from prospective guests. If you do the screening yourself, prepare your own checklist, adapting the items listed here to reflect what your bed and breakfast home is set up to provide. This can then be used in your brochure, and copies can be ready by the telephone.

Always find out the reason why a visitor is coming to your area, because the location of your home could be an important factor. A teacher coming to attend a seminar at a university will want to be near the school. A couple coming to look at houses because they plan to relocate to the area will most likely want to stay in the neighborhood they are scouting. If your home is not in a good location for some of the people who contact you, tell them so. Then if they decide to stay at your B&B anyway, they will know what the situation is.

Your location could also be an issue if your home is not anywhere near public transportation. If this is the case, make it a point to find out whether guests will be bringing their own car or plan to rent one during their visit. If not, make sure they understand that transportation will be a problem if they choose to stay with you. At times like these, it's good to be a part of a local network of bed and breakfast homes. The guests whose needs you cannot meet will appreciate a referral to another area B&B that can.

Finding out the reason why guests will be visiting can also help you discover whether their activities will be compatible with your own routine. One host reports that she did not accept a guest who was coming to the area on a work assignment that meant he needed to sleep days. This would have been disruptive to the normal routine of her home. And one Florida host whose home is located near a popular beach says she decided against hosting a group of people "who were obviously looking to party over Easter break." This would have disrupted her normally peaceful lifestyle, so she steered them, instead, to an area motel.

It is a good idea to keep on hand, right by the phone, a list of alternative lodging for people who obviously would be more comfortable in a hotel or motel. And be aware, too, that it is not uncommon for bed and breakfast hosts to sometimes receive misdirected calls from people who are seeking a shelter or some sort of transient housing. If there are shelters, youth hostels, a YMCA or YWCA, or other low-cost temporary housing in your area, keep their numbers handy.

When prospective guests contact you, find out what the composition of the party will be—how many people, whether there are children (and if so, their ages), and whether they hope to bring along a pet. Use this information to determine whether you can accommodate the guests. If there is a party of six traveling together and you have accommodations for a maximum of four, then you should discuss the possibility of using the sofa bed or setting up cots in the rooms (some people will think this is fine; others won't). If necessary, refer them to another, larger bed and breakfast home. If there are children under the age of ten, and you accept only those children who are ten or older, then you'll need to screen out these particular guests. If someone wants to bring a Doberman pinscher along on the trip, and you have a cat that would object, explain that you cannot accommodate the pet; the guest will go elsewhere or leave the pet at home.

How many nights the party wishes to stay, and the dates of the visit, are additional pieces of information you must obtain not only to make your home "guest ready" for their arrival but also so that you can block out those dates on your calendar in case other prospective guests inquire about those dates. If rooms are reserved, then this means no vacancy if others call. Be especially careful not to double-book a room, or to overlap dates. You don't want to have one party of four still in residence when the next party of four shows up. Keep a good calendar!

Some hosts screen out guests who wish to stay for longer periods of time than the hosts would find comfortable. "A couple wanted to be here from three weeks to three months," says Marjorie Lindmark, owner of Bed 'n' Breakfast in Phoenix. That was too long, she felt, so she chose not to accommodate them. For most hosts, the pleasure in offering bed and breakfast comes largely from the variety of people who come and go, plus the ability to schedule some time where there are no guests in residence at all. A guest who stays for a long time could being to feel more like a roommate. So consider what your feelings are about long-term guests before agreeing to accommodate anyone looking for that type of situation.

You will need to explain to prospective guests what kinds of beds are available in your bed and breakfast (twins, full, queen, or king) to see what they would prefer. And describe the bathroom facilities. If there is a shared bath only, expect that some people will immediately envision a line of guests going clear out the front door and down the block as they each wait their turn. Assure them that this is not the case by letting them know that the bathroom is shared by only one or two other people, that it is right next to the room they would be using, that there is a second bathroom available if necessary—any piece of information that would help dispel the image of long waits and lack of privacy. For those who still seem uncomfortable about the shared bath, don't press the issue. "Attitude toward sharing the bath" is one of the ways that the owners of the Prince George Inn Bed and Breakfast in Annapolis, Maryland, screen prospective guests. Some people really would be happier somewhere that offers a private bath.

If there are aspects of your bed and breakfast that could pose a problem to certain guests, be sure to bring them up: You have a cat or dog, which rules out guests who have allergies to animals. You have rooms on the second and third floors only, and no elevator, which rules out guests who have difficulty walking up stairs. You have a strictly nonsmoking household, which rules out any guests who want to be able to smoke wherever they stay. You have mattresses that are only six feet in length, ruling out anyone over six feet tall. Ask prospective guests if they have any special requirements that you should know about, such as diet restrictions or allergies.

The bottom line is that there should be no surprises. You should know exactly what prospective guests are looking for, and guests should know exactly what they'll be getting if they stay at your bed and breakfast. A good screening process will cover all of the necessary information.

Meeting your own needs

The screening process is intended not only to determine whether your bed and breakfast offers the kind of accommodations that a guest is seeking; it is also for the purpose of helping a host find out whether or not a prospective guest is a "bed and breakfast person." This refers to just about the most wonderful species of human being that ever walked the earth. People of this type stand out in a crowd: They smile at babies, say "thank you" to clerks and waiters, and hold doors for people who have their arms full of packages. They give money when someone asks for spare change, help little old ladies across the street, and cheerfully give up their seat on the bus to someone who needs it more. They are kind to animals, they often give presents for no reason, and they love sunsets. Or in the words of one host from Indiana, bed and breakfast people are "the best in the world."

Now, how can you be sure that every person whom you allow to stay in your home is a "bed and breakfast person"? The truth is that you can't, no matter who does the screening—you or a reservation service organization—and no matter how carefully the process is followed. There is just no way to accurately assess someone's character through answers given on a form or through a telephone conversation. You can try, and you should try; just realize that no screening method is foolproof. Still, the guidelines given here should help to weed out the most obvious cases.

First of all, ask how the prospective guest heard about your bed and breakfast. This can tell you a lot. "My Aunt Gertrude stayed with you last summer" is a good piece of information. If you remember Aunt Gertrude fondly as the sweetest lady, then you can feel confident that she wouldn't refer her niece to you unless she, too, was just as sweet. If, on the other hand, if you didn't enjoy Aunt Gertrude's visit and found yourself counting the hours until her departure, then perhaps you should tell her niece that you have no vacancies for the weekend she

Jack Argenio, the director of Bed & Breakfast Ltd. in New Haven, Connecticut, enjoys telling the story about a reservation he claims he once handled for a woman calling ahead from a hotel in Boston. She made a point to impress upon him that she was used to the very best. "She mentioned three times that she was staying at the Ritz," Jack recalls. Although she was clearly fussy, Jack was confident that she would be happy with one of his hosts who had an exceptionally elegant home, so arrangements were made. The woman gave her permanent address as Heaven, California. Familiar with California, but not with this particular city, Jack asked her where "Heaven" was. "That's what we who live there call Beverly Hills," she replied. So the reservation made and the host forewarned, the day arrived when a limousine pulled up to the bed and breakfast home. A well-dressed woman emerged and came to the door, where she said not one word to the host while she looked around. Still with no words exchanged, she then turned and walked out of the house, got back into the limo, and drove away. At this the host, who had been standing there the entire time, became quite upset. She called Jack and told him how insulted she felt by this woman's flagrant show of disdain for her fine home. Jack was sympathetic but philosophical. "My dear," he said, "your home is very nice, but let's face it: It's just not Heaven!"

would like to visit. The longer you are in business, the more you will be contacted by people who were referred to your bed and breakfast by friends and relatives who have already stayed with you. Accommodating "a friend of a friend" is usually safer for you because you already have a character reference.

For the total strangers who contact you as a result of your inclusion in a guidebook or a brochure sent out by a tourist office, it's an excellent idea for you to ask for a reference. This can be an employer, minister, banker, business associate—someone you can call to verify the prospective guest's reliability. Yes, this will mean a toll call for your phone bill, but it is an expense that is necessary for your own protection and peace of mind. If someone refuses to give you a reference, then it's best not to accommodate that person.

Another piece of information you should require is a business address and telephone number, in addition to the prospective guest's home address and number. (Unless the guest gives the employer's name as a reference, most hosts will not have occasion to contact the guest's place of work. This is good information to keep on hand in the unlikely event of a problem.) Anyone who is vague or evasive about his or her occupation or place of work, who gives incomplete information about a home residence, or who refuses to give you the names of all the members of the party should be screened out. And because this information is the only concrete way a host has to check up on any prospective guest, some hosts will not accept last-minute reservations that simply do not give them enough time to make reference checks. And some hosts will never, never take anyone who comes to the door without having first called to make a reservation. If you are advertising your bed and breakfast home (and its address) in guidebooks and in paid advertisements, you can expect this to happen every once in a while. It does mean that you have to turn away some business, but as long as yours is not a commercial enterprise but, rather, your private home, it's best to institute the safeguards that you can and adhere to them, with no exceptions.

Experienced hosts say that they try to draw out the people who contact them by telephone, getting them to talk about themselves a little bit so that the hosts can learn something about their personalities. Questions like "Have you ever visited our city before?" "Is this your first time staying in a bed and breakfast?" "Why are you coming to the area?" will help get them talking. See how they handle themselves on the telephone. "Occasionally, I do not like the sound of a voice and we are magically full," says one Maine host. Anyone who is not friendly or seems too demanding or critical is not the "bed and breakfast person" that a host is looking for as a guest. You can simply say that you do not have a vacancy.

Hosts who accept reservations by mail might want to include a place on their reservation request form for prospective guests to write down their interests or hobbies. Some hosts will add a note: "Tell me a little bit about yourself." This gives you something to talk about if you like to confirm the reservation by telephone, and it gives some insight into your guests' lives. The form is also a good place to request the license number of a guest's car (if he or she is bringing it). Some hosts report that they feel uncomfortable about asking for the license number on the telephone because it gives the impression that they are suspicious of the guest; they will just make a note of it when the guest arrives, at a time when the guest will not notice. This is one more piece of information that is good for you to have on file in the unlikely event that the guest turns out to be of unsavory character.

One final note on the screening process is that it should absolutely *not* be used as a form of discrimination against anyone on the basis of race, color, religion, or sexual preference. If you have irreconcilable differences with people for any of these reasons, you should think twice about becoming a host, and not just because you fear a lawsuit. To be a good host, you've got to love people in all their varieties. If a personal prejudice is going to interfere with your role as a friendly and hospitable host, then offering bed and breakfast is not a good idea.

Confirming a reservation

Once you and your prospective guest have decided to go ahead and make a reservation, there are a few matters to arrange, preferably by telephone. (Note: If you list your home with a reservation service organization, some or all of these details will be handled through the agency.)

Always settle on a definite arrival time that is convenient for both you and your guest, and impress upon the guest that the arrival time is important to you. If the guest says that he or she may be late, request a courtesy telephone call to let you know. If you are willing to pick up your guests at the airport or at the bus or train station, make plans to do this as you note the arrival time and flight/train/bus number.

Now is also the time to explain the prices and ask for a deposit, to be sent to you in advance. Some hosts ask for an amount equal to that of one night's stay; others ask for a percentage of the total projected amount (usually 25 percent). Mention that the balance is due upon arrival and go over what forms of payment you accept.

You will need to decide upon a cancellation policy because you will get cancellations, as well as no-shows. Generally, hosts will make a refund if a cancellation is made seven days prior to the originally planned date of arrival. A service charge is deducted from the refund (hosts charge anywhere from $5 to $10). This charge compensates you for your time and effort to process the reservation. Hosts generally do not make a refund of the deposit for cancellations made at the last minute or for no-shows who later contact them. This is because they have had to hold the rooms, possibly turning away other guests. To avoid conflicts over your cancellation policy, print it on your reservation request form or in a confirmation letter sent after a reservation has been made. This makes it the responsibility of the guest to notify you according to your guidelines if there is a problem and he or she cannot honor the reservation. (Note: If you list your home with an RSO, that agency will have a cancellation policy that guests must follow.)

A confirmation letter stating the dates that have been reserved and the prices, plus the expected time of arrival, is a good idea because it acts as a reminder to the guest about points you have already gone over. It can also act as an invoice in case the guest has not yet sent the deposit by the time the letter is received. Include with the letter a map and directions to your home.

The role of the RSO

A reservation service organization can make a host's life much easier when it comes to screening guests. You can literally let the RSO do all the work for you, taking calls from prospective guests, asking them the right questions, and obtaining the right information from them. (See "Reservation Service Organizations" in chapter 4.)

The managers of reservation service organizations take thousands of calls and, therefore, have considerable experience in weeding out those who do not fit the model of a "bed and breakfast person." "In dealing with people over the telephone day in and day out, you quickly learn to spot potential problems. Then we ask lots and lots of questions, and if we think there will be a problem, we don't place them," says the manager of Bed 'n' Breakfast Ltd. in Washington, D.C. Danie Bernard, manager of B&B Suncoast Accommodations in St. Pete Beach, Florida, says, "I have twenty years in personnel, know what to say and ask, and have a 'feel' for a good customer." "We ask a lot of questions in order to find out what the caller is looking for," says Nancy Jenkins, former manager of Bed & Breakfast Exchange in St. Helena, California.

"We eliminate about 15 percent of potential guests and on the basis of nine years' experience know that it is foolhardy for any individual in a private home to try to do his or her own screening. Our credo is 'Our hosts are more important than the guests.' Homeowners should find out how an agency screens their guests," says Jean Brown, manager of Bed & Breakfast International in Kensington, California. Is it typical for RSOs to turn away a percentage of the people who contact them looking for bed and breakfast accommodations? "Of course. It's our job," says Kate Winters, manager of Bed & Breakfast Rocky Mountains. Some reasons prospective guests are turned away:

"Many people just call to find out prices," says Irmgard Castleberry, manager of Pacific Bed & Breakfast in Seattle, Washington. "Those are the ones looking for a one-night cheap room, and we do not want those guests. They are better off in a cheap motel."

Mary McAulay, manager of Urban Ventures in New York City, has turned away those who were "too cranky" or whose address and telephone number did not check out. Ruth Wilson, manager of Bed & Breakfast Texas Style in Dallas, says, "I ask for references, business and personal, also credit card references. I *have called* the references!" Arline Kardasis, co-owner of Bed & Breakfast Associates, Bay Colony, Ltd. in Boston, has screened out those who "could not or would not provide information on an employer, occupation, reason for visit, full home address, work telephone number, home telephone number, and names of all members of their party."

Some reservation service organizations, such as The Traveler in Maryland, will not accept mail reservations. "Chatting on the phone really helps you know the type of person," says Eileen Wood, manager of Bed & Breakfast Guest Homes in Algoma, Wisconsin. The manager of the Bed & Breakfast League, a national RSO based in Washington, D.C., says, "We make reservations by telephone only so that we may talk with the potential guests. If they are polite, give personal information easily, and seem flexible, we'll book them. If they are rude, pushy, or demanding, we won't."

The manager of Pineapple Hospitality in New England has turned away people who were "not wanting to have to meet people." A bed and breakfast is not for anyone who wishes to spend a few days in total privacy and anonymity. Jack Argenio, manager of Bed & Breakfast Ltd. in New Haven, Connecticut, has turned away those who were "too fussy," and the manager of Bed & Breakfast Down East in Maine turned away one caller who was "obviously intoxicated."

People who call at the last minute are not often placed. "With last-minute requests we do not have enough time to get background information," says the manager of Eye Openers Bed & Breakfast Reservations in Altadena, California.

Gary Winget, manager of the Bed & Breakfast Registry, based in St. Paul, Minnesota, lists a number of reasons for not placing some of the people who have contacted that RSO: Some wanted to have friends over for a party; some wanted to know "how liberal" the hosts were; some wanted to sneak people into their rooms; some had no idea what a bed and breakfast was.

If you list your home with a reservation service organization, find out how that agency screens the people who write or call looking for bed and breakfast accommodations. If you are going to relinquish this important process to someone else, you must be sure that the screening is done very carefully.

The reservation service organization provides an additional service for the hosts it represents—that of "matching" certain guests with certain hosts, based on mutual interests. This is a service that can help you enjoy offering bed and breakfast even more because guests with whom you share something in common will be directed to your home. One Boston host who loved to run especially enjoyed the visit of a woman who also loved to run: "We ran together every morning," she says. "It was hard to see her leave."

New hosts usually wonder how the placement process works and at what point they get involved in it when guests make their initial contact with the reservation service organization. RSOs keep on hand information about your bed and breakfast home based (usually) on a home visit. This is the same kind of information that you would include on your own screening checklist if you were to handle the process yourself: the bedroom and bathroom set-ups, the kinds of beds, special restrictions (such as no pets, or children over the age of twelve only), special features (such as a swimming pool, or a fireplace in the bedroom), and potential problems (such as a pet in residence or stairway access only to second-floor rooms). With all of this information, the RSO manager can easily answer the basic questions that a prospective guest will have about accommodations. Thus far, you need not be involved in the process at all. If the guest decides that your bed and breakfast would be the best choice, and the RSO manager is satisfied with the reliability of the guest, the RSO will get in touch with you before confirming the reservation.

Screening Form

Name ______________________________
Address ______________________________
Home phone ______________________________
Occupation / job title ______________________________
Employer's name ______________________________
Work address ______________________________
Work phone ______________________________
Reference's name ______________________________
Reference's address ______________________________
Reference's phone ______________________________

Composition of party:
Number of adults (list names): ______________________________
Children (list ages): ______________________________
Pets: yes ___ no ___

Date of arrival ______________ Number of nights ________
Last night of visit ______________
Time of arrival ______________
Expected time of departure ______________

Accommodations desired:
___ Single room
___ Double room
___ Private bath
___ Shared bath
___ Twin beds
___ Double bed
___ Queen- or king-size bed
___ Extra cot in room

Location desired: ______________________________

Arriving by:
___ Air
___ Bus
___ Train
___ Automobile (license number):

____ Rental car
____ Desires pickup at airport or bus or train station
____ (Note arrival time and identifying number of flight/bus/ train): _______
____ Needs parking for car
____ Needs access to public transportation

Special requirements:
____ Smoking
____ Nonsmoking
____ Diet restrictions
____ Allergies
____ Needs room on ground floor or elevator
____ Over six feet tall
____ Medical alert

Costs:
$_______ room per night × _____ nights = $____________
Deposit due in advance . . . . $____________
Balance due upon arrival . . . . $____________

Form of payment accepted:
____ Cash
____ Traveler's checks
____ Personal check
____ Credit card

Refund policy for cancellations: ______________________________
Purpose of visit: ____
Where guest heard about this B&B: __________________________
Has guest stayed in a B&B before? ___________________________
Guest's special interests/hobbies: ____________________________

The RSO manager will tell you about the guest and the dates that he or she wishes to visit. "If a host has questions about a particular request, we will get the answers to their questions. We do drop or refuse reservations where the questions are not answered or are not answered to our or the host's satisfaction," says Gary Winget of the Bed & Breakfast Registry. This is fairly common among reservation service organizations; the host has final approval or refusal of a prospective guest. If the dates of the visit are not good for your schedule, you can turn down the guest, and the RSO will place the person elsewhere. If you choose not to host a single man because your husband will be away on business the particular days the guest wants to visit, you have the right to turn down the reservation and ask the RSO to place him somewhere else. Keep in mind, though, that even though each individual host does have the final say-so on each reservation, the RSO does expect a spirit of cooperation; if you wish to continue to list your home with the RSO, you've got to have a good reason for any reservation you do turn down.

One particular advantage enjoyed by hosts who list with a reservation service organization is the high number of guests who have used the services of the RSO before and who either come back again or refer their friends and relatives to the RSO. Rest & Repast Bed & Breakfast in Pine Groves Mills, Pennsylvania, for example, reports that approximately 50 percent of the guests placed by this RSO are repeat customers. And Orleans Bed and Breakfast in Massachusetts reports that more than 50 percent of its new guests have been referred by people who have been accommodated in the past. This is definitely an advantage for hosts who want to be sure that every guest is a "bed and breakfast person." Rest & Repast even makes a point of placing some of its seasoned guests with brand-new hosts in order to make the hosts feel more comfortable in their new role! Guests who are personally known to be the right kind of persons for B&B are a treasured commodity. "Selected guests are notified on an annual basis of the new host directory," says Gary Winget. "A preferred-guest club is now being organized and will provide regular contact with selected guests."

Whether you choose to list with an RSO, which will handle the screening of guests for you, or whether you choose to stay independent and handle the screening yourself, the important thing is that it be done. As bed and breakfast becomes more and more popular in North America, more and more people are seeking out B&B accommodations, sometimes for the wrong reasons. The screening process can help educate prospective guests about bed and breakfast, making sure that the people who do come to visit your home understand the difference between a B&B and a hotel or motel. And those people who would honestly not enjoy the unique experience of bed and breakfast can be directed to another type of accommodation.

One-night guests

There are many, many hosts out there who require a minimum stay of two nights for any guest who stays at their bed and breakfast home. There are good reasons for this, and they will become quite obvious to you once you start hosting. The main reason is that one-nighters are a lot more work than people who stay two or more nights.

Consider that you have to make both the guest room and the bathroom "guest ready" between the departure of one guest and the arrival of the next. And consider that each guest uses an entire set of towels and an entire set of sheets and pillowcases—which means that the bed has to be stripped, the laundry done, and the bed remade. Someone staying two or three days can use the same towels and sheets during his or her visit, and the bathroom needs only a few touch-ups to keep it clean. For a series of one-nighters, the whole process of cleaning is a never-ending one. That's a lot of laundry and toilet bowls. The fact that you're doing this because you love people can get to be pretty remote under these circumstances.

Still, it is unlikely that your rooms will be booked every single night of the week by people who wish to stay only one night. Usually, they will be sprinkled among the number of guests who stay longer, giving you some respite from the amount of work that providing for a one-nighter causes. Keep this in mind before deciding to turn away *all* short-term guests.

There are a number of travelers who want and need accommodation for only one night. People driving great distances could spend one night in Ohio and the next in Illinois and the one following who knows where? They have someplace to go and have no intention of lingering at a B&B just to fulfill the two-night minimum. Yet, long-distance travelers sometimes prefer to stay in a bed and breakfast home just to have a little human contact on their trip. If no host will take them, they will end up in the nearest motel. Business travelers, too, sometimes need to be in town for only one or two days to have a meeting, go for a job interview, or attend a conference. They, too, will go elsewhere if no host will accept them for one night only.

If you are just starting out with your bed and breakfast or have trouble attracting as many guests as you would like even though you've been hosting for a while, do not be hasty in turning away one-nighters. Word-of-mouth is one of the most effective ways to publicize your bed and breakfast, so that one-night guest who was treated so well at your home means a lot more than just the laundry and clean-up time for you. The investment may be worth it for the future business you might enjoy as a result.

Some hosts do take steps to ensure that they don't end up losing money by taking a guest for just one night (think of the costs of detergent and electricity for the laundry, the breakfast ingredients that must be purchased, even gasoline if you offer a ride to or from the airport or train station). They ask for a surcharge as part of their system of pricing. (See "Pricing Your Bed and Breakfast" in chapter 3.) So if you normally ask $30 for a single room, you might add $5 or $10 to the cost for anyone who does not stay a minimum of two nights. This way, all your time and energy are counterbalanced to an extent, and the guest understands that you will make an exception under these terms.

Single travelers

It has long been a tradition that people who travel alone are punished. They are given the smallest, most uncomfortable rooms in hotels and the worst tables in restaurants, and they are charged disproportionate prices for them. This is such a problem that a number of people who have suffered the indignities forced upon a single traveler feel moved to fight back, in the only way they can—by taking business away from the establishments that sin. As far back as 1891, a group of women who were fed up with second-class treatment when they traveled alone formed what was then called the Women's Rest Tour Association. Its members devoted themselves to keeping detailed records of where they were treated well during their travels—and where they were not. The membership used this information as a guide, winning for some establishments a loyal following, losing for others the patronage that they did not deserve to have.

Today, the Women's Rest Tour Association still exists under the name of the Traveler's Information Exchange. And it is not the only organization of its kind. More and more, travelers are evaluating the accommodations they use and are spreading the word—good or bad—faster and more efficiently than ever before. The point is that there are a lot of people who do travel alone for various reasons, and the kind of treatment they receive in your bed and breakfast will determine whether you win, or lose, their patronage.

As a host, you will be contacted by single travelers. They are drawn to bed and breakfast homes because of their reputation for atmosphere, comfort, safety, and friendliness, qualities that are sometimes valued by someone traveling alone even more than by those traveling with family or friends. Yet, it is not unusual for a bed and breakfast host to fall into the same pattern of thinking that has been plaguing the single traveler for much too long. Consider the following incident:

Upon arrival at a bed and breakfast home, a woman was shown to a tiny bedroom (a "single") off the kitchen, with the bathroom down the hall. The tour of the house had included a peek at another, larger guest room that had a queen-sized bed, a sitting area with a comfortable chair and table, and an adjoining private bath. This more comfortable room was vacant, and the woman would have much preferred that choice, but the host didn't even ask. Why? It was a "double." Surely no single person should have all that space to herself.

This is exactly the kind of thinking that could get your bed and breakfast home stricken from recommended lodging lists for single travelers. Of course, some people traveling alone are budget minded; they will find a tiny room with the bathroom down the hall just fine, if the price is right. But many single travelers want to enjoy their accommodations. They are willing to pay a little more for a larger space and a private bath, perhaps even a more pleasing décor, a more comfortable bed, and a better view. (Unfortunately, these differences are too often the case when comparing singles with doubles.) This is not to say that people traveling alone are willing to pay the full price that would normally be charged for double occupancy. Many consider this another type of punishment for the single traveler, and you can bet that it will be duly noted.

Instead, think about the following compromise as a way to encourage single travelers to stay at your bed and breakfast home. Say you have a single room and a double room available for guests. No matter which room is used, you've still got to wash a set of sheets and clean the bathroom. Does it really matter whether the sheets are twin size or queen size? Does it really matter that one bathroom is off the hallway and the other adjoins the larger guest room? Of course, the answer is no. The work is essentially the same for you. The real difference is in the price. Let's say that your single room is priced at $25, your double at

$50. This is only fair—more people, more money. And if the double is booked for two people at full price, so be it. But if it's not, why not give your single traveler a choice of rooms instead of assuming that he or she "should" automatically get the smaller room? Now, obviously the double room is worth more than the single room because it offers more. (See "Pricing Your Bed and Breakfast" in chapter 3.) So adjust your price accordingly. If the double is available, why not invite a single traveler to use it for a reduced rate, say $35 or $40? This way, your visitor makes the decision and will be much happier for the choice.

Realistically, this choice can be extended only at the time a guest arrives at your door, unless he or she does want to reserve the double room in advance, either at full price or at a small reduction that you determine (perhaps $45 for a room priced at $50 for double occupancy). This keeps you from losing money if you get a call in the interim from someone else wanting to book the double at full cost and you have to turn them away. (The $5 reduction covers the approximate cost in food and drink that you would have had to supply for the second person.)

Do your best to make the single rooms in your bed and breakfast comfortable and homey. For some reason, single rooms end up on the bottom of the priority list for many hosts. This is just not good business sense. A guest will notice immediately and feel that you do not consider his or her comfort as important as the comfort of guests who are not alone. Make the quarters as spacious as possible by removing unnecessary furniture or rearranging what you have in a better way. Get rid of that big bookcase and install a few wall shelves on brackets instead. Put the floor lamp elsewhere in the house and substitute a space-saving lamp that hangs from the ceiling. Is that massive oak bureau the only one you've got, or can it be switched with a smaller bureau, maybe even one that fits neatly inside the closet? (Don't forget that some platform types of beds have drawers underneath. This is good in a small room.) Ask yourself if the room seems too dark—which will make it seem even smaller than it is. Paint the walls and ceiling white to open up the space. Take down the heavy, dark drapes and hang white or light-colored ones instead. Make sure that your light bulbs have a high enough wattage to make the room feel bright and cheery. A small single room can be quite charming if you put the time and energy into making it that way.

Beyond making their accommodations as comfortable as possible, ask yourself whether you are being as hospitable to your single travelers as you are to couples or families. There is an unfortunate stigma attached to being alone, and sometimes the attitude that there is something wrong with anyone who is alone comes through unintentionally. Obvious discomfort when the single traveler joins a group of other guests who are in couples; different seating times at the breakfast table; a general feeling of being left out of activities that include other guests—you must guard against all of these. (But don't go overboard in the other direction either, making a single traveler uncomfortable by giving him or her *too* much attention.)

Did you hear about the host who married her very first guest?" asks Arline Kardasis, co-owner of Bed and Breakfast Associates, Bay Colony Ltd., in Massachusetts. She tells the story of a host, whose home was located in an outlying area of Boston, who registered with her reservation service organization a few years back. Her inconvenient location and her restriction of "no single men" unfortunately meant no visitors. Then one day Arline was contacted by a company inquiring about housing for an executive coming from Sweden to do some consulting work for the firm. The host's home was very near the company, but the gentleman was unmarried. After some discussion, the host decided to relent on her rule about single men. Talk about the perfect guest. The couple was married within the year, and the host now lives in Sweden with her husband.

Some hosts who live alone do not want to accommodate single travelers of the opposite sex. If you live alone, this is a consideration, and you will have to make a decision. Some hosts are apprehensive about their personal safety or about how it might appear to the neighbors, or they are just plain uncomfortable about the idea of sharing a roof with a stranger of the opposite sex. Any of these reasons are good ones to screen out members of the opposite gender. It's your home, and you have a responsibility to yourself to feel comfortable and safe in it. If your bed and breakfast is registered with a reservation service organization, ask the manager not to place any single traveler of the opposite sex with you. If you handle your own reservations, you need to come up with something to say when someone wants to make a reservation with you and you prefer not to accommodate that person because of the decision you've made. You can always say that you have personal plans for that particular night (or nights) that prevent you from accepting any bed and breakfast guests at that time and give your apologies graciously. (See "Screening Your Guests" in this chapter.)

If you are set up to accept single travelers at your bed and breakfast, you can play an important part in extending the kind of hospitality to them that they have long been denied. And you can be sure that the good word will spread like wildfire.

Hosting children

If you're a parent, you are well aware of how disruptive and destructive children can be at times—but you also know how sweet and obedient they can be at others. They are not necessarily all terrors who should be unconditionally banned from bed and breakfast homes. Rather, children are guests of a special sort who need a different kind of hospitality. As a bed and breakfast host, you have to decide whether you wish to accept children. Many people travel as a family, and if you choose not to allow children—of any age—to stay in your home, then you will most certainly narrow your market. This is especially true if your home is well situated near an attraction geared toward young people—Sea World, Disneyland, amusement parks, special museums (such as the one devoted to Buffalo Bill)—or in an area where they can hike or swim. So consider the following points carefully before making your decision.

Some hosts feel that they are simply not set up to accommodate children as overnight guests, when in fact it might be easier than you think. For an infant, a crib is not the only solution, although it's great if you already have one from the days when your children were small. "One couple, when I told them I had nothing for their one-month-old daughter, said, 'No problem.' They pulled a drawer out of the dresser and made a bed for her. That's where she slept," says Lona Smith, owner of Summerwood, a bed and breakfast home registered with a reservation service organization called Leatherstocking B&B of Central New York. A host registered with Pineapple Hospitality, an RSO in New England, says this about sleeping arrangements for young children: "If they are little, we set up the playpen for them in the parents' room, and they seem to sleep quite nicely." And sometimes parents are quite comfortable about the idea of placing their infant on the double bed between them, where he or she can sleep peacefully and safely with Mom and Dad right there.

At Leftwich House in Graham, North Carolina, a small child can use the crib, and an older child can be accommodated in a small room with a bed that adjoins the parents' room. Patricia Boettcher, owner of 3B's Bed & Breakfast in Spring Valley, Ohio, puts older children right in the parents' room: "We can set up cots for children, as our rooms are spacious."

One couple traveling with a baby and a four-year-old were happy to locate a bed and breakfast home in Mystic, Connecticut, that had adjoining bedrooms that shared a bath. The family could be together, bother no one else in the bed and breakfast, and have some privacy and space as well.

Another idea for accommodating an older child is a hammock or an inflatable mattress with a sleeping bag. (Older children might enjoy the opportunity to sleep in a tent pitched right outside the house, if the parents approve.) And a small inflatable plastic swimming pool is great for an infant; it's as comfortable as an air mattress, and the child can't fall out. So if you are contacted by parents who have children, explain what kinds of "beds" you can provide for the youngsters and see if the parents think they're suitable.

Some hosts accept children of a certain age only—infants only, toddlers only, over twelve only—depending on what they're used to or what they think their home can best endure. "Because of goosedown quilts, etc., I accept only eight years or older," says the owner of Spindrift Bed & Breakfast in Bandon, Oregon. This is an important consideration. How "child proof" is your home? Do you fear for your quilts, your antique furniture, the original paintings on the walls? Do you have a lot of knick-knacks around, just the right size for a two-year-old to throw? If so, then accepting children only eight or older isn't such a bad idea, or else infants who can't yet manage to get a good grip on your favorite figurines. Be aware that denying someone accommodation on the basis of age may be interpreted as a violation of civil rights. (A California case brought by a family denied B&B accommodation because of their child is pending.) Therefore, it is wiser to adhere to the more negotiable guideline of "Children under twelve are discouraged because the premises are not child-safe," rather than the black-and-white rule of "No children allowed!" The latter shouts discrimination.

If you have a child yourself, chances are you've already made your house "safe" for little ones. This involves covering electrical outlets, putting up gates at the top and bottom of staircases, and locking cabinets, among other things. If you don't have a child but wish to host children, you've got to take whatever measures are necessary to ensure the well-being of your young guests. A host registered with Eye Openers Bed & Breakfast in Altadena, California, has this house rule: "No children under twelve because of the swimming pool." Children over twelve should be able to handle themselves in a strictly adult environment, knowing to stay away from a swimming pool if they can't swim (or knowing enough to heed Mom and Dad's telling them to stay away from it). Take a close look at your home and evaluate its features in view of different age groups. Should you accept young visitors of certain ages only, as some hosts do?

Of course, a lot depends upon the parents. George and Barbara Painter, owners of Turkey Nest Rest in Gatlinburg, Tennessee, admit that "our town's a great place for children," but they will accept them "only if parents can manage them." Ellen Madison, owner of Woody Hill Guest House in Westerly, Rhode Island, says she accepts children "reluctantly," based on "parents' assurances that other guests will not be disturbed." A frank talk with parents before they show up at your B&B, or when they first arrive, should be on your agenda. Make it clear that the parents are expected to supervise their youngsters during their stay, that babysitting does not come with the price of the room. If you wish, you can offer to babysit so that the parents can go out alone to dinner, shopping, sightseeing. This is a terrific amenity to offer parents who are likely to be experiencing more family togetherness than they might be used to; a chance to get away by themselves for a while might be very welcome. Make it clear, though, that your babysitting services are *by arrangement only*. You can charge a fee for this service if you wish. (See "Pricing Your Bed and Breakfast" in chapter 3.)

Do your best to think of ways to entertain the children (bored children are often the ones who go looking for something to do that maybe they shouldn't). Meadowview Guest House in Lancaster, Pennsylvania, keeps toys and games on hand. At Leftwich House in Graham, North Carolina, "there is a playroom upstairs with toys." Ocean View House in Santa Barbara, California, even advertises its special "amenity" just for kids: "Children are delighted with the backyard playhouse." A San Diego man traveling with his young son was happy to find a swing set in the yard at a bed and breakfast home in northern California. (A strong rope and a tire hung from a tree branch can keep kids entertained sometimes for hours; so can a makeshift sandbox—a discarded tractor-sized tire filled with sand.)

"It was great to find children's books sitting on the night stand next to the bed," said one mother traveling with her two small children. Books to read, or coloring books and a box of crayons, are good items to keep on hand for your young visitors. Consider preparing some "fun baskets" for children who will be indoors a lot during their visit—filled perhaps with old costume jewelry to play with; an assortment of old hats, purses, shawls, scarves, and other clothing with a lot of character (like a safari shirt or fancy dress with sequins and sparkles) for "dress up"; a variety of tinker toys, building blocks, and erector set materials; stuffed animals; even a rock collection (fascinating for an older child, but hide this basket from younger kids).

It's a nice touch to give the child a farewell gift when the visit is over; if you see that a youngster is becoming especially attached to any item in a "fun basket," consider giving that item as a present—a string of beads from the costume jewelry, a small stuffed animal, a great-looking hunk of quartz—something small but valued by the child and appreciated by the parents for your thoughtfulness. (Be sure to check with the parents before giving an item to a child to keep.)

How will your other guests, the ones without children, react to sharing the bed and breakfast with youngsters? Chances are that there will be few problems if parents supervise their kids closely. Many people enjoy being around children and think of the opportunity as a highlight of their stay, rather than a liability. One father who was staying at a B&B with his three-year-old son makes this report: "The other guests, rather than being put off by having kids present, responded more like grandparents and seemed to like it. Everyone was very supportive." The couple who owned this particular bed and breakfast home had two small children themselves, so there was already a family atmosphere. The home was already "child proof," and the kids all played together. If you have children yourself, consider that they might enjoy the chance to meet a variety of kids their own age. This is one way to make bed and breakfast truly a family project; give your children some of the responsibility for hosting the younger members of a visiting family.

If you decide to go ahead with allowing children to stay at your bed and breakfast, you will have to deal with the problem of preparing and serving food just for them. The welcome snack upon arrival and the evening snack should include milk, cookies, and fruit—items that adults usually enjoy as well. The parents of infants should supply their own formula (make this clear in advance), but you'll be responsible for the breakfast of children older than this. (See the section "Especially for Children" in chapter 8, "A Memorable Breakfast.")

Your success with hosting children has a lot to do with your feelings about them to begin with. If you really don't like kids, you probably shouldn't have them in your home, even if your location is a two-minute walk from Sea World and you'll be passing up a lot of guests who are bringing their kids to see Shamu the Whale. One couple tried it, but it just didn't work out: "We have on occasion accepted children but will no longer. Children want special food—are fussy eaters, leave crumbs on the floor, are noisy." Yes, they are all of these things. But they are more as well, and you've got to be able to see this. One father sensed this right away about the hosts with whom he and his child stayed for a wonderful visit. "Mostly, it was more the attitude of really being glad to see kids at the place," he says. The hosts simply loved kids and enjoyed having them around. If you feel the same way, your bed and breakfast can reach out to the family market that so many hosts are turning away.

Four-legged guests

Hosting pets is not for everyone. No way should you allow a full set of paws to pad around your home if there are priceless oriental rugs on the floor, heirloom crystal on the table, and museum-quality *objets d'art* on display. Of course, it's not worth the risk. There are plenty of guests who do not travel with their pets, and it's safer for your lovely home to host human beings exclusively on the assumption that they will be more careful.

Yet there are a large number of people who do travel with their pets. These may be people who are relocating or just on vacation, but they want the whole family together—and this includes Bowzer. Pet owners do not have an easy time of it when trying to locate overnight accommodations. There are some hotels, motels, inns—and bed and breakfast homes, too—that accept pets, but most do not. "A problem we have is finding hosts who will take pets," says Ashby Willcox of Bed & Breakfast of Tidewater, Virginia. "Sorry, none of our hosts accept pets," reads the literature printed by Orleans Bed & Breakfast Associates on Cape Cod. Pet owners must go elsewhere.

If you choose to accept pets, you can definitely attract a market by offering this privilege. But before you decide, evaluate the space that would be used to accommodate the animals. It must be "pet proof," able to handle the presence of animals with a minimum of wear and tear. Lincoln Alden, owner of Watercourse Way Bed & Breakfast in Stratford, Vermont, allows guests to house their dogs in the barn that is on his property. If you have a secure, separate space like this, you can easily accommodate the animals that your guests might want to bring with them. Keeping a dog outside on a leash, with no shelter, is not a good idea even in good weather. Little Fifi might never have been outdoors on her own in her entire life, and this will be uncomfortable for her. *Never* leave an animal outdoors in rain, snow, or sub-zero temperatures.

The ranch manager of Anchor Hill Ranch in Rogersville, Missouri, welcomes guests with horses. The place already has box stalls, with runs, to accommodate horses, so there is no problem. Guests are charged $5 per horse per night. This rate includes hay and oats, stall cleaning, and watering.

Most of us don't have this kind of space, so if a guest wants to bring a pet, this means that the animal will have to stay inside the house. This rules out horses, but cats and dogs can work out fine if the individual guest room can be made "pet proof." Ideally, the floor should be tile or linoleum instead of wood, and there should not be wall-to-wall carpeting because it's too hard to clean thoroughly between visits. A throw rug next to the bed is nice for the owner's comfort, and it can be washed easily after each furry guest checks out. There should be no knickknacks on dresser or table tops (they can tempt even the most well-behaved pet into a game not unlike handball).

During your initial conversation with them on the telephone, ask guests to bring the animal's own feeding and watering dishes, food, a leash (for dogs) and a "pooper scooper" if you wish to require that one be used for clean-ups, and a kitty-litter box and litter. Ask where the animal usually sleeps and try to extract an honest answer. Some pet owners might be reluctant to tell you that their pet sleeps on the bed, but it's much better that you know this in advance. If Cuddles is used to being on the bed, that's probably where the little darling will end up no matter what you or his owner thinks about it. You're much better off just asking the owner to bring something along to protect the blankets you will be providing. Just in case this item is forgotten, keep on hand a washable cover that can be placed on top of the blankets to protect them from shedding hair.

Some animals are used to sleeping on their own special pillow or blanket; if your guest's furry friend usually sleeps alone on its own bedding, ask the owner to bring it along. (Janet Turley, owner of The House of Amacord in Buckland, Massachusetts, says she doesn't usually allow pets in her bed and breakfast, but she did agree to accept a dog once because he had his own sleeping bag!)

If the owner cannot bring along all of the items you request for the pet's comfort (guests arriving by plane or bus might not be able to transport everything), find out what exactly you need to have on hand, such as the brand of food that the animal usually eats, or kitty litter and a box (a sturdy cardboard one is fine if placed on top of a sheet of plastic). Add the cost of any items to the guest's bill, along with the surcharge you decide upon for the pet (usually $5 to $10 per night).

Also ask the guests to clip the nails of their animals before arriving at your bed and breakfast. (It might be a good idea to invest in a pair of those special scissors available at pet stores just in case an owner forgets.) Then if the animal decides to scratch something, the damage will be limited.

Once guests arrive, tell them the "rules" for the pet: Never leave pets alone and unrestrained in any room of the house. (They might get overzealous in their exploration of new territory.) Never let cats roam the grounds. (They're very good at sneaking off and hiding.) Never let dogs roam the grounds unless they are accompanied by the owner and restrained on a leash. (They might get lost or run into a belligerent animal who thinks he owns the territory.) And point out to the owner where the dog may relieve himself.

If you wish, you can require that a guest confine a cat to the kennel most owners have to transport their animals. (Make sure you inform the guest of this in advance.) If the guest room has an adjoining "pet proof" bathroom, you could also give the owner the option of putting Rambo in there if he becomes emotional (destructively so) about being in a new environment.

You might want to add your own rules to this list that are tailored to the needs of your own home—keep the dog away from the swimming pool, the pet ducks, and the flower bed. Keep the cat away from the fishbowl, the baby's toys, and the turkey defrosting in the kitchen. Make it clear to pet owners that it is their responsibility for supervising their animals at all times. So when the dog starts frantically scratching at the door to go outside, it's the guest (and not the host) who takes the animal out to answer the call of nature. Most problems are caused because the host just didn't lay down the law right in the beginning. Don't make this mistake.

Every state requires a general health certificate for dogs and cats coming in from other states, and you must comply. In fact, you should require a health certificate even for pets that are traveling within the same state, just to be sure, according to Doctor of Veterinary Medicine John Bujalski. Pets can carry communicable diseases and parasites, and you have a right to proof that any animal staying in your home is healthy.

At the time that pet owners are making reservations with you, inform them that you will expect them to produce a health certificate for their animal upon arrival. According to Dr. Bujalski, it should be issued by their own veterinarian within ten days prior to their visit with you, covering the following items: For dogs, the animal must be current on its vaccinations against distemper and Parvo virus disease (yearly shots are required), as well as rabies (after the initial inoculation, shots are needed every three years). Dogs should also have a negative stool sample, ensuring that they carry no parasites. (Parasites deposited in stools can live up to a year in the ground.) A health certificate for cats should show that inoculations are current for rabies, upper-respiratory viruses, and cat distemper (called Feline Panleukopenia). If the owner does not produce a health certificate, it's best to refuse the animal, especially if you have animals of your own that run the risk of picking up a parasite or contagious disease.

To be on the safe side, the guest room in which an animal has stayed should be thoroughly cleaned and disinfected after each use. Vacuum well to pick up any hair. To disinfect tile or linoleum floors, Dr. Bujalski recommends a solution of one part chlorine bleach and ten parts water. (Don't use the solution on wood, as the bleaching action might affect it.) There is also a sanitizing spray called Asepticare that has been recommended to kill bacterial germs and viruses.

After disinfecting the room, use a "premise spray" to kill fleas. "Every animal potentially carries fleas," Dr. Bujalski says. The spray is colorless and water-based, so it can be used freely without harming furniture. He also suggests placing flea powder inside the vacuum cleaner bag to prevent any fleas that may be drawn inside from venturing back out again.

Dogs and cats are big on territory rights, and their natural inclination is to "mark" new territory. This is a difficult problem to control, but you can take measures to discourage marking behavior. Dr. Bujalski suggests placing mothball flakes in the corners of the guest room (not enough for humans to detect the odor). Animals usually head for the corners first to begin exploration of a new environment. "They hate the smell of napthalene," says Dr. Bujalski. Maybe, just maybe, they'll hate it enough to leave the room alone.

If you live in either Hawaii or North Carolina, you should check current health department regulations meticulously before accepting pets. Hawaii has a stringent 120-day quarantine period before pets can be admitted to the state. North Carolina has a law (Chapter 72–7, Volume 2C) that expressly forbids inns and hotels from allowing dogs to stay in any sleeping rooms. Both the proprietor and the guest can be fined $50 or imprisoned up to thirty days for a violation. Unless you find out differently, you should assume that this law applies to bed and breakfast homes in that jurisdiction as well.

If you have a pet yourself, you probably know that most pets are healthy most of the time and also fairly well behaved most of the time if they have been trained properly. Generally speaking, allowing guests to bring pets to your home will cause you no trouble at all. "They're very considerate of my home," says a host registered with Kingston Area Bed & Breakfast in Canada. Requiring a health certificate, cleaning and disinfecting the room after each use, and making the rules clear in advance will all provide that extra insurance for you that all will be well. Further precautions you might want to consider are limited stays for guests with animals, a restriction to small dogs only, a written statement that clearly spells out that the pet owner is liable for any damages caused by the pet (ask the guest to sign it), and a refundable deposit (payable in advance) that is in addition to the fee charged for accommodating the pet.

To court business from pet owners, you can do several things: Include "cats and dogs welcome" on your business card or brochure. Make sure that your reservation service organization knows that you welcome pets. And mention this fact in the information you provide for any guidebook listing.

You can also send notification to the editor of *Touring with Towzer*, a nationwide directory of accommodations that permit guests with dogs. This publication is produced by the Gaines Dog Care Center, 250 North Street, White Plains, New York 10625. Most of the listings are hotels and motels, but there are some bed and breakfast homes included. Ernest and Edna Shipe, for example, list their bed and breakfast home (called Valley View Farm), located in Mathias, West Virginia, in this publication. Animal lovers throughout the United States who order this directory to help them plan their travels will then have the information about your bed and breakfast.

Hosting foreign visitors

People who live in Europe, or who have traveled there from other countries around the world, are familiar with the idea of bed and breakfast. They are delighted to find that B&B is now available in North America, and when they plan their travels here, foreign visitors often seek out the type of accommodations that they have enjoyed so much elsewhere. A bed and breakfast host whose home is located in an area that attracts foreign visitors (such as a large city, a popular resort, or a base for a large international corporation) is in a good position to reach out to this market.

You can expect that many foreign visitors will speak English very well indeed, and many will have acquired enough English to communicate on a basic level. Still, there will be many more who do not speak the English language well, or at all. If you hope to attract the variety of foreign visitors who come to your area, it's a good idea to polish the language skills you might already have (remember high school French?) or work on acquiring a new language so that you can make the most of your opportunities.

"We have multilingual host families, with French, German, and Spanish the major second languages. We believe this is not only more comfortable for foreign travelers but is also advantageous for those who are interested in other cultures," reads the brochure issued by Bed & Breakfast Tropical Florida, a reservation service organization based in South Miami. By advertising the fact that some of its hosts speak other languages, the RSO can attract those visitors who are looking for that special amenity. Pacific Bed & Breakfast, an RSO located in Seattle, Washington, also advertises the language skills of its hosts. "*Wir sprechen Deutsch*" reads its brochure as a way to attract German-speaking guests. One host registered with Bed & Breakfast Center City, an RSO in Philadelphia, finds that people are especially attracted to her B&B because of her proficiency in languages: "I have traveled extensively, am familiar with various cultures, and speak several languages," says Marjorie Amrom, owner of Trade Winds. This has had a positive effect on her bed and breakfast business.

If you already speak one or more languages besides English, you can start using this fact immediately to reach out to foreign visitors. If you list with an RSO, ask the agency to include a note on its brochure similar to those printed by Bed & Breakfast Tropical Florida and Pacific Bed & Breakfast. If you print your own brochure as an independent host, make sure to include your language skill somewhere in the copy. (You might even want to print a bilingual brochure.) Then make your brochures available to tourist bureaus, embassies, consulates, international corporations, the chamber of commerce, car-rental companies, and any other places you can think of in your area that might have frequent contact with foreign visitors. And if your B&B is listed in any guidebook, be sure to include your language proficiency in the description.

If you do not speak a language other than English and you find that large numbers of foreign visitors to your area are passing by your bed and breakfast because of it, then it might be wise to consider learning another language. It's not as difficult as you might think. "It's largely a matter of attitude," says Lee Riethmiller, director of the Intercontinental

Foreign Language Program, a school for foreign languages located in Cambridge, Massachusetts. "American education doesn't emphasize language learning as school systems in many other countries do, so we grow up thinking that learning another language is impossible when actually it's easy. We're all natural mimics; we love to make new sounds because it's fun. Once you realize this, you can get rid of that mental block and learn as many new languages as you want." Fluent in ten languages himself, Mr. Riethmiller ought to know. His special course in which students learn six languages *at once* has been going strong for six years. So monolinguals take heart. If your bed and breakfast is suffering because you don't know *hola* from *adios*, then give it a shot. Buy some tapes, take an evening course, practice with your kids. Mastering a second—or third or fourth—language can open up opportunities for you to meet some very interesting people from the rest of the world as they visit you right in your own home.

An accessible B&B

There are an estimated 36 million people in the United States who have some kind of physical disability. For them, impairment of mobility, hearing, or vision rules out a number of commercial accommodations that have not modified their facilities to allow easy access for people with handicaps. Some hotels (especially the newer ones) have followed state and federal codes for making their bedrooms, bathrooms, common areas, entrances and exits, hallways, and parking facilities accessible. Still, a traveler with special requirements is usually faced with a narrow choice, and often at a price higher than desired. A selection of accessible bed and breakfast homes can offer a welcome alternative for people with physical disabilities whenever they travel.

What does it take to make a bed and breakfast home accessible? Clearly, some houses are structured so that they cannot be easily adapted for people with impairments in mobility. "I have a spiral staircase in a three-story townhouse in the city, which would be difficult for someone who cannot ambulate well," says a Philadelphia host. If this sounds like your own situation, making your B&B accessible is probably not feasible. But if your home has a bedroom, a bathroom, and a dining area on the ground level (with no steps up or down between the areas), then you should give some serious thought to making the necessary renovations to accommodate people who use wheelchairs to get around.

How extensive would renovations be? Be advised that most houses are not constructed with anyone but the able-bodied in mind. The fact that your bed and breakfast has ground-floor accommodations will be enticement enough for some travelers who can get around with the aid of a cane, crutches, or a walker. But you may have to make major modifications if you want to accommodate travelers who use wheelchairs. If you intend to renovate your home anyway, these modifications should be included in your plans.

A big problem for people without full mobility is getting through doorways that are too narrow—and in many private homes, they are. A person in a wheelchair needs more width to maneuver than typical doorways allow. How wide are yours? Measure the doors to the guest rooms, the bathroom, the dining area, and any common space that guests are invited to use (such as the living room or TV room), as well as the front door. Unless you've got French doors throughout the house, you very well might have to widen your doorways (a minimum width of thirty-two inches is the standard recommendation). And was your home built during the period when thresholds were in vogue? A threshold is a piece of wood positioned at the bottom of a doorframe as a cross piece—attractive maybe, but a real annoyance to someone who needs a clear path. The thresholds will have to go.

A clear path is essential for people with an impairment of mobility or vision. Unnecessary furniture and decorations—extra chairs, tables, desks, pole lamps, throw rugs, knick-knacks—should all be moved out of the guest room in favor of more floor space. Hallways, too, must be free of obstructions and wide enough to accommodate a wheelchair comfortably. (A width of thirty-two inches is usually okay for a doorway, but it's a tight fit for a hallway; wider is better.)

In the guest room, furniture should be arranged so that each piece has ample floor space near it to allow access by wheelchair (the thirty-two inch guideline is a good one to follow). And remember that everything must be reachable from a sitting position. This includes light, heat, and air conditioning switches. Hooks for robes should be placed low enough on doors or inside closets for your guests to reach easily. The horizontal pole in the closet should be lowered (or a second one added beneath the first) so that clothes can be hung on hangers, and removed, with no trouble.

Bathrooms tend to be small, which can pose a problem for someone who needs lots of floor space. Remove unnecessary furniture or decorations to make the area as roomy as possible. A person using a wheelchair should be able to turn around, open and close the door, and reach the sink and toilet easily. Grab bars for the bathtub and shower are recommended for the safety of *all* your guests. In addition, an accessible bed and breakfast should have grab bars at the toilet. (A grab bar in the guest room at bedside is also a good idea.) The sink can be more easily reached if it is twenty-seven inches or less in height and is the type that allows knee clearance under the basin.

Getting in and out of your home needs to be as easy as getting around within it. Steps up or down to the "ground level" can be a problem. The owners of Spindrift Bed & Breakfast in Bandon, Oregon, have installed a wheelchair ramp as a solution. If you need to install a ramp, have a professional builder do it so that it is sturdy, made of a nonskid material, rises at a *gradual* gradient, and is wide enough to allow ample clearance on each side of a wheelchair. If your bed and breakfast is located in a building that has an elevator, check to see if the buttons can be reached from a sitting position, and if the doors are wide enough (thirty-two inches or more) to facilitate wheelchairs; also check to see if there are Braille symbols to indicate floors.

The path to your B&B's entrance needs to be absolutely free of obstructions. Parking must be near the entrance, and parking spaces have to allow ample room for a guest to get in and out of a car easily. This means a width of about thirteen feet.

Extensive renovations are not necessary to accommodate individuals with impairments in vision and hearing, but you will have to make some modifications for your guests' comfort and safety. Smoke alarms, for example, must be equipped with a flashing light as an emergency signal for the hearing impaired. Special telephone systems are also available to enable hearing- or speech-impaired individuals to communicate via telephone lines with other users of the same type of equipment. A telecommunications device for the deaf (known as a TDD or a TTY) resembles a typewriter with a small viewing screen; amplified phone handsets are also available.

These are some of the major considerations you will have if you wish to make your bed and breakfast home accessible. For more detailed guidelines, check your telephone book under "Disabled Services" for agencies in your area. Each state and major city has an Office of Handicapped Affairs, as well as additional agencies that specialize in the concerns of individuals with specific impairments. These offices can provide you with more information and perhaps even direct you to a local architectural center that has a program devoted to creating barrier-free environments for people with physical disabilities. Or, write to the Paralyzed Veterans of America, 801 Eighteenth Street, N.W., Washington, D.C. 20006; phone (202) USA–1300. This organization has extensive detailed resources, including house plans.

These same government agencies can be very helpful in spreading the word about your accessible bed and breakfast home. They sometimes publish an access guide to the area or collaborate with other organizations to provide information to both residents and visitors about accessible lodging, restaurants, attractions, and transportation. The local office of the Easter Seal Society can also be very helpful to you as you seek out resources and ways to publicize your B&B. And you might find it useful to obtain a copy of the *International Directory of Access Guides*, published by Rehabilitation International U.S.A. (1123 Broadway, Suite 704, New York, New York 10010, for $5.00) to identify guides written about your area. Ideally, your B&B should be listed in updates of these guides, so get in touch with the publishers with information.

There are two national organizations that provide travel information to disabled individuals. You should make it a point to contact both with information about your bed and breakfast: One is the Society for the Advancement of Travel for the Handicapped (SATH), 26 Court Street, Brooklyn, New York 11242, phone (718) 858–5483. The other is the Travel Information Service, Moss Rehabilitation Hospital, 12th Street and Tabor Road, Philadelphia, Pennsylvania 19141, phone (215) 329–5715.

There are also a number of tour operators that organize tours for travelers with disabilities. Send information to: Whole Person Tours, P.O. Box 1084, Bayonne, New Jersey 07002–1084, phone (201) 858–3400; Flying Wheels Travel, P.O. Box 382, Owatonna, Minnesota 55060, phone 1–800–533–0363 (in Minnesota, 1–800–722–9351); Wings on Wheels (Evergreen Travel), 19505(L) 44th Avenue W., Lynwood, Washington 98036, phone (206) 776–1184; Nautilus Tours, 5435 Donna Avenue, Tarzana, California 91356, phone (818) 343–6339; Anglo California Travel Service, 4250 Williams Road, San Jose, California 95129, phone (408) 257–2257; Directions Unlimited, 344 Main Street, Mt. Kisco, New York 10549, phone 1–800–533–5343; and Doral Travel, P.O. Box 545, Brick, New Jersey 08723, phone (201) 840–0084. For an updated list of tour operators, contact the Information Center for Individuals with Disabilities, 20 Park Plaza, Room 330, Boston, Massachusetts 02116; phone (617) 727–5540 Voice or (617) 727–5236 TTY.

The Itinerary is a magazine directed to travelers with physical disabilities. The focus is to help readers learn of travel opportunities, resources, and experiences. Advertising in this publication is a good way to let the community of people interested in accessible lodging know about your B&B. Write to *The Itinerary* for an advertising rate card: P.O. Box 1084, Bayonne, New Jersey 07002–1084, phone (201) 858–3400. You might also send a press release for a possible article about your accessible B&B.

Be sure to include appropriate information on your brochure. If you have a TDD or TTY for the hearing impaired, list the number. If you are adept at sign language, mention this fact. If you have a ground-floor room, say so. If the bed and breakfast is wheelchair accessible, publicize this information. Ask any reservation service organization that lists your B&B to include this important information in its literature. Southern Comfort B&B Reservation Service in Louisiana, for example, has this note in its brochure: "In Baton Rouge, there are available suites of living / dining / bed / bath / kitchen that meet all state and federal codes for handicapped."

Not every bed and breakfast owner will be able to make the premises accessible. Indeed, one host reports that she learned this the hard way, when she suffered a leg injury and found that there was nothing she could do to help herself up and down the staircases in her three-story house. But other houses are more suited to adaptation. (Bed and breakfast homes that have already been adapted to accommodate a host or family member with a physical disability are in an ideal position to court this specialized market.) Although there are some bed and breakfast homes that are accessible, the amount of attention given to this issue is still quite minimal. This places any B&B owner who takes the initiative to offer this special feature out in front of the developing bed and breakfast industry.

7
The Perfect Host

The welcome

The front door was already open and the host was waving a welcome as my taxi stopped in front of her Hyannisport home, my bed and breakfast for the night. I was in a very bad humor, no question about it. I was tired after a three-hour ferry ride from Nantucket and exasperated by the confusion of bus schedules that had stranded me on Cape Cod until the next morning's bus to Boston. I was hot, my hair was sticky with ocean spray, I longed to wash my face, and I was worried about arriving on time for my mid-morning appointment the next day. I had been very fortunate in finding a host registered with House Guests Cape Cod who was willing to take a guest on such short notice (I had called from the bus station) and for one night only, but I sure didn't feel lucky. This was an emergency layover and no more. I was determined to be miserable.

My host showed me immediately to my room for the night and asked if I would like to have a glass of wine while I got settled. I suddenly realized that this was exactly what I wanted at that very moment. A chilled glass of chablis quickly appeared, and my host (who had heard my sad story already from the manager of the reservation service organization) quietly disappeared into another part of the house. A short time later—face scrubbed, hair combed, and clothes changed—I was following her directions to the nearby private beach to watch the sunset. Before long I found myself enjoying how peaceful it was there and thinking of little more than the plate of home-baked cookies waiting for me when I returned from my stroll.

As a bed and breakfast host, you'll be welcoming all sorts of people in all sorts of moods into your home. Some could very well be the way I was that evening in Hyannisport, wanting to be left alone but still needing just enough attention to bring me back to my normal, cheerful self. Other guests (most of them, we hope) will be in high spirits when they arrive.

If possible, you should find out in advance why your guests are visiting the area. You need not acknowledge the reason when you meet them for the first time, but it will help you to tailor your welcome to the occasion. Those guests on vacation or celebrating a wedding, birthday, graduation, or anniversary will most likely be quite cheerful when they arrive at your doorstep. They will definitely contrast with those who are in town to visit a friend or relative who has taken ill, or to attend a funeral. And those who are relocating or traveling on business are in another category: They have business to take care of and that is probably the first thing on their minds. Although a smile and a warm handshake are always appropriate to welcome anyone under any circumstances, try to "read" how your guests are feeling when you open the front door—exuberant, sad, worried, rushed, joyful, tired, angry, happy, preoccupied. It's your job to make *all* your guests feel comfortable immediately, using your "antennae" to sense what should or should not be said, and what should or should not be done, in order to accomplish this. And leave your own problems behind when you open that door. You might have had a rough day, but don't let your guests see it on your face. It's time for a smile and a warm handshake, no matter what.

As a host, you will find that one of your major responsibilities is to make sure that you're home when your guests are scheduled to arrive. Always agree upon a definite arrival time when a guest is making a reservation. Then, when that day and time comes, you be there waiting to welcome your visitors. It's incredibly disorienting for a guest to arrive at the right place at the right time and find no one home. A woman visiting the Big Apple reports such an unsettling experience: "The host was not home all day, so I was unable to gain access until dark—a little scary on my first solo trip to New York City."

Put yourself in your guests' shoes. You've just arrived in a strange city for the first time, and you're on your way to the private home of someone you've never seen before in your life. You're a little nervous about all this bed and breakfast stuff anyway, but your Aunt Mavis has traveled the world over and swears that you'll love it. So the taxi leaves you and your two heavy suitcases off at the address you've been sent to. Right on time. But why is the house dark? Why does no one answer the doorbell? Should you run after the taxi? Should you sit down on the doorstep to wait, in the rain? Should you start looking for a phone to call the host just in case she really is in there but is asleep? Or too sick to come to the door? Or did she perhaps just forget about your reservation and fly to Switzerland to take in a little skiing?

This is no way to welcome a guest. Of course, things can come up unexpectedly, calling you away from home (to get your daughter's scraped knee checked after she fell off the swing; to pick up your spouse after the Volvo sputtered and died; to retrieve the purse you left on top of your desk when you ran out of your office so that you'd be home on time to welcome your guest). Whenever something like this occurs, try to find a friend or neighbor who is willing to come to your home and welcome your guests in your place. It's wonderful if you can find someone who loves people as much as you do and will invite your guests inside, offer them a cup of coffee or glass of wine, and even get them settled into their rooms if the delay will be lengthy. If a guest was referred to you through a reservation service organization, get in touch with the RSO manager if you have a problem finding someone to stand in for you. The RSO manager will help if possible because the problem reflects on that agency's service.

If you absolutely cannot find someone to welcome the guests who will be arriving while you're gone, do *not* leave the door unlocked with an open invitation to come inside pasted on the door. Your guests might very well be the trustworthy, but who knows who else might come to your door while you're away and find the house empty and the door unlocked? Besides, new arrivals will feel uncomfortable about coming inside when no one is home, and you should really be there to satisfy the questions in your mind about any guest before you permit that person inside your home. Some hosts leave a note on the door addressed to the expected guest by name. (If it's placed inside a sealed envelope, the contents will not be seen by anyone else who happens to come to the door.) In the note, apologize for the inconvenience and say you'll be back shortly. You might also want to make a suggestion about how to spend the intervening time: "There's a lovely pond out back—please feel free to walk around and enjoy the scenery. And help yourself to the lemonade I've left in the thermos on the picnic table." Or: "There's a café at the end of the street that makes a terrific cappuccino. I've already told Tony to put it on my tab!" Do your best to turn the inconvenience into a pleasant experience.

If you are home when your guests arrive, open the door wide when you hear them coming, before they have to ring the doorbell. Opening the door not only resolves the question in their minds of whether or not they have, indeed, found the right place, but it's also just a friendly thing to do. It will give them a good feeling about your bed and breakfast.

Ellen Madison has a pet in residence at the Woody Hill Guest House B&B in Westerly, Rhode Island. She recalls the day her furry friend decided to welcome some new guests. "I was not home when some of my guests arrived a bit early, and they were not sure that they had come to the right place. My fat, black, lazy cat ambled out for a pat. Very quickly my guests rushed back to the car, grabbed the book in which I am written up, consulted it, and found out that I had a cat named 'Treasure.' They tentatively addressed the cat by the name and were rewarded with an affirmative leg rub." Relieved, the guests immediately made themselves at home until their host arrived.

To help your guests identify your home easily, display your house number clearly so that it is visible from the street. Some hosts affix a plate carrying their family name on or near the front door.

The difficulty that guests sometimes have in figuring out which home on the street is the bed and breakfast they're looking for prompted the owners of a bed and breakfast home in Michigan to design and sell flags that say "B&B" on them. A host can display the flag whenever guests are expected to help guide them to the right place easily. (For information on the B&B flags, write to The Parsonage, 6 East 24th Street, Holland, Michigan 49423.) One note of caution: Check any regulations governing the use of signs and/or flags in your community; they could be prohibited in a residential area. Consider, too, that use of a sign or flag does declare in a public way that you are in the bed and breakfast business; some hosts prefer to protect their privacy more closely. Are you one of them?

To make your home look inviting to a guest who is expected to arrive after dark, Rick Madden, the former director of a reservation service organization called Bed & Breakfast Colorado, says, "The outside light *must* be on." (It's also a good safety measure to light the way to your door.) Danie Bernard, owner of an RSO in St. Pete Beach, Florida, says that guests in residence appreciate "a light left burning outside while they are out at night." Even though they might no longer need assistance to locate your home again, the light makes them feel more welcome to come back inside.

Leaving the light on as a warm welcome is a nice touch even if you will be picking up your guests at the airport, the bus station, or the train station. Many hosts are willing to do this, if it's convenient for them. It's a wonderful amenity to offer guests who would otherwise have to take a taxi or public transportation to your home. This means that your first contact with some of your guests will be at the plane, bus, or train. Please don't be late. Finding that no one is there to meet you is just as unnerving as finding no one at home at the bed and breakfast where you have a reservation. Make a good impression and be there waiting for your guest to disembark. Have you ever been welcomed after a trip with a bouquet of flowers? Suddenly, the discomforts of traveling disappear. You will most likely be placing fresh flowers in your guests' room anyway; why not meet them with the bouquet when they arrive?

During the drive back to your home, use the time to find out a little more about your guests and their plans for their visit. It's very helpful to orient them to the area as much as possible during the drive; point out landmarks as you pass them. If you arrive at your home during the evening hours, the light that you left on for the event will present a much cheerier welcome than will a dark house.

Once you have invited your guests inside your home, the best thing to do is show them directly to their room and point out where their bathroom is. Then if something is not as it should be (they wanted twin beds; you have a double, for example), they can decide then and there whether they wish to leave. With luck, good communication between your guests and you at the time a reservation is made will have prevented misunderstandings from happening—but they do happen. For these times, you will need to have a clearly stated refund policy. (See "Confirming a Reservation" in chapter 6.) If a guest does wish to leave, don't make a scene. Even though you may not think that the complaint is deserved, let this be your guide: "The customer is always right." Smile, say you're sorry that your bed and breakfast isn't quite what he or she was looking for, give any refund due according to your policy, and wave good-bye. It's just possible that what didn't work out for this guest would be perfect for that same guest's friend, acquaintance, or relative. For this reason, you want all of your guests (even the ones who decide to leave) to remember you kindly.

Once you're sure that the room is agreeable to your new guests, offer to help them with anything that might need to be taken care of immediately: Show them where they may leave their car for the night; help bring their belongings into the guest room; take their ice chest into the kitchen so that they may place perishables in your refrigerator after they've gotten settled. In the guest room itself, point out the light switches and explain how to operate the privacy lock on the door, window locks, the pull drapes, the heat, the air conditioner, the electric blanket, and anything else that might be there for their comfort. Show them where the extra pillows and blankets are kept.

Be aware that people who have been traveling will most likely want to freshen up a bit immediately after they arrive, so allow them this time before you start socializing. Always offer your guests a "welcome drink," but preface the offer with something like this: "You'll probably want a few minutes to get settled. Then I'd love for you to join me for some coffee or a glass of wine. Why don't you just come into the living room when you're ready? Then I'll show you around the rest of the house and the grounds, too."

Make your living room as inviting as possible. Create an *atmosphere*, using your resources to best advantage. Should you open the drapes so that your guests will have a view of the sunset over the beach? Should you close the drapes and light the two small lamps (instead of the overhead) to give the room a soft appearance? Should you open a window to let in a little fresh air? Should you put on some background music? Should you light a fire in the fireplace?

"It is incredible how many homes are fortunate enough to have a nice, homey fireplace and then neglect to use it," says Mary Gill of Be Our Guest, a reservation service organization in Plymouth, Massachusetts. She makes a comparison between two similar bed and breakfast homes. At the first one, guests come out of the cold night and "they see a cheery fire burning in the fireplace." The host invites them to join him for a drink before the fire. At the other B&B home, however, "the fireplace is stone cold," which gives guests the impression that "they are not important enough for the host to go to the trouble," says Gill. "It's obvious which host has the best chance over the years of building up a steady, repeat business, and a lot of word-of-mouth recommendations. Keep in mind that some experienced travelers who use bed and breakfast have seen the best and the worst of B&Bs. Naturally, they will tell their friends about their best discoveries and the B&Bs to stay away from." Make yours a discovery that your guests will want to share.

Depending on the time of day and the season, offer your guests something to drink—hot chocolate, hot or cold cider, mulled wine, tea, hot or iced coffee, juice, soft drinks, a liqueur. Many hosts also offer a snack at the time of guests' arrival—cookies, cheese and fruit, cake, or a "dessert" type of bread such as banana or cranberry. A snack is always a good idea because your guests have most likely been traveling for a while, leaving them little time to eat. If it's late, they won't be able to go out to dinner before they retire; and if it's earlier in the day, it could take some time before they're ready to go out and look for a restaurant. Either way, some cookies or fruit would be a very welcome sight indeed.

The occasion of a "welcome drink" also gives you and your guests a chance to get acquainted with one another. Here, you can find out a little more about your guests' plans and make suggestions to help make their visit more enjoyable. This can be a good time for "orientation," or directing your guests to the best that your area has to offer. (See "Orientation" later in this chapter.)

Afterwards, take the time to show your guests the house and the grounds. As you do this, make it clear what areas of the house they are welcome to use: "This is the family room. Please feel free to come in here to watch television or select something to read from the bookcase. And we've got a deck of cards and Trivial Pursuit over there on the shelf."

At the same time, point out (in a nice way) any parts of the house and grounds that are off limits: "This is the bathroom that is used only by family members. The master bedroom is through that door. If there's some kind of emergency at night, that's where you can find me. Otherwise, once I'm in there for the night, I prefer not to be disturbed."

Your tour should include any other light switches or door locks that your guests will have to deal with. If you wish to give your guests keys to the front door or to their bedroom (see "Safety Precautions" in chapter 9), now is the time to do it. And go over any "rules" that you expect your guests to follow: "After 11:00 P.M., we have 'quiet hours' so that the people who want to sleep aren't bothered by any kind of noise. And if you're the last one up, please turn off the light in the living room."

Introduce all family members and other guests in residence so that the new arrivals will feel at home. If someone is not home at the moment, at least mention that Sonny is at school and that the young couple staying in the Sunshine Room are out hiking. Also introduce your pets and explain any idiosyncracies that they might have: "Foofie likes to bite toes, so be careful when she's in your room and you want to change your shoes."

The end of the tour is an opportune time for you to part company with your guests if you want to get on with other things, and it's a perfect time to take care of collecting the balance due. Bring it up now: "We like to get payment out of the way on the first night. This is the bill for the balance due on the three nights you've reserved. Why don't we do this now?"

Many hosts feel uncomfortable about asking for payment; it's like putting a price tag on hospitality and just doesn't feel right. Still, you've got to finance that hospitality. It's your responsibility to bring up the issue of payment and get it taken care of right away. Otherwise, you'll be suffering over it for days. If the bill is paid at the outset, you and your guests are free to proceed with one of the most enjoyable aspects of bed and breakfast—becoming friends.

Orientation

A New England woman visiting a town in Newfoundland for the first time decided to stay in a bed and breakfast home instead of a hotel or motel. Why? "In order to talk to a 'native,'" she says. The host answered her questions about the area and suggested some sights to see that she hadn't known about.

A medical worker from Wisconsin was relocating to Boston to take part in a one-year training program at a city hospital. "I wanted a human resource other than a front-desk clerk," he says. So he made arrangements to stay at a B&B registered with Bed and Breakfast Brookline/Boston that was within walking distance of the hospital. He found the host a valuable source of information, advice, and comfort as he got oriented to a new city and located his own apartment. "Who better than a resident to help you out?" he asks.

"I'm not much of a tourist," says a woman from Pennsylvania who traveled the B&B way on a recent trip to Canada. "I wanted to visit a certain area and get a feeling for how it might be to live there. I wanted to meet people." It so happened that her hosts were involved in organizing a local festival that was to take place in the town during her stay. She was invited to help out and did just that. "I never had my thumbs in so many bowls of chowder in my life, but it was great," she says. "I found the people to be extraordinarily friendly."

These three guests are typical of people who prefer to stay at bed and breakfast homes instead of hotels and motels. They want an inside view of the area that they're visiting, something only a resident can give them. For your guests, a good orientation to the area is one of the key assets of staying in a bed and breakfast home, so be prepared to share your knowledge of local activities.

Keep on hand any books written about your region to lend to your guests—a guidebook or two, plus books devoted to its history, architecture, or flora and fauna. Books suggesting interesting walks, hikes, or bicycle trips are also of interest to many people. And it's always fun for a guest to read a fictional story set in the area he or she is visiting; these will make a welcome addition to your bookshelf.

Your guests will need to get around while they're staying with you, so stock up on schedules of buses, trains, subways, and ferries, plus the business cards of any car-rental companies in the area. (It wouldn't hurt to inquire about obtaining rental discounts for your guests. Some hosts have successfully negotiated this benefit.) A good map that can be borrowed is always in demand. Check with your local tourist office or chamber of commerce about obtaining a supply of maps that can be given to your guests. Because both organizations are in the business of promoting the area, they will often make quantities available to bed and breakfast hosts at a discounted price or even for free. (It helps if you're a member.)

These organizations are also real gold mines when it comes to more general information directed to visitors. They produce brochures and pamphlets dealing with major tourist attractions, as well as calendars of cultural and community events coming up. Get on their mailing lists and find out what the benefits of membership would be for your bed and breakfast.

Shopping is usually on the agenda for many visitors, so start collecting business cards from the various shops in your area that sell arts and crafts, clothing, souvenirs, and regional items. Keep track of sales so that whenever a guest wants to know where to get the best deal on an item, you can make some suggestions.

In addition to the business cards, start collecting brochures, pamphlets, and flyers that promote any type of event or service that could be of interest to your guests. Many stores, restaurants, and even supermarkets keep stacks of promotional literature from community businesses available to the public. Whenever you see something that looks appealing to a visitor, take a few copies. You'll soon be surprised at how quickly your collection of resources can grow. Now, where to keep them? Host consultant Ellie Welch Ramsey suggests placing all of the information in a large basket and inviting guests to sift through it themselves. She also has an excellent suggestion for augmenting your basket's supplies. "I tell my guests that I'm trying to fill the basket and ask them to bring back extra literature from any of the places they'll be visiting," she says. Of course, many of your guests will be trekking off to the museums, the observatories, and the historical sites. Ellie has found her guests very cooperative about bringing back some extra brochures for other guests.

For those events that are here today and gone tomorrow, you might want to put all of those notices inside a folder so that they can be sorted and thrown away easily whenever the event is over. These include those announcing films, museum exhibits, concerts, festivals, art exhibits, dance performances, theatre presentations, and sporting events.

If you don't already subscribe to a daily newspaper, you should think about doing this for the benefit of your guests. It enables them to see what is going on around town for entertainment, and it helps keep them up with the news of the day. A subscription to any magazine published as a guide to the city, state, or region is also a good idea.

While your guests are staying with you, they might want to attend religious services or have a desire to get some exercise if these are a part of their usual routine. Obtain the schedules of services from the houses of worship in your neighborhood, as well as information about any drop-in classes or open exercise periods at local gyms, health clubs, and dance studios. Also keep on hand information regarding the rental of recreational equipment such as bicycles, roller or ice skates, skis, boats, or anything else that visitors would be likely to need.

Your guests will be seeking out their own lunch and dinner, so start collecting menus from restaurants that you like. The managers of most restaurants will be more than happy to give you a copy because your bed and breakfast could bring more business to their establishments. One host makes up his own personal restaurant guide for his guests. He calls it "The Blue Wax Farm Zero Base Guide to Eating." It includes eight favorites in the East Burke, Vermont, area—how many miles away each is located from the farm, and a short description of the food, the décor, the clientele, and the prices. (The owner of Blue Wax Farm also offers his own updates on the hiking trails in his area.) You don't have to produce anything as elaborate as this, but do take the trouble to point out the good (and the not so good) restaurants when your guests are planning to go out to eat.

If there are any pizza parlors or delicatessens nearby that will deliver (especially any that are open late), make sure to have their menus on hand for the convenience of guests who arrive at your home after the usual dinner hour is over. At these times a large pizza to go, delivered right to your door, can be a very welcome sight.

If you should notice that any restaurants or stores are advertising discount coupons for particular items, clip and save these, adding them to the basket. There's no reason why your guests shouldn't enjoy their pizza at half-price or buy their souvenirs at a two-for-one sale. They'll appreciate the thought.

Once you've got your "orientation basket" full of information, place it where all your guests have access to it, perhaps in the living room or family room or in the foyer between the guest rooms. You'll soon find that having your resources available in this way is a great time-saver for you. You won't have to draw the same little maps over and over again for different guests, and you won't have to check and double-check the hours of operation for that great restaurant down the street. For many questions dealing with orientation to your area, you can direct your guests right to the basket for the information they seek. You might even want to help them locate the right brochure or map, as you do not want to give the impression that they're annoying you with their questions and that that's why you're pointing to a basket.

There will be times, though, when your guests will want information that is not contained in your trusty basket. Ellie Welch Ramsey tells of spending an entire evening mapping out an itinerary for some guests who wanted to conduct their own walking tour of Boston's most notable Victorian houses. Expect that you will get requests like these for which you'll have to draw on your personal knowledge to give advice and make suggestions. If you enjoy pointing out what your neighborhood has to offer to visitors, you'll enjoy this aspect of your bed and breakfast business very much. This is exactly what will bring many guests to your door.

Orientation checklist

- ☐ Books of interest:
  - ☐ Guidebooks
  - ☐ History
  - ☐ Architecture
  - ☐ Flora and fauna
  - ☐ Fiction set in local area
  - ☐ Legends
- ☐ City/state/regional magazines
- ☐ Daily newspaper
- ☐ Calendar of events
- ☐ Festivals:
  - ☐ Art exhibits
  - ☐ Dance performances
  - ☐ Sports
- ☐ Business cards for local businesses
- ☐ Menus from restaurants
- ☐ Discount coupons for stores/restaurants/rental cars/tours

- ☐ Maps
- ☐ Transportation schedules:
  - ☐ Subway
  - ☐ Bus
  - ☐ Train
  - ☐ Ferry
- ☐ Car-rental information
- ☐ Brochures/flyers/schedules for current events:
  - ☐ Theatres
  - ☐ Films
  - ☐ Museums
  - ☐ Concerts
- ☐ Sightseeing information:
  - ☐ Tours
  - ☐ Brochures for tourist attractions
- ☐ Equipment rentals:
  - ☐ Skis
  - ☐ Boats
  - ☐ Bicycles
  - ☐ Roller/ice skates
- ☐ Schedules:
  - ☐ Religious services
  - ☐ Dance studio drop-in classes
  - ☐ Health clubs

Guest letter

You have some decisions to make about how you wish your visitors to conduct themselves while they are guests in your home. And then you have the job of communicating these guidelines to your guests in a way that is "firm but nice," according to host Linda Nichols. The initial orientation tour of the house and grounds is an opportune time to point out some of the "rules" that you expect your guests to follow. Still, there will be some guidelines that will not come up naturally during the course of the tour. And, too, you don't want to overwhelm your guests with a voluminous list of "dos and don'ts" when you first meet. A good way to outline what your guests need to know is to put your guidelines into a welcome letter. This is left inside the guest room, usually on the tray that contains the drinking glasses. This one-page letter (try not to make it longer) can be quickly scanned by your guests for the information that pertains to them. It can include the following items:

Welcome

Begin your letter by welcoming your guests to your home. The Bed & Breakfast Registry of Maine suggests this opening: "Welcome to your home away from home. I am pleased to have you as a guest and would like you to enjoy your stay. How can I help you? Do you need information about sightseeing? transportation? entertainment? Just ask. If I don't know the answer, I'll be glad to find out."

Breakfast

If you would like to establish a preferred time to serve breakfast, make this clear. The Bed & Breakfast Registry of Maine offers this model: "Breakfast will be served between 7:00 and 8:00 A.M. If that time is not convenient and you would like to serve yourself at a later time, please make arrangements with me before you retire." Catherine Hatala, a host registered with Bed and Breakfast Center City in Philadelphia, includes this note about breakfast: "In most cases, I will have the pleasure of eating with you. When I cannot and leave food warming in the toaster oven, kindly remember to push the lever down after you remove the food. If there is anything on the table that requires refrigeration, I would be grateful if you could return it to the fridge. Of course, I will take care of the dishes."

Food and drink

Most hosts provide a snack (a fruit basket or other goodies) and complimentary drinks for their guests. Some guests will have no idea that these are available unless you tell them: "Please help yourself to some fresh fruit or a soft drink in the evening. Both can be found in the small refrigerator in the hallway just outside the kitchen door," reads the welcome letter provided as a model by the Bed & Breakfast Registry of Maine.

Keys

You will have to decide whether you wish to give your guests house keys. The best advice for your own safety is *not* to do this if it can be avoided; however, there could be times when it's simply unavoidable given the incompatibility of your own schedule with your guests' comings and goings. Folkstone Bed & Breakfast Registry in Boylston, Massachusetts, suggests to its hosts that they ask for a deposit for any house key that is lent to a guest. The deposit is refunded when the house key is returned.

You may have to explain how the lock works. One host with a tricky lock adds this note to her welcome letter: "On your tray, you have probably found your set of keys. Please lock both the top and bottom locks when you leave. The bottom can be locked from the inside by simply putting the center piece in a vertical position."

Lights

Your guests will have to know what to do about the lights if they are the last ones up at night, or if they leave the house, so Covered Bridge

Bed & Breakfast, an RSO located in Connecticut, suggests covering this matter in the welcome letter. A simple "Please turn out the lights if you are the last one up at night" will make the responsibility clear to your guests.

Quiet hours

It's a good idea to give guests some idea of the normal routine of the house so that they can fit themselves into it: "The hours between 11:00 P.M. and 7:00 A.M. are 'quiet hours' so that we can all get our rest. We ask that if you wish to use the radio or television between these hours, you keep the volume low." If there are unusual hours kept by any member of the household on a regular basis, it's considerate to let your guests know this: "Our college-age son, Tommy, has a summer job with late hours. If you hear the back door opening at about midnight, it's Tommy. He is very quiet when he comes in, so unless you are already awake at this hour, you probably won't hear him at all."

The telephone

Be *very* clear about what you expect from guests regarding local and long-distance telephone calls. Many hosts have been unpleasantly surprised by phone bills arriving a month after guests have let their fingers do the walking. It's especially important that you set guidelines for long-distance calls: "If you need to make long-distance calls, kindly charge them to your credit card or your telephone number," reads one host's welcome letter.

Evaluate the type of local service that you now have to see if you need to add a similar note regarding message units for local calls that are out of the "unlimited call" area provided by your service. One host cuts out the page in the telephone book that explains how many message units are used for calls to nearby locales and asks her guests to leave the appropriate amount of change. If you have an answering machine, explain how to disengage it if a guest wants to use the phone when you aren't around: "Because of my schedule, I must have an answering machine. You need not answer the phone when it rings. If you are expecting a call and do not reach the phone before the tape begins, push the 'Start/Stop' button when you pick up the phone. Upon completion of your call, depress the button again."

You can, if you wish, acquire telephone equipment that restricts out-going calls to local areas. Another option is to offer long-distance service by credit card charges only. Special equipment is available for purchase that automatically adds a small amount for each call made as extra income for the host. A host who accommodates a good number of business travelers needs to weigh all of these options very carefully as phone access is vital to these guests.

House and grounds

According to the manager of City Lights Bed & Breakfast, Ltd., an RSO in New York City, the biggest mistake that new hosts make is "giving guests the run of the entire apartment instead of setting reasonable limits." Your tour can point out some of the areas that guests are welcome to use, or not; your welcome letter can clarify these further: "Feel free to use the pool and deck, and make yourself comfortable in the living room any evening after 8:00 P.M. to watch television or join us for conversation. Please walk around the farm if you wish, but we ask that you not go inside the barn or into the pasture."

Care of the room

Because every host handles "care of the room" differently, you might want to explain what guests can expect from you regarding it while they are in residence. Some hosts will not enter a guest room during its occupancy. If the beds are left unmade, they'll stay that way. The idea here is that the room is like a private bedroom in their own home. A note in the welcome letter indicating this would be a good idea: "This room is 'yours' for your stay, and I will not enter it except to change the linens every two days." Other hosts get right in there every day and change the sheets, make the bed, vacuum, dust, and water the plants. If you are this kind of host, your note can say: "I like to straighten the guest room after breakfast, so please make sure that any of your belongings are not left on the bed at this time."

Check-out time

If you have an established check-out time (which is a good idea so that you can be sure that you'll be home when your guests will be leaving), a reminder in your welcome letter is not a bad idea: "We would appreciate your leaving by noon on your last day with us. If there is a problem, please let us know."

Smoking

You have probably screened out any guests who are not compatible with your policy governing smoking in your home, but you still might want to include a reminder in your welcome letter: "We prefer that you do not smoke in this room, but you may smoke in the family room if you wish."

Alcohol

If you choose not to allow alcohol, specify this in your welcome letter: "We ask that you do not use alcoholic beverages while a guest in our home." Otherwise, a host usually provides complimentary wine as well as ice for those guests who wish to bring in their own alcoholic beverages.

Laundry

If you have laundry facilities and do not mind your guests using them, or if you are willing to do a load of dirty clothing for them, mention this in your welcome letter: "I will be glad to show you how to operate the laundry equipment if you should need to use it." If you wish to charge a small amount for the detergent, water, and electricity, specify it: "We ask for 50 cents per load to cover costs."

Pets in residence

Always make an effort to introduce your pets to your guests when they arrive. However, if Frisky likes his afternoon romp and he's often not around when you're ready to make introductions, it might be a good idea to include a note about the little rascal in the welcome letter. This way, there will be no surprises for your guests when they find a large, furry creature curled up at the bottom of their bed. A Philadelphia host includes this note about her pet: "Our dog, which my son named at two, is Puppy. She is a lovely pet. Her only flaw is that she is too friendly. If she is bothersome to you, you may put her in the back yard for a bit. Actually, she has her own routine and will probably not disturb you at all."

Emergencies

Few hosts have thus far included "Emergencies" in their welcome letters, but it is recommended so that your guests know what to do in case there is a problem of an emergency nature. You might want to say something like this: "Should a problem of an emergency nature develop, there is a list of emergency telephone numbers right by the telephone. And should you need to get ahold of me during the day for any reason, my telephone number at work is ______ . Our next-door neighbor, Harry Jones, is a close friend of the family. He is usually at home during the day and will be glad to help should the need arise. His phone number is ______ ."

The closing

End your letter with something friendly, like: "Wishing you a pleasant stay," or "I hope you enjoy your visit. Please let me know if there's anything else I can do to make your stay more enjoyable."

In your letter, include only those items that are absolutely necessary. Of the items discussed here, it's possible that you need mention only three or four, depending on how well you orient your guests to your house and grounds when they arrive. Again, keep the letter short—one page if possible. If it's too long, your guests won't take the time to read it, and they might also begin to feel that there are so many rules and regulations that maybe they should have just spent their vacation at Fort Dix. Leave out the obvious information. Some hosts tell guests what they already know, or what common sense would tell them anyway. "Your room is on the second floor." (No kidding. The guest had to get to his room on the second floor in order to read the welcome letter—which tells him that his room is on the second floor.) "If you smoke, please use the ashtray." (Are there other options?) "The bathroom adjoins the guest room." (It surely does, just as the host pointed out during the tour.)

There could be items that you need to add to your list of "rules," tailored to your own household situation: "Please do not use the pool after dark. . . . Please do not leave your children unattended. . . . Please make sure that your pet is kept on a leash if you wish to take him outside."

Keep the tone of the letter upbeat. Although you are laying down guidelines for guests to follow, you do not want to sound nasty, sarcastic, or patronizing—even when you're discussing your pet peeve. Pretend that you are writing the letter to your best friend, who will be staying with you for a few days. In fact, you might want to give a draft of the letter to your best friend to see what he or she thinks of the tone and the content.

Type the letter onto an $8^1/_2'' \times 11''$ sheet of paper, and check for spelling errors. Then photocopy it onto the paper of your choice so that you can use the same letter for all of your guests. It's a nice touch to make your copies on good-quality paper, which does not cost much more than regular copy paper, or even copy the letter onto your own stationery. Sign each letter individually (instead of duplicating your signature) for a more personal touch. Fold the letter in half and address it to each guest by name before placing it on the tray in the guest room.

Some hosts have gotten into the habit of leaving little notes in the guest room, the bathroom, and throughout the rest of the house to instruct their guests what they can, and cannot, do. Other hosts feel that these detract from the home-like atmosphere of their bed and breakfast and interfere with the décor. A welcome letter keeps all the information together in one place and avoids all those sticky notes on the refrigerator, windows, doors. A welcome letter is definitely preferable, and much more friendly.

The visit

Many new hosts wonder just how much time they are expected to spend with their guests. Strictly speaking, a host need see a guest only when that person arrives, when breakfast is served, and when it's time to check out. But the reality for most hosts is that they do see their guests more often than just at these times. This is by choice. Getting to know the people who visit you is one of the advantages of being a bed and breakfast host.

Try to arrange your day so that you can join your guests at the breakfast table. "Remember that the hospitality you extend will be more than repaid to you by the warm conversation and friendship that often develop at the breakfast table," says Arline Kardasis, co-owner of a reservation service organization in Boston known as Bed & Breakfast Associates Bay Colony.

For many guests, part of the attraction of staying at a bed and breakfast home is the opportunity to experience a life that is different from their own. Invite them to watch you milk the cows or help you pick blueberries. Show them how you refinish antique furniture or make a quilt. Your line of work or hobby could be very interesting to someone who knows little about what it involves. (Who knows? You might even get some help with your chores.)

As you carry out your daily activities, see if you can fit your guests into your routine somehow. If you're driving downtown to do a little shopping, consider asking your guests if they would like to come along

> "You might not have so much, but the plain simplicity of your life is what appeals to so many people who live the fast pace of the city," says Edna Shipe of Valley View Farm, a bed and breakfast in West Virginia. One guest who returns to the farm every so often is affectionately called "Manhattan Maude." She writes: "Edna, I am missing your pies. I also am missing the butterflies, the squirrels, the calves and sheep on the hill, the smell of the forest. I do not remember how many years since the last time I saw butterflies."

for the ride. (They can explore while you're busy with errands.) If you're walking down to the drugstore for a newspaper, you might want to ask your guests if they would like to walk along with you. (They could need to purchase some personal items themselves, or maybe they would just enjoy a stroll around the neighborhood.) If you're planning to watch a movie on your VCR in the evening, consider asking your guests to join you. (Maybe they'd prefer some company to spending the time in their room alone reading.)

Of course, you need not extend any of these invitations unless you want to. The idea is to allow yourself the freedom you need to go about your business but still be as helpful and hospitable to your guests as you can. In most cases, you do want to leave yourself open to more social contact than what is possible over the breakfast table—provided that your guests want it as well. Some will, some won't, and some won't be sure. How much, or how little, a host gets involved can vary greatly, depending on the guest.

"Maybe it's meddling, but I love it," says one host who is registered with Bed and Breakfast Associates Bay Colony. To him, being a good host means getting involved, "giving a guest more than breakfast and a smile." To illustrate his point, he tells of a woman from Toledo, Ohio, who was in Boston for a convention and away from her husband and children for the first time in her married life. She was clearly afraid to venture beyond the house, so the host decided to help her out, literally. "I sent her to the grocery store for milk," he says. Next came a trip together across town for fresh produce, at which point he left her with directions on how to use the city's subway system. Before two days had passed, the host found the guest confidently instructing a new arrival from Texas on how to get around in Boston. "If left to her own devices, she would have read those three library books she brought with her instead of exploring the city," the host says. Sometimes guests need a gentle nudge to get more out of their visit. A good host can help get things rolling, as did the "meddling" host who helped his rather timid visitor explore a new city and enjoy it, in spite of her apprehensions.

For some people in an unfamiliar area for reasons that are not at all pleasant—like visiting a relative in a hospital—be aware that they might want and need more social involvement than those guests who are merely interested in sightseeing. For these people, the everyday activities of your household are comforting; they bring some semblance of normalcy back into their lives. One woman staying with host Ellie Welch Ramsey on such an occasion took it upon herself to wash the dishes every day. This is certainly not a task that a host expects a guest to do, but Ellie let her alone. "It made her feel better to be busy," she says.

You'll find that you have a lot in common with some of your guests, and the desire to spend time together will be mutual. One gentleman tells of returning to the town where he had been born and raised to attend his fifty-year high school reunion. He felt lucky to find a bed and breakfast home ten minutes away from the high school, where the reunion would be held. It so happened that the hosts remembered his father, who had been the county superintendent of schools when they had attended grade school. "We were able to compare memories about various mutual acquaintances and events," the guest recalls, even though they had not known one another as children. They indulged in long, nostalgic conversations that made the guest's return ("my last") to his hometown very special.

A young couple who spent their vacation in a rural coastal area found it enjoyable to be with their hosts a great deal of the time. "We spent a lot of time talking together and occasionally shared things like cooking and washing dishes. We ate all of our meals together and spent most evenings together, chatting over wine or coffee." They also went sailing and hiking together.

This much togetherness is not the norm, but it's wonderful when it happens naturally and spontaneously, laying the groundwork for a lasting friendship. Just how much "togetherness" is the right amount is sometimes a difficult thing for a host to figure out, especially at first. There can be too much. Here is what some reservation service organization managers say about the biggest mistake that new hosts tend to make: "Trying to do too much and spending too much time with their guests. There is a middle ground and it takes a little while to find it," says the manager of Bed 'n' Breakfast Ltd., of Washington, D.C. "A few will suffocate the guests with attention," says the manager of Mi Casa Su Casa in Tempe, Arizona, or "hovering over a guest, not leaving enough private space," as the manager of Pacific Bed & Breakfast in Seattle, Washington, puts it. She goes on to advise new hosts to "be gracious, available, but know when to pull back. Don't talk a guest to death." "New hosts, if anything, might try to do too much for their guests," says the manager of Greater Boston Hospitality. "If they are overly concerned for their guests' well-being, they could be perceived as intrusive and make their guests uncomfortable. A good feel for this comes with a little experience."

How do guests react to too much attention? "I like the helpfulness and friendliness of a local contact," says one California resident who enjoys traveling the B&B way. "But a few times I have encountered hosts who were too inquisitive. A friendly interest is one thing; being 'nosy' is something else. At one place I remember we were more or less asked to account for all our activities of the day: 'Where did you have dinner,' and so forth. Harmless but irritating."

An east coast couple enjoyed their Canadian host (whom they describe as "a nice, talkative guy") very much, but they were quite tired upon arrival after their long trip and just wanted to rest. "Although we enjoyed his enthusiasm, he did hang out in 'our room'—which was clearly 'his room'—a bit too long. He didn't pick up on our weariness."

"You have to be able to tell when people want to visit, and when they want privacy," says the manager of Southern Comfort Bed & Breakfast in Baton Rouge, Louisiana. When you aren't sure what they want, fish a little: "Would you like to join me for coffee, or are you tired? Maybe you'd just like to rest for a while?" Extend invitations, but don't come on too strong. Make yourself available, but let your guests seek you out.

There will be times when the shoe will be on the other foot, when you'll have an overly friendly guest who wants to spend a lot of time with you, but you just don't have the time or inclination for so much togetherness. At times like these, you'll have to take it upon yourself to be firm but courteous to stop your guest from following you around. "I have to finish vacuuming the living room and then rush off to pick up Junior from baseball practice. Maybe we can get together for a glass of wine late this evening when the day is over"—this is one way of letting your guests know that you have other responsibilities at the moment but would be happy to resume the conversation later. If you are expecting friends for a dinner party, you might want to announce the event to your guests ahead of time so that they understand that it is a private affair and that there is no open invitation: "Some of my friends will be coming over this evening for dinner, and I hope we won't disturb you. Please feel free to go into the family room and watch television if you wish and help yourself to some soft drinks from the refrigerator in the kitchen."

Discouraging lengthy conversations might be difficult at first, but it is a necessary skill to acquire so that you can balance your bed and breakfast business with your personal life. You might want to develop a few all-purpose ways to end conversations and practice role playing with a friend: "I wish I could have a second cup of coffee and just sit here and relax for a while but I'm afraid I can't. Now, is there anything you'll be

The Host Commandments

I. Thou shalt clean thine home until it likens itself unto a precious jewel that doth sparkle and shine.

II. Thou shalt stick to thine home, yea as a fly to flypaper, when thou dost expect the arrival of guests.

III. Thou shalt welcome with good cheer all guests who should cross thy threshold seeking bed and, yea, breakfast.

IV. Thou shalt make ready coffee aplenty upon the waking hour and invite thy guests to partake freely and abundantly thereof.

V. Thou shalt treat thy guests as thou wouldst thine own self be treated.

VI. Thou shalt not speak an unkind word, yea though thy guest's puppy doth relieve itself, yea merrily, upon thy floor.

VII. Thou shalt not chitchat with thy guests when they long only to bury their weary heads in yon goosedown pillows.

VIII. Thou shalt not smack the hindside of thy guest's offspring when, lo, thou dost behold what havoc the little ones have wrought upon thy cherished home.

IX. Thou shalt collect thy rightful tithe, yea in full, before thy guest taketh his leave and forgetteth to pay.

X. Thou shalt bid thy guests a fond farewell with hope that the friendship between ye may grow like a bud that blooms to full flower in the warm spring.

The Guest Commandments

I. Thou shalt show up after thou hast made a reservation and thy kindly host hast worked for seven days and seven nights to prepare for thine arrival.

II. Thou shalt call thine host if thou art delayed.

III. Thou shalt pay thy bill upon arrival.

IV. Thou shalt ask thy host, yea in advance, if there be room at the inn for thine four-footed companion known unto thee as "Fluffy."

V. Thou shalt not liken thyself unto a herd of stampeding camels when thy host hast lain down his weary head to rest.

VI. Thou shalt not imbibe freely of spirits at thy host's hearth so that thou falleth flat upon thy face.

VII. Thou shalt leave the pieces of silver in thy host's silverware drawer and abscond not with them or with other precious goods into the dark of night.

VIII. Thou shalt harken unto the commandments decreed by thine host.

IX. Thou shalt do unto thy host's home as thou wouldst do unto thine own.

X. Thou shalt bounteously thank thy gracious host for welcoming thee with good cheer into his home.

needing before I excuse myself?" One host admits to setting the timer on her clothes dryer for 10:00 A.M. so that when it rings she can excuse herself gracefully from lingering at the breakfast table.

The best advice is to recognize that no two guests are alike. Don't compare one with another. You'll like some more and others less. Some will like *you* more, others less. Each relationship between a host and a guest is unique. Try to let each one follow its natural course (making adjustments where necessary for both your privacy and your guests') and see where it leads. For many, it's a lasting friendship.

The farewell

"I can't believe that any motel or hotel manager would have hugged and kissed me good-bye and sent me away with a pint jar of rhubarb jam to take home with me," says a gentleman from California, describing the farewell he received from the couple who own a bed and breakfast home in Webster, South Dakota, called Lakeside Farm. These hosts made a lasting impression on their guest. "They are on my Christmas list for sure," he says.

How you say good-bye to your guests is just as important as how you say hello. A warm welcome can make your guests feel at home immediately and can even help to start a friendship; a hearty *bon voyage* confirms that your guests are welcome to come back and can help that budding friendship grow. You would take the time to say a personal good-bye to friends who had been visiting with you and who were about to take their leave; extend the same courtesy to your bed and breakfast guests. Be there, if you can, when they are packing their things and getting ready to drive off. If it is not possible for you to be home at this time (which could be the case if you have work or family responsibilities that take you out of the house), make it a point to say your farewells the last time you will be seeing your guests, perhaps the evening before their departure.

Many hosts like to give their guests a small gift when they leave. Food is always a good choice. Your guests will be traveling away from your home just as surely as they traveled to it. A box of your oatmeal cookies or a loaf of your zucchini bread will certainly help your guests to remember you fondly a few hours later when they're still on the road—and hungry. Attaching or enclosing the recipe has two advantages if you write it on the back of one of your brochures: It gives your guests a lasting memento of their visit (which they will enjoy over and over again each time they follow your directions), and it also leaves a permanent calling card with your guests (with your bed and breakfast's address and phone number on it) that you know they won't throw away!

If a guest especially enjoys something that you serve for breakfast or a snack, consider giving it as a gift. This is exactly how the Californian ended up with a pint of jam from his host at Lakeside Farm: "I raved about her home-made rhubarb jam, and so she had it on the table every morning," he recalls. When it came time to take his leave, what better remembrance of his happy visit could there possibly be?

A product of your region also makes a good gift—a small jar of honey, a bunch of red chili peppers, a corn-husk doll. The "city folk" who visit bed and breakfast homes in the country might especially appreciate seasonal produce from your garden—a container of strawberries, a pumpkin, a bag of apples, some ripe corn.

If you enjoy any type of arts or crafts, consider making small gifts for your guests—a ceramic bead, a pot holder, a postcard-size sketch or watercolor of your B&B.

If you do decide to give gifts, don't do anything elaborate, time consuming, or expensive. The gift should be a memento, nothing more. Think about your own resources and talents and see if you can come up with "a little something" that your guests would appreciate as a parting gift.

Before your guests make their final departure, conduct a last-minute inspection of their room and bathroom for forgotten items. "Shortly after opening, I learned that one must always look under the bed when guests leave," says Lona Smith, owner of Summerwood in Richfield Springs, New York. "I have found quite an assortment of things—money, baby bottles, Cheerios." Under the bed, inside the drawers, in the closet, on the hooks in the bathroom, inside the medicine cabinet—all of these places should be checked. Still, you won't find everything until it's too late, no matter how diligently you search.

Whenever you do find a lost item, follow the advice of Kate Winters, manager of a reservation service organization called Bed & Breakfast Rocky Mountains. She tells the hosts registered with her RSO to write a note to the guest who left the item behind, saying: "You left [specify the article] in your room during your recent stay with us. Please let me know how you would like to handle it. If you desire to have it sent by parcel post, or otherwise, I will prepare it for mailing and send you an estimate of the cost." One further suggestion to this good advice is to find out before you write the note how much it would cost to send the item parcel post and include that information in your communication. This way, you have to write only once, and the guest can send you a check in the right amount to cover the cost.

If you have lent anything to your guests during their stay, their check-out time is the right time to make sure you get it back. You can quickly lose a guidebook, your best map of the area, or your only umbrella when a forgetful guest makes a hurried departure. Your "inspection" of their room should tell you whether the borrowed items have been left for your future guests to use; if you don't see something, ask (*tactfully*, of course, or they might feel that you're accusing them of stealing). Also, if you gave your guests a house key or a key to the door of their bedroom, collect it at check-out time.

Perhaps your guests have extended their stay beyond their originally planned visit. (This is not uncommon.) This means that the "payment in full" that was taken care of upon arrival is no longer enough to cover everything that is now owed. The evening previous to their check-out is a good time to remind your guests about the balance due: "I've made up the bill for the extra two nights you added onto your visit. It might be hectic in the morning when you're trying to get packed and out of here in time to catch the train, so this evening might be a better time to take care of it." Some hosts prefer to place the final bill inside an envelope and set it near the guest's plate at his or her final morning meal with you.

Keep in mind that some of your guests will need a ride to the airport or the bus or train station. Is it convenient for you to do this? Guests always appreciate the offer.

Just as your welcome is tailored to each guest's mood and reason for visiting, so should your farewell be tailored. In a way, trying to say good-bye in an appropriate manner is easier because you've had some time to get to know your guests. There's not as much guesswork involved. For each farewell, follow your observations and intuitions about the person. Don't embarrass a guest who spent most of her time in her room with little social contact during her one-night stay by producing a lavish show of affection and a gift upon her departure. Don't hug someone who is obviously not a "hugger." Don't give a gift to anyone whom you simply did not hit it off with. For these people, a warm smile, a hearty handshake, and a word or two of good will are all it takes to leave them with a good feeling about your hospitality. For those guests who did become friends, bring on the hugs and the gifts. Enjoy this precious benefit of being a bed and breakfast host to the fullest.

Guest comments

So now you've done everything you thought possible to make your guests' visit comfortable and enjoyable. You cleaned like crazy, cooked up a veritable feast for breakfast, tried the right tests on the mattress and pillows to make sure that they weren't "dead," bought new designer sheets, and offered friendly conversation but did not intrude on your guests' privacy. So how did you do? Were you really a good host? Was the bed and breakfast experience everything your guests expected?

There's one sure way to find out—ask. Not person to person, of course, because few guests will tell you straight out if anything was wrong. The best way to solicit honest comments from guests is to ask them to answer some questions on a form that you supply. They should do this before they leave—usually right before they leave so that they don't have to explain anything that they wrote, which is as it should be unless you're really up for a long session of criticism/self-criticism. No—what you want are the comments written down, short and to the point, so that you can evaluate the critique in your own way after your guests leave.

Different hosts have their own ways of devising evaluation forms that work for them. Some ask guests to rate the food, hospitality, cleanliness, comfort of the room, and other features on a scale of "Excellent," "Good," "Fair," "Poor." Other hosts think that this kind of rating scale really does not give enough useful information to upgrade anything that is indicated as less than "Excellent." A better way to get what you need is to ask more open-ended questions that allow guests to say more clearly what's on their minds. A question like "If you could change one thing about this bed and breakfast, what would it be?" really provokes thought from both the guest who was dissatisfied with some aspect of your service as well as the one who was very satisfied but will think a little harder to come up with an observation that could help you improve your service and hospitality even more. This is what you want.

A sample evaluation form is provided here to use as a guide in developing your own form. Give a copy of the form to your guests the evening before they are scheduled to check out, or place a copy in their room. Ask them to leave the form in the guest room when they check out, or suggest that they mail it to you later. (It's nice to provide a stamped envelope for this purpose.)

If you are listed with a reservation service organization, it is possible that the RSO already has forms or postcards available for the pur-

Evaluation Form

You're important to us! We try hard to make every guest's stay comfortable and enjoyable. We would appreciate any suggestions you have to help us do our job well. Please take a few minutes to answer the questions below and leave this form for us when you check out. Thank you! We hope you enjoyed your visit!

What did you like most about staying at our bed and breakfast?

Were there any disappointments?

If you could change one thing about our bed and breakfast, what would it be?

Please add any comments that you wish.

pose of soliciting comments from guests who were placed with you. Of course, the RSO needs to know that any guests who booked a reservation through it found their accommodations satisfactory—and if not, why not. The quality of each bed and breakfast home it lists reflects upon the RSO itself. Sally Godfrey, the manager of a reservation service organization in Maine known as Bed & Breakfast Down East, supplies her hosts with copies of a short form to give their guests, who are asked to mail them directly to the RSO. The form includes the following method of evaluation: "Please rate our service, on a scale of 1 to 10, for promptness, courtesy, and efficiency." Other questions are: "Did you find your accommodations clean and attractive?" "Were your hosts congenial and helpful?" "Were there any surprises?"

Postcards are given to guests who register through Historic Charleston Bed & Breakfast in Charleston, South Carolina, and through Bed & Breakfast of Maine. (The RSO in Maine even pre-stamps the cards to encourage guests to reply.) If your RSO does solicit comments from guests, ask that these be shared with you.

Remember that your bed and breakfast will be compared on the evaluation forms with any and all accommodations that your variety of guests has ever experienced. In a way, this is good; you'll find out how you compare with hotels, motels, inns, even a weekend at the in-laws'. But you can also expect from guests who are still suffering from a bad case of "hotel mentality" comments about the problems of sharing a bathroom and lack of room service. Read them all and forget about the ones that don't apply, but take to heart those that do. For a new host especially, feedback from your guests will help you to improve upon the comfort and hospitality that you want to characterize your bed and breakfast.

Memories

"We stayed in the loveliest B&B last summer! (What *was* the name of that little town?) And we had the nicest hosts! (What *was* their name?)"

Few of us have a perfect memory. Nor are we as organized as we would like to be. While traveling, we certainly intend to write down all those important details that we want to remember for "next time"—mileage, rental costs, admission charges, names and addresses. Sometimes we don't. (Where *is* that pen when I need it?) Sometimes we do. (Have you seen my journal from last year's vacation anywhere?) And, of course, we collect brochures, maps, business cards, and postcards. (Are they in that box up in the attic?) The reality is that often we just can't remember the information we thought we would never forget.

This could mean trouble for a bed and breakfast host. As unbelievable as it might seem, a guest who had a wonderful visit at your B&B might very well have difficulty remembering your name six months hence. This very common, and very human, quirk can directly affect your business. There goes the possibility of a return visit in the near or distant future. If it is too much trouble to locate you again, a former guest could decide to try another B&B.

Worse, a guest's friends, associates, or relatives who might be planning to travel to your area will not be able to find you. A lead that consisted of no more than "I think her last name starts with a 'B' and she lives somewhere on the Cape" would be a challenge for the best investigative reporter, never mind the average person trying to settle arrangements for a vacation that is supposed to make life easier for a while, not harder.

Return visits and personal recommendations from satisfied customers can bring you a considerable amount of business that could be lost to you unless you take steps to safeguard against it.

What's in a name?

Name your B&B. A short, catchy name gives your B&B more of an identity, and it will be more likely to remain in a guest's memory long after your street and house number have been forgotten. There are, of course, no guarantees on this point, but it sure beats expecting former guests to come up with the right combination of details to locate you once again. Then, if you choose to list your B&B in the telephone directory, you are just a phone call away. If you list with a reservation service organization, it will be a lot easier for its representatives to respond to an inquiry about "Hill House" than to pinpoint "some house on Beacon Hill—with black shutters, I think" as the certain B&B that the guest desires.

It is a good idea to adopt a designation that gives useful information about your B&B, but any name is better than none at all. Selecting a name like Jenny's Place or Maggie's Farm ensures that if they can remember your first name, former guests will have a good handle on your B&B's name. A surname can work effectively if it is not too long or too difficult. Using rhyme or alliteration will make it even easier to remember (Craven's Haven, for example, or The Henderson House).

Some hosts opt for an abbreviation: Mrs. K's B&B in Kennett Square, Pennsylvania, is one of these.

Or consider including information about the location of your home. Identify the city or town where you reside, or specify a landmark nearby: Collegeville Digs, East Lake George House, Hill Pond House, The Old Forge. If former guests are able to recall the name of the landmark, then they'll remember your B&B as well.

Some hosts tie in the name of their B&Bs with the surroundings. Mention a special feature of the area, its geography, its flora or fauna: House on the Hill, House Among Trees, Rock Ledge Manor, Cliffside, The Lake House, The Beeches, Twin Maples, Corner Birches Guest House, Blueberry Bush, The Berry Patch.

Others refer to a special characteristic of their homes, such as the age, color, or architecture: Centennial House, A Century Old, Victorian Rose, Brass Bed Victorian Guest House, Blue Shutters, The Yellow Cottage, Stone House Inn, The Farmhouse, The Four Gables, Widow's Walk.

Or you could try to impart a sense of the general atmosphere of your B&B, as in Radnor Charm, Country Comfort, or Country Cupboard. But watch out for unintended references. Chestnut Hill Serenity and Fair Meadows may sound appealing for their tranquility—but isn't Pleasant Acres the name of a cemetery out on Route 9? And Red Light Rooms could sound a little racy to someone who has no way of knowing that the name refers merely to the lovely scarlet-colored curtains in the guestrooms.

Still, do not be afraid to be innovative or playful with your selection. An unusual name, like A Doll's House, The Phoenix, or Mon Rêve, will raise questions about how you thought up the name in the first place. And the story behind it will make the name even more memorable for your guests.

Remember me?

Within a month after a guest's visit, it is safe to assume that the person has either recorded and filed the necessary information about your B&B in a safe place or has hopelessly lost it despite all good intentions. A note from you, with your B&B's name and address on it, could be as welcome a sight as lost treasure that's been recovered.

Consider your note to follow up a guest's visit one of the most important elements of your hosting, even though the visit itself is over. If

Lona and George Smith recall the most embarrassing incident at their bed and breakfast home in Richfield Springs, New York, as perhaps also the funniest. It occurred when they were hosting their very first guests, three couples who were good friends. On their third night at Summerwood, the group returned home about 11:00 P.M., after their hosts had gone to bed. "Shortly, I heard a lot of running and laughter," says Lona. "Not wanting to embarrass them, I stayed put. Things settled down in fifteen or twenty minutes. The next morning when I got up, I found my house had been somewhat rearranged." Plants had been moved. Potatoes and onions, which were kept in baskets in the kitchen, were dumped on the kitchen table. And the baskets were in the dining room. Some kind of game? the host wondered. The mystery was solved when the first guest came downstairs. There had been a bat in the house! The women had retreated upstairs and watched from the banister while the men (one a policeman), with baskets on their heads (they had heard that bats got into your hair), vanquished the bat with a broom. Quite an adventure to tell! "They promised that with the telling, the tiny bat would grow into a large vampire with a five-foot wingspread," says Lona.

done well, it will leave a positive, final impression of your B&B with your guests and may, perhaps, help to finally secure a place for your B&B in their permanent address books.

Although the note can be brief, under no circumstances should you send the same message to everyone indiscriminately. "Hope you enjoyed yourself while you were here!" may be fine for the couple on their second honeymoon, but it will not do for the man who came to visit his sister in the hospital. "We loved your company!" may be terrific for the aspiring comedian who liked to try out new jokes at the breakfast table, but it does not ring true for the rather shy young lady who spent most of her time alone in her room.

In your note, try to reach out to address something in each guest's personal experience. Refer to a special interest or hobby: "I saw a program by the American Ballet Theatre last night, and it got me wondering how your dance classes are coming along." Recall a particular incident that occurred during the time a guest stayed with you: "Today was a beautiful sunny day, much like a day you went out into the fields with the neighbor's children to pick blackberries."

Keep the message upbeat, even when writing to someone who stayed with you under less than pleasant circumstances. You should not hesitate to show genuine concern about a guest suffering from an illness or recovering from the loss of a loved one: "I've been thinking about you and just wanted to drop you a note to send my best wishes." You might want to bring up a subject that would not act as a reminder of the problem: "Your favorite B&B companion, Fluffy, just had five wonderful little kittens yesterday!" However, if you find that you have serious doubts about finding the right thing to say to people in these kinds of situations, then forget the note. Sometimes it is more sensitive and caring to say nothing at all.

Remembering the details of why different people visited you could be difficult, especially if you have a parade of guests all at once. So make sure that you record on your guests' reservation forms what you will need later—"here for computer programming seminar" or "attending niece's wedding." This way, when you write your notes a month afterward, you will not have to rely solely on your own faulty memory. "On the back of guests' registration cards, I will write special personal data to remind me of who they are—job information, hobbies, interests, anniversaries, etcetera," says the owner of Singleton House in Eureka Springs, Arkansas.

If you have the time and energy, jot down the contents of the follow-up message on the back of each guest's reservation form, along with the date it was sent. It will serve as a handy reference in case you have further contact with the guest or need some inspiration before writing to someone else.

One final caution about content: Never, ever, write a note that is not tailored to the person you are sending it to, or with the transparent purpose of drumming up more business. Your grace and style will attract more business than will appearing insistent, desperate, or insincere.

From the first moment a former guest lays eyes on it in the mailbox, your note should stand out as something special. It should not resemble a business communication but should give the feeling of being very personal. Purchase matching envelopes and note paper that in some way coordinate with the appearance or atmosphere of your B&B. If your home is painted blue, seek out blue paper near that shade. If your home is decorated with antiques, look for off-white or grained paper that looks like parchment. Keep an eye out for stationery sales and stock up in advance. Stock up on stamps, too. At the post office, request commemorative stamps. The designs change frequently and can make your envelope even more attractive.

If you wish to go to the expense, personal stationery with your B&B's name and address imprinted on it can be made to order. This is not necessary, however. (See chapter 5, "Publicizing Your Bed and

Breakfast.") And do not type your message, even if your best penmanship would not win any awards. A typed message is too formal. Your note should be a very personal communication.

Your own newsletter

If you belong to a reservation service organization, it's likely that it will take care of keeping in touch with your former guests by various means. (Be sure to ask how this is done.) This is one very important advantage of affiliating with a good RSO. A number of RSOs produce their own newsletters and send them to former guests of all their hosts.

There are some, however, that do not publish a newsletter or that do not maintain connections with your former guests to your satisfaction. If you find yourself in this situation, or if you are an independent host unaffiliated with an RSO, consider publishing your own newsletter.

If you've never done anything like this before, the idea can sound intimidating at first. But in this age of word processors and desk-top publishing, putting together a newsletter two or three times a year might be easier for you than writing all those personal notes.

The newsletter need not be elaborate—one page printed on both sides is all it takes. "News" items you could include are updates on yourself, your family, and your pets; favorite recipes; upcoming dates to remember (such as festivals, concerts, football games—whatever interests your guests); funny stories about your B&B; and facts about the area. Basically, the newsletter should look and sound like you, giving former guests a fond remembrance of their visit.

A thousand words

Some hosts like to take a photograph of each guest at some point during the visit and mail it with the follow-up note as a memento. This is a great idea, providing that the timing and occasion of taking the picture are appropriate.

Choose the moment well: as your guests are happily loading up the station wagon with towels and picnic baskets for a day at the beach, for example, or donning their wraps for a night on the town. Toasting a successful job interview. Romping with the family dog in the yard. All of these are special memories that your guests would love to have captured on film.

On the other hand, there are moments to avoid. When a guest is rushing to the airport, it is hardly the time to make him stop and pose for you. Or when someone has just come through the door after a grueling day of sales presentations. Or before breakfast—ever! If taking a picture seems forced, unnatural, a problem in any way, don't do it. The last thing you want to do is make a guest uncomfortable.

Your photograph will be even more treasured if it comes in the mail as a surprise a month after the visit. So, if possible, keep your intention to send it a secret from your guests. "Photography is a hobby of mine" and "We want to make a photo album of all our guests" are good lines, but if you have trouble making little white lies like these believable, then it is better to tell the truth and be done with it: "I'll send you a copy when I get the film developed." You could run the risk of giving the mistaken impression that what you are really doing is collecting mug shots just in case the family silver disappears. The photo should remind your guests of what a wonderful time they had at your B&B.

A book exchange

Even people who do not read much in their normal, everyday lives often find themselves reaching for a book when they are on a trip. At last they have the time to read for pleasure over a leisurely breakfast, while relaxing at the beach, or before retiring for the night. And a good paperback seems to have become the universal solution for those long hours of waiting for bus, train, or airplane connections.

A good host will, of course, invite guests to use the family library and keep on hand guidebooks as a resource for guests. But a separate "book exchange" will not only indulge your guests' immediate desire for new reading material; it will also help your business once your guests have long since departed.

A good number of books read by people during their travels fall under the category of "light reading." Because of this, people are not inclined to keep these books once they have finished reading them. They would welcome the opportunity to trade them for other new or used, but unread, books. Your book exchange is the place to do just that.

Start your book exchange by seeding it with material that appeals to a wide variety of reading tastes—mysteries, science fiction, short stories, romance novels, and perhaps some plays or poetry. Stay away from anything too long, too dense, or too eclectic. It's not likely that many vacationers will feel like curling up with *War and Peace* or *The Political Implications of Dialectical Materialism*. And if your B&B accepts children, add some children's books and comic books as well.

All of these can be obtained inexpensively at flea markets, yard sales, thrift stores, and bookstores that have special discount sections. And you might be pleasantly surprised at what a request to friends for old, unwanted books can generate. One host found herself the happy recipient of a neighbor's entire library when he decided to retire, sell his house, and move to a sunnier climate!

Set aside a small bookcase or a few shelves for your book exchange, keeping the area separate from the library of books that you do not want leaving the house by mistake. You might even want to label it "Book Exchange," "Book Bar," or "Trading Post" just to designate clearly that these are the books that can be traded.

On the inside front cover of each book, write your B&B's name, address, and telephone number. Then, wherever a book may go, so does a calling card for your B&B.

Explain to guests that there is only one rule as far as the book exchange is concerned: For every book taken, one must be donated. Inside the cover of the donated book, in addition to the information about your B&B, a guest writes his or her name, the date of visit, home town, and any message he or she wants to pass along to future guests.

For those who protest that they do not know what kind of message to write, be ready with some suggestions based on their interests and activities while visiting you. A runner who just finished his first marathon might write a few words of advice for others who come to do the same thing next year. Someone who bravely faced, and mastered, the tangle of subway lines in the city might want to write down some helpful hints for someone else about to use mass transit for the first time. The key to interesting personal messages is imagination. For guests, thumbing through the books to read messages from all kinds of people can be part of the adventure of staying at your B&B. They will feel a part of the special community of people who have enjoyed your hospitality. A book taken from the book exchange will act as a memento of their visit, something they want to keep. And it's also something they can easily refer to when they want to locate your name and address once again.

Holiday greetings

The season of Christmas, Hanukkah, and New Year's is the time to get in touch with friends. A card from you at this time is a good way to keep in touch with your former guests.

If you buy holiday cards, stay away from those with religious themes, as your guests will undoubtedly be of a variety of faiths. "Seasons Greetings" and "Happy Holidays" are good, universal messages. Economize by purchasing cards right after the season is over, when there are half-price sales on leftover holiday merchandise. Thinking ahead for next year can save you money.

A photo card—with a picture of your B&B on it—is preferable to the regular cards. Obtainable at most photo-processing stores, photo cards do not cost significantly more than regular holiday cards bought in season, but they are much more personal.

Take a photo of your home, either inside or out. Better yet, have a friend take the photo so that you can be in the picture yourself. For former guests, it will be fun to see their host all bundled up, standing ankle-deep in snow in front of the house they last saw in hot August sunshine, or sitting by the familiar living room fireplace, now decorated with Christmas stockings and pine boughs.

The best type of photo card to purchase is the kind that has a cut-out window where you can insert the photograph. It allows removal of the photo to be kept after the holiday season is over, which makes it preferable to those with the photo printed directly on them.

The neighbors

New hosts usually wonder what kind of reception they're in for from the neighbors when they open their homes for bed and breakfast. They wonder if they should make some sort of public announcement. As a new host, should you take a full-page ad in the local paper, stage an open house, rent a loudspeaker? Need you do anything at all to let the neighbors know that you are now offering bed and breakfast to guests?

The answer is no. You need not parade up and down Main Street proclaiming that you operate a B&B any more than a writer, a seamstress, and a graphic designer do to herald the fact that they have opened home-based businesses. Bed and breakfast is the gentle art of hospitality, and as such it is as unobtrusive as writing, sewing, or sketching. It will not bother anyone in the neighborhood. Possible problems arise only when neighbors don't understand that this is the case. Bed and breakfast is such an innovative concept in this part of the world that it is sometimes met with suspicion. Because of this, some hosts never mention their B&B operation to any of their neighbors.

You might find it hard to believe at first, but it's quite possible that your neighbors won't notice anything at all that might suggest to them that they are living next door to a bed and breakfast. One California host says this of her neighbors: "They don't know I'm a hostess. There's no indication that the couples who stay here are different from our own houseguests and family members." "We are so low-key that many [neighbors] weren't even aware of it for over a year," says a Massachusetts host.

A Florida host says, "I just say I have friends visiting." And hosts in rural areas report that their neighbors are so distant that they never notice a thing, or if they do, they don't care.

The key to keeping a low profile is to guard against anything that might bother the neighbors—such as noise or taking their parking spaces. "We try to get our guests' cars into our driveway so that the neighbors don't get a chance to complain. We did it for a year before I told anyone I was doing it," says a host from Kingston, Ontario. A Pennsylvania host says, "My driveway holds six cars, and there is ample parking in front of my house. Also, my guests cause no undue disturbance in the neighborhood."

If your neighbors do notice and you feel that an explanation is in order, or if you hope to use your community ties to draw visitors to your bed and breakfast, you can hardly keep the low profile that works best for some hosts. You'll have to tell people what you're doing, which means that you've got to be prepared to educate them in what bed and breakfast is all about—many will have no idea. Lisa Hileman, owner of Countryside in Summit Point, West Virginia, recalls her experience with the neighbors when she first began hosting: "Countryside was the first small B&B in the entire state of West Virginia. The local folks thought I was having an *orgy*—'Breakfast in Bed with Lisa.' They thought I was going to put up a flashing neon sign—'Eat and Sleep, Truckers Welcome!' We had to educate the local people and the tourists as to what we were doing here. In the beginning they were negative because it was something new and different. Now they accept us and see that we are not a blight on the neighborhood and that our guests are nice people."

Once your neighbors do understand what bed and breakfast is, chances are that they will be quite receptive. "They send their visiting relatives to stay with us, so it is a convenience for them," says Carol Emerick, owner of The Cottage in San Diego, California. "Several neighbors use me when they have out-of-town guests," says Robert Somaini of Woodruff House in Barre, Vermont. In fact, one of his neighbors takes his overflow in busy times. Another host reports that her neighbors love the idea of her having a B&B so much that they often come over to meet the guests!

Catherine Hatala, a host with Bed and Breakfast Center City in Philadelphia, says that one of her neighbors "will often walk a guest down and make him feel at home if I am not available at the guest's arrival time." She goes on to say that her neighbors are very kind and courteous to her guests when they encounter them anywhere in the neighborhood: "If my neighbors see my guests on the street, they greet them and sometimes answer questions for them and make recommendations," she says.

Because their bed and breakfast home is the only one in the village of Richfield Springs, New York, Lona and George Smith, the owners of Summerwood, have found that their neighbors "have been extremely supportive and encouraging to the point that they send us many guests who are out-of-town visitors coming for weddings, etc."

Roy Mixon, too, has found that his neighbors more than accept the presence of Rockland Farm Retreat in Bumpass, Virginia. "They send guests, come to socials, and enjoy the benefits—the employment and the money the guests spend in the area," he says. Rockland is a former plantation that has been restored. In West Virginia, the owner of a grand old house that she restored as a bed and breakfast also found that her neighbors approved of the project, viewing it as a contribution to the community: "They are very proud," she says. Another host, living in Eureka Springs, Arkansas, has had a similar experience with her neighbors. "They love it, since restoration improved the value of property," she says.

In one case, it was the neighbors who suggested that the host open her home for bed and breakfast in the first place! For some years, the owner of a lovely home in Leaburg, Oregon, had allowed people to visit her extensive landscaped grounds with its many beautiful flowering plants. So that guests could enjoy the park-like atmosphere even more, as well as the home that was constructed especially to enhance the natural surroundings, both neighbors and guests urged the owner of Marjon, Margie Haas, to open her home for bed and breakfast. In 1982, she did just that.

The support of your neighbors can be especially important to you if you encounter any problems with zoning boards regarding the operation of your bed and breakfast. (See "Zoning" in chapter 9.) A host in Graham, North Carolina, found her neighbors taking her side when she needed them. "I had to have their approval initially because the block had to be rezoned from residential," she says.

If you decide that you wish to have a visible presence in your neighborhood, you've got to take steps to garner support for yourself and to foster the understanding of what bed and breakfast is and what kind of a contribution it can make to the community. An open house might not be a bad idea—invite some of the neighbors over for coffee and to meet a few of your guests. People seem to fear what they don't know, so take it upon yourself to dispel the mystery. Let your neighbors find out what a good neighbor a bed and breakfast can be.

8
A Memorable Breakfast

For many of us, eating breakfast is something we get through quickly so that we can move on to the more important business of the day. The setting doesn't really matter, as long as we have what we need on the table. Sometimes the food doesn't even seem to matter, as long as it can be prepared quickly and will hold us until lunch.

But there are days when we do make the time to have a leisurely morning meal with those special touches—a tablecloth, the "good" china, a vase of flowers, those terrific blueberry pancakes made from scratch. Sunday brunch—how wonderful it is! For your bed and breakfast guests, every day is Sunday. Your job as a host is to make the breakfast experience enjoyable not only with what you serve, but also how you serve it.

Scenic settings

Okay, we all learned that the fork goes to the left of the plate and that the knife and spoon go to the right on top of a plain white napkin that has been folded in half, then in thirds. The salt and pepper shakers go dead center, next to the sugar and cream.

This little lesson may have helped us set the table for our own meals throughout the years, but when it comes to bed and breakfast, it's not enough. Of course, there's nothing wrong with the common table setting we all use, but, face it, it's so very ordinary. (When was the last time you sat down to eat in your own home and said, "Ooh! Just look at that setting"?)

Think of the space where your guests will eat breakfast as an "environment." Everything in the area should contribute to the pleasure of the meal. You must first decide where the best place is for your guests to eat their breakfast. The dining room is an obvious choice, but there could be other options that would make the experience special. Does your home have an area outdoors where guests could enjoy their meal in good weather—a patio, a balcony, a deck, a flower garden, a lawn? What would it take to set up a picnic table and chairs or patio furniture under the willow tree or next to the duck pond? Would it be easy enough to carry the food to the outdoor setting?

Moselle Schaffer, the owner of Camel Lot in Westfield, Indiana, offers bed and breakfast on her exotic animal farm. Her brochure includes this note: "Breakfast is served on the terrace overlooking the tiger compound, or the sunroom or—on bleak days—beside a crackling fire in the library." Who could resist the chance to have a morning meal with a prince of the jungle?

Another alternative setting (for those of us who do not have a tiger compound) is the guest room itself, but only if the space is large enough and can be divided easily so that the sleeping area and the dining area do not interfere with each other. A suite or separate guest house is perfect for such an arrangement, but a small single or double room will not work—too cramped.

Keep in mind, too, that confining the dining area to the guest room does distance you from your visitors. Couples might enjoy the opportunity to have a more private breakfast, but single travelers might not want to eat alone in their room. Some hosts decide against setting up a separate breakfast area for guests for this reason; others do but let guests know that they're welcome in the dining room.

If you do want to set up a breakfast area in the guest room, first imagine that the room has no furniture at all in it. Then look at the shape of the room. Is there a particular section of it where a table and chairs would fit quite naturally? Next to the bay windows? In front of the fireplace? Near the sliding glass doors? Inside the alcove? What kind of a "view" would your guests have if you were to place the table and chairs where you think they would go best? (You don't want your guests staring straight at the unmade bed while they have their soufflé.) A window or fireplace will draw their attention; you can also create a view (of sorts) by placing an interesting piece of art near the table.

Now that you've identified where in the guest room a breakfast area would go best, take a look at the room in the morning during the different hours (both early and late) that your guests will be having breakfast. From where does the light enter the room and from what angle? Can you position the table and chairs in your chosen spot without the strong morning sun shining directly into your guests' eyes? Can the window shade or curtain be adjusted to block the light but still offer a view?

Too little light is just as bad as too much. If the table and chairs would fit best inside a dark alcove or corner, is there an electrical outlet near enough to connect a small lamp? (A full or partial canopy of sheer or netted material can be draped above the dining area to separate it somewhat from the "bedroom." Don't use material that is opaque; it will make the environment feel too small and confined.)

Most hosts simply use their own dining room to serve their guests' breakfast. It's the most convenient place, requires no extra decorating, and provides a common area where hosts and guests can share breakfast and get to know one another—one of the treasured advantages of bed and breakfast. Perhaps your dining room has been arranged the same way for years, but try to look at the room with new eyes. Evaluate it the same way you would if you were about to create a completely new dining area. Consider the shape of the room, the light source, the view, and the general comfort of the guests who will be joining you at the table. Should you make any changes? Perhaps the table and chairs actually go better over by the window or farther away from the kitchen door.

After you've determined the best place to serve breakfast, it's time to concentrate on how to make your table setting special. There are a few touches that make any table more appealing: a "real" tablecloth (instead of a plastic one), cloth napkins (instead of paper ones), and the "good" china and silver that you usually save for special occasions. Add to these a centerpiece and an interesting presentation for the napkin, and you're all set.

The main thing to remember is that you want the table to look attractive. For this, use your imagination. Maybe the fork, knife, and spoon should all go to the right of the plate in order to better display the beautifully folded napkin at the left. Or maybe the silverware looks best placed together at an angle on a napkin that has been folded end to end into a large, imposing triangle. Forget the rules we were all taught about setting a table. Be daring. Experiment. And enjoy yourself.

The centerpiece

Many of us get through life just fine with nothing more in the center of our dining room table than the salt and pepper shakers. And it's true that you need not go to the trouble of buying or creating a centerpiece just because you'll now be hosting bed and breakfast guests. But it's a nice gesture. The presence of a strong, imaginative centerpiece shows your guests that you consider breakfast to be a special event. This, they will remember.

A vase of flowers is a very common centerpiece, but always a very lovely one. Fresh flowers are especially attractive in season for their fragrance; a sprig of flowers from the arrangement can be placed on each napkin for a special touch that unifies the total table setting. (Be aware that guests may suffer from hay fever, though.) A permanent presentation of dried flowers is also appealing and has the advantages to a host of involving no work after the arrangement has been created, and costing nothing beyond the initial expense. If you coordinate the colors in the flower arrangement with those in your tablecloth, placemats, napkins, and dishware, the most basic table setting can look quite elegant.

If you enjoy decorating and wish to do more than this, creating an unusual centerpiece can be a lot of fun for a host and can make the breakfast experience at your home quite memorable for your guests. You can develop an entire table theme around your centerpiece based on the season, a holiday or special occasion, or even your guests' personal interests.

For the fall season, consider a centerpiece of polished gourds piled high in a basket, along with a selection of dried flowers in autumn reds, golds, browns, and oranges. For the Christmas season, fill a basket or clear glass bowl with tiny wrapped packages. These can be empty, but it's fun to wrap matchboxes, scented soaps, or miniature candles; then a package can be placed on each napkin or plate as a gift and to unify the table setting. For New Year's, turn a large party hat on its side (or place it upside down, using a transparent vase for a base) and fill it with noisemakers, streaming ribbons (the kind that curl are good for this), and maybe a balloon or two; place a noisemaker on each plate or napkin as a gift (and, again, to unify the setting).

You should always try to coordinate any colors used in your centerpiece with those in the rest of your table setting. Of course you're not going to run out and buy a whole new set of tablecloths, placemats, napkins, and dishware for every season and every holiday. This is not necessary to achieve the effect you want. You can change the entire look of your table quite inexpensively by choosing a white tablecloth that you can use year-in and year-out, and merely changing the colors of your napkins or placemats. (If you sew, these can be made easily at a very reasonable cost.) Or buy napkin rings in different colors and use those to accent the colors that dominate your centerpiece. (Doing this involves even less expense than buying or making several sets of napkins.)

If your dishware seems to clash with any of your seasonal color schemes, often all you need to do is simply add an accent of that color to the centerpiece (a dash of turquoise among the autumn colors), and the problem is solved. Or adapt the colors in the centerpiece to suit your dishware. (Sacrifice the "Valentine red" for a "Valentine pink," the color of the floral design on your dishes.)

If you want a real challenge, but a very rewarding one, think of how you could tie in the theme of the breakfast table with some personal aspect of your different guests' visits.

Many people travel on special occasions as a means of celebration—a birthday, anniversary, wedding, graduation. You will know this in advance from your screening process; you can make the event especially memorable for your guests by taking the time to create a table setting just for the occasion. Now is the time to put that old mortarboard from college or dolls saved from atop your own wedding cake to good use as part of the centerpiece. And place a card with your good wishes on the plate of the visitor who is celebrating the event. (You might want to keep an assortment of cards on hand for this purpose.)

Some hosts have even surprised their guests by making a birthday cake. If the spirit moves you, by all means do it. There's no question that the thought (and the cake) will be greatly appreciated, but know that this is above and beyond what a bed and breakfast host is expected to provide.

For guests who are visiting you for other reasons, you might see where that leads you with centerpiece ideas. Are you hosting some fans come to cheer on their favorite team? (Maybe a pennant placed in a tall, slender vase would look better to these folks than any flower arrangement.) A few fishermen about to try their luck? (The goldfish bowl could be moved to the table for the morning.) A musician in town to give a concert? (What's to stop you from getting that old violin out of the attic, arranging a few flowers in its center, and placing it on the table on top of some sheet music?) A runner warming up for the big race? (Perhaps some new decorative shoelaces would make an appropriate napkin ring and a fun gift from you "for luck.") A teacher come to address the National Education Association? (How about your son's lunch box, with the lid open, filled with a couple of schoolbooks, some pencils, a box of chalk, and a few tall flowers towering over it all?)

You get the idea. You'll find that you can tailor-make centerpieces quite easily once you get started. Your guests will certainly remember you for highlighting their special moment. This works, of course, only when the reason for a guest's visit is an uplifting one. If a teacher has come to your bed and breakfast for a few days to escape from the schoolbooks and the pencils and the chalk, she probably won't want to be reminded of them at her breakfast table. Use your good judgment about when to go for something out of the ordinary in a centerpiece, and when to use just a nice vase of flowers.

Always try to draw from what you already have instead of spending extra money to create individualized centerpieces. Yet, if your location happens to draw a certain type of visitor (football fans, skiers, honeymooners, fishermen), it's easier to plan ahead for the "unusual" centerpieces. In this case, you can use the items over and over again. Maybe a goldfish wouldn't be such a bad investment.

Especially for children

No one needs to tell you that children usually can't wait to get away from the table. There are too many rules ("Don't talk with your mouth full!"), too many things that can break ("Be careful with that glass!") or spill ("Watch out for the milk!"). Eating may be necessary, but it's sure not much fun when Mom and Dad are worried about your every move. It's even worse in someone else's house, where parents are more concerned than ever that their children behave.

If you accept children at your bed and breakfast, there are some things you can do to help cut the tension so that both the kids and their parents can relax and have a good time.

You are most likely using your best china and crystal for the adults. Do not feel that you are obligated to use these for a child who is old enough to sit at the table but still likely to break and spill. It will be a big relief all around (for you, for the parents, and for the child, too) if the youngster's place setting contains attractive, but unbreakable, dishware. (Take care, though, not to insult a well-behaved eleven- or twelve-year-old with the kid stuff.)

This doesn't mean merely trotting out the "old" plastic dishes imprinted with designs of fronds and rosettes. Doing this will make it embarrassingly obvious that you fear for the safety of your "good" things. (They may not be safe, but parents can sometimes be sensitive about this.) Instead, give some attention to creating a special place setting just for the child.

Brightly colored dishes, and perhaps a colored or patterned napkin as well, are a good start. You can make the setting interesting by folding the napkin in a way a child might enjoy, or placing it in the arms of a small stuffed animal.

Do you have any toy soldiers, monsters, superheroes? Why not give Godzilla a fork to hold or put Spiderman in charge of the spoon?

Do you have a small train set? Why not put three or four cars in a half-circle above the child's plate and load them up with the silverware, the napkin, and the salt and pepper shakers?

If you are hosting more than one child, or if you have children yourself who will be eating breakfast with the guests, it might be fun to set up a "children's table" near the "adults' table," where they can be watched but still enjoy their breakfast in peace. Just as for the adult table, you'll need a centerpiece and a theme for the table setting. You can do this easily with stuffed animals. Set up a few extra chairs at the table with Teddy in one and Garfield in the other with their own place settings. If you have some plastic fruit, place a selection on each plate. (As a centerpiece, how about an empty honey pot with a small bear poking his nose inside?)

Other ideas: Place a tiny table-and-chairs set from a doll house on the table as a centerpiece. Or display a toy tea-party set. Or create a miniature farm right in the center of the table, and use some of the pieces for the place setting: Put a cow next to the glass of milk. A tractor can haul the spoon. (Maybe a large green placemat would make a good field for the tractor.) Or think about a jungle theme, with toy lions, tigers, bears, elephants, and maybe a Tarzan model. (And how about a napkin made of black and yellow tiger-striped material?) Or perhaps a prehistoric theme would be fun, with a few dinosaurs roaming the table.

If a holiday is near, work it into the child's place setting. For a Halloween centerpiece, put a mask on the teddy bear and a toy jack-o'-lantern in his lap. For Christmas, try a Santa's hat on Teddy and place the silverware inside a red stocking, along with a candy cane.

The child should be able to touch the things that you place on the table for his or her amusement and, yes, even play with them. For this reason, all items you use should be touchable—that is, unbreakable. And of course, you must always take a child's age into consideration when planning a place setting. Some very small children could get so totally distracted by the toys that they forget to eat altogether, or Raggedy Ann ends up face-down in the oatmeal. Use your judgment about what's possible, and appropriate, for youngsters of different ages. And consult with a child's parents the evening before as you plan the breakfast. Respect their wishes regarding their youngster's meal.

And, too, you shouldn't spend a lot of money buying stuffed animals and other toys for the table setting. Look at what you might already have and use your imagination. Your own children's toys are your greatest resource. (Ask them to help you design and set up place settings for visiting children—it's a good way to make them feel part of the family B&B business.) Remember that a child's table setting does not have to be elaborate, just something that says, "This is for you!"

One more thing to keep in mind is that if kids like what they see, they might want to take it home with them. Plan for this. Check with the parents first, then have a little something on the table that the youngsters *can* take with them—a monster of their choice, one of the farm animals, the Christmas stocking, the toy jack-o'-lantern, the Halloween mask—something that does not cost you a lot of money and that will make them happy. The children who visit you will be sure to remember their special breakfast. And their parents will appreciate the trouble you took for their children. If you want to attract families with children to your bed and breakfast, this is absolutely one way to do it. The good word will spread.

The coffee

If the development of the bed and breakfast industry in this part of the world is any indication that people here are becoming more interested in enjoying the finer things in life, so is the parallel development of a more refined taste in another area—coffee. What we were satisfied with at the breakfast table ten or fifteen years ago no longer satisfies. As a nation, we've collectively developed an educated palate. Today, there's no excuse for serving anything but a great cup of coffee. We know it, and so do our guests. "Better coffee" went at the top of the list of desired improvements suggested by one guest for the bed and breakfast home she had visited. This is how your guests will be judging you. Can you make your coffee any better than it is now?

The quality of your coffee depends upon a number of things. The first is the method you use to brew it (and I do mean "brew"—never use an instant coffee for your guests). If you are using an electric percolator, you're not alone. An estimated 60 percent of the people who drink coffee continue to use this method in their homes. It does have the advantage of keeping the coffee hot for that second or third cup. In recent times, though, popular opinion is running against percolators because the pot has more control over the brewing process than you do. This type of pot can produce under-brewed or over-brewed coffee, depending on the temperature of the water—which you cannot control. So if you're looking to make "the perfect cup," you've got to look elsewhere.

A number of people have been turning in their percolators for an electric drip pot. (The type with an automatic timer to start the coffee brewing even before you get up can make a host's life a little easier.) This type of pot matches the advantage of the percolator in keeping the coffee hot while you linger at the breakfast table, but it generally brews a better cup of coffee if used correctly. This is due in part to the filtration method of brewing. Here, hot water is poured over drip grind coffee that has been placed in a filter (usually made of paper). The water goes through the coffee once, unlike in a percolator, which pumps the same water over the same grounds again and again. This is considered the crucial factor in the superiority of a drip pot over a percolator. Non-electric drip pots make excellent coffee but present a problem in keeping it hot. You can put the pot over a low flame to heat, but this must be done no later than fifteen minutes after the coffee has been brewed, or no longer than thirty minutes at a stretch, or the flavor will be altered. As a general rule, "old" coffee should never be reheated. It's just not the same.

Another brewing method that has taken hold in this country is steeping in a French Melior pot. This method involves adding freshly boiled water directly to ground coffee and steeping the mixture for five full minutes (no more and no less). The grounds are then separated from the finished brew by means of a plunger device. This method is favored by some because the resulting coffee is rich and flavorful, and it can be brewed fresh right at the table. A disadvantage is that the coffee can cool off during the steeping process, but you can now buy a "coffee cozy" modeled after the traditional "tea cozy" but designed to fit snugly over the Melior's glass cylinder to help trap the heat inside. (A cozy—which is sort of a jacket for a pot of hot liquid—is easy enough to make out of quilted material.) The pot (with or without its cozy) is so attractive that it makes a nice addition to the breakfast table or an early morning wake-up tray.

A more elaborate (and more expensive) pot that employs steam pressure to produce an espresso or cappuccino is wonderful if you already happen to have one, and it provides a good amenity for your guests, but it's not necessary to buy one just for this purpose. The best advice is to make sure you have a good, basic pot (drip is really the most reliable for the quality it produces) and care for it well. If you are buying a new pot, select one made of glass, as a metallic surface will alter the taste of the brew somewhat (stainless steel is the best choice of the metals). The pot must be scrubbed clean after each use; a quick rinse will not remove the oils that form an invisible film on the pot's surface—and this film will change the taste of the coffee.

The size of your coffee pot also affects the taste. An eight-cup pot is designed to brew eight cups of coffee to its peak aroma and taste. If you use this same pot to brew only one or two cups of coffee, you won't get the same quality. You should not brew less than three-quarters of a pot's maximum capacity. So for an eight-cup pot, don't make any less than six or your brew will lose some of its flavor.

If you're buying a new pot, don't select one that will produce more coffee than you need at any one time. (Remember, you lose quality when you reheat. It's better to make several smaller pots of coffee at different times during the day than one large pot in the morning.) You might want to have two pots, one small and one large, that you can alternate depending on the number of guests you have staying with you.

The choice of the coffee itself is another major factor when it comes to creating the best possible cup of coffee. Find out which is the proper grind of coffee suited to your particular coffee maker (look in the directions or ask someone in a gourmet store). If the grind is too fine or too coarse for your pot, the quality of the coffee will diminish. It's best to pass by the shelf in the local grocery store that contains all those cans of vacuum-packed, pre-ground coffee and head instead to the specialty section or to a gourmet store where you can see, and smell, the coffee beans you are buying. The best coffee is made from newly roasted beans (some stores guarantee that theirs have been roasted within twenty-four hours of sale) that are ground immediately before brewing. You may wish to purchase a small grinder to use at home; devices that will do this can usually be purchased at the same place you find whole coffee beans. If you don't choose to become this much of a purist about the coffee you serve, you can have the beans ground to the right consistency for your pot right at the store. Even decaffeinated coffee beans are available for purchase this way. (It's a good idea to keep some decaf on hand for those guests who like coffee but not the effects of caffeine.)

If you store it properly, the coffee you have had ground just right for your pot will not lose any of its taste. Coffee can become stale. You wouldn't think of serving bread that has lost its freshness; neither should you serve coffee that has suffered a familiar fate. To guard its freshness, store your coffee in an airtight container in the freezer compartment of your refrigerator. It can be used directly from the freezer (it won't crystallize, so you don't have to "thaw" it). It will keep here about a month, compared with ten days (tops) in the regular part of the refrigerator. Keep the coffee away from moisture and food odors, as these will destroy its flavor.

When serving your delicious coffee, do it justice by providing either whole milk or cream instead of skim milk, an imitation cream, or a powdered substitute. Offer sugar and a good low-calorie sweetener for those who prefer it. These items are most attractive when served in a creamer and bowl instead of the cartons in which they were originally packaged.

The serious coffee drinkers among your guests will thank you for a good cup of coffee in the morning even more if you offer to bring a wake-up tray to their room before they have to face anyone across the breakfast table. Some people really rely on that first cup to get them on their feet at the beginning of the day. Ask your guests before they retire if they would like their coffee in the privacy of their room. If so, prepare the tray with a small thermos (coffee stays hot best in a thermos), cups, spoons, napkins, milk or cream, sugar and sugar substitute, and perhaps a small vase with a flower in it. For this, your guests will always remember you fondly.

You might want to consider an international variation for the coffee you serve in the afternoon or evening. This can be done easily by adding any number of flavorings to the finished brew: a few cinnamon sticks, chocolate syrup, or even a little hot chocolate and an orange slice mixed with the coffee. A topping of whipped cream is a favorite touch. This can be sprinkled with a little nutmeg, shaved chocolate, grated orange rind, or cinnamon. For coffee with a little punch to it, any of these liqueurs can be successfully added to the brew: anisette, white crème de menthe, cognac, and amaretto. Experiment and see what you like best.

Iced coffee is a wonderful drink to serve on hot, lazy afternoons or evenings. Too many people have given up on making iced coffee after one or two bad experiences—too watery, not cold enough, not enough taste. There are a few tricks to creating good iced coffee. First, always brew extra-strength coffee if you plan to pour it over ice cubes (the ice dilutes the coffee to regular strength). Or freeze some newly made coffee in the ice-cube tray and use the cubes instead of ice (less dilution, more taste). Freshly brewed coffee whipped with a few scoops of a good, creamy brand of coffee ice cream, with maybe a little chocolate syrup, and topped with whipped cream if you wish makes a terrific drink. Where most people have made their mistake with iced coffee in the past is using leftover coffee to make it. Coffee that has been chilled in the refrigerator or that has even been sitting at room temperature for a few hours just does not have the taste that freshly brewed coffee has. When you're making iced coffee, start at the beginning with a new brew, just as you would if you were preparing to serve your guests hot coffee. It makes a world of difference in the finished product.

For tea drinkers

Expect that some of your guests will not want coffee at all but a nice cup of tea instead. Keep different kinds of teas on hand to suit the different tastes of your guests.

There are some helpful hints for making the perfect cup of tea, just as there are with coffee. One of the most common mistakes is that we tend to use up whatever water might already be standing in the tea kettle. Boiling this water might ensure that it's safe to drink, certainly, but "old" water gets flat, just as your soft drink does if you leave its bottle or can open for a while. You can't notice the de-aeration as much with water, but it's still there, and your tea will suffer for it. Always start with fresh, cold water brought to the boiling point.

An earthenware or porcelain teapot is superior to any made of metal (as with coffee, a metallic surface affects the taste). Preheat the teapot by rinsing it with some of the boiling water. This will help maintain the temperature of the tea once the brewing begins. Some people claim that loose tea mixed directly with the water, or contained within a tea ball or leaf basket, is superior to using tea bags; some say it doesn't matter. Let your own taste buds guide your choice.

Don't judge the finished brew by its color; rather, time the brewing to determine when it's ready. Tea should be left for at least three minutes, but usually no more than five or you run the risk of bitterness. Then remove the tea bags or the tea ball or leaf basket to stop the brewing process. Never reuse teabags or leaves.

To keep the tea hot while your guests enjoy lingering over a few cups, place the pot inside a tea cozy to trap the heat. Some people love their tea served with a little honey, lemon, sugar, or milk. A wake-up tray containing these and a teapot with freshly brewed tea is a considerate amenity to offer your guests in the morning.

The food

When it comes to food, everyone's a critic. We're always evaluating what we eat, judging its merits for taste ("This is a teeny bit overcooked"), amount ("It was great but I'm still hungry"), nutrition ("Does this have sugar in it?"), price ("I expected something better than this for what I paid"), calories ("This is much too fattening"), and eye appeal ("What in the world is this green stuff?"). As a bed and breakfast host, you not only have to be aware that your guests are judging the food you serve according to these criteria, but also that the meal you're responsible for also happens to carry with it the reputation of being the most important meal of the day. As if this weren't enough, it has to be "special" in keeping with the bed and breakfast tradition. The pressure's on. How are you going to make your guests (*all* of them) happy when they join you at the breakfast table?

First of all, give them a choice—but not too much of a choice. According to Marguerite Swanson, the director of a reservation service organization in Texas called Bed & Breakfast Society of Houston, the biggest mistake made by new hosts is asking, "What would you like for breakfast?" An open-ended question like this could get requests for anything from fried ostrich eggs to oatmeal. *You* decide what the options will be and list them for your guests. It's a good idea to type or hand write the choices and leave a copy of this "menu" in the guest room. Ask your guests to note which items they prefer and to give the menu back to you before they retire for the night.

Some hosts even print menu choices on their brochures so that anyone considering staying at their bed and breakfast homes knows exactly what to expect. Prentice Strong, the owner of Penury Hall in Southwest Harbor, Maine, lists these items on his brochure: juice, fruit compote, melon, seasonal fruit, eggs Benedict, blueberry pancakes, "penurious" omelet, date-walnut French toast, poached eggs 'n' hash, "favorite eggs" and muffins, plus homemade jams and jellies, pure maple syrup, and coffee, tea, or milk. This sure lets guests know that they're in for quite a gastronomical treat if they decide to stay at Penury Hall. An interesting, varied menu like this can be used, as Prentice Strong does, to attract people to his B&B. The brochure for Dairy Hollow House in Eureka Springs, Arkansas, also describes the pleasures of eating a delicious "from scratch" breakfast. "A Dairy Hollow House Breakfast is a leisurely affair. Coffee, tea, herb tea, or café au lait, in your room if you like (the morning paper is by your door), is followed by fresh fruit in season or just-squeezed orange juice served in our sunny parlour. Next comes a basket of fresh-baked whole-wheat butterhorns and a loaf of sweet bread, or a generous helping of our famous German baked pancakes, puffy and golden, hot from the oven. Of course, there's more coffee (or whatever) to go with the meal, as well as homemade jam and real butter."

Notice that the choices at Dairy Hollow House are limited to basically two—one a "continental" type of breakfast, the other a "full" breakfast. Here, a guest can decide how much, or how little, he or she wants to eat. And because there's a set menu, the host does not have to scramble to buy ingredients and prepare a variety of items for breakfast. This is especially important if you have a number of guests staying with you at one time and you give them too wide a choice. You could end up spending hours in the kitchen preparing an assortment of omelets, oatmeal, quiche, and pancakes.

Some hosts choose to serve a continental breakfast only. This is fine as long as guests are told in advance that this is the case. According to the manager of a reservation service organization called Greater Boston Hospitality, a continental breakfast usually includes fruit, juice, rolls or muffins with butter and jam, and fresh coffee, tea, and/or milk. Some hosts also offer croissants and individual cold cereals. The owners of an RSO in Plymouth, Massachusetts, known as Be Our Guest, suggest adding to the selection small containers of assorted yogurts, foil-wrapped wedges of cheese or any type of quality cheese, and a package of cream cheese that can be used on bagels, toast, or bread. Hard-boiled eggs and slices of cold ham are also tasty items to include.

Serving a continental breakfast appeals to many hosts because it's less trouble and generally less expensive than preparing a "full" breakfast. It's a great alternative for hosts who have to leave for work early in the morning, often before their guests have gotten out of bed. A continental breakfast can be prepared the night before and left for guests to help themselves. Be advised, though, that some of your guests may not be satisfied with a continental breakfast unless you have made the effort to make it hearty enough for those who consider breakfast an important meal of the day. "If you want repeat business, and word-of-mouth praise, you'll not be able to get away with the skimpy continental breakfast of low-cost rolls, doughnuts, coffee, and canned juice," say the owners of Be Our Guest.

All items served in a continental breakfast must be of high quality and plentiful: Your own home-baked breads, muffins, or scones or products from a good bakery are absolutely necessary. (Stay away from those quickie, pre-packaged mixes. Your guests will no doubt recognize them for what they are and will not be impressed.) And provide real butter, fresh-squeezed juice, and brewed coffee (not instant) with real milk or cream. A toaster oven or microwave oven that guests can operate themselves in your absence to heat their croissants or muffins is a nice touch if your schedule does not allow you to serve the breakfast yourself.

Including an offer of a continental breakfast as a choice on your menu is a good way of accommodating those guests who prefer to eat lightly in the morning. If at all possible, though, you should also offer the option of a full breakfast—which could include a main dish like quiche, omelets, casseroles, French toast, blintzes, soufflés, waffles, or pancakes—as well as servings of ham, bacon, or sausage and other side dishes if you wish, plus items that normally constitute a continental breakfast. Offering a full breakfast is especially important if your bed and breakfast business is based in a resort area where your guests will be leaving for some kind of demanding physical activity afterwards—skiing, boating, hiking. They need that hearty breakfast and will most likely choose to stay at a B&B that will provide it.

The best advice is to settle on a few main dishes that you're particularly good at preparing and offer those on your menu. One couple always offers a baked apple pancake because it's a sure hit every time. Some of the items that guests have reported that they particularly enjoyed while staying at bed and breakfast homes are "good coffee cake" (from a Pennsylvania couple), "homemade sourdough biscuits and fresh blueberries" (from a Canadian woman), "homemade breads, muffins, Scotch ham, oatmeal pancakes, Swedish pancakes, and quiche" (from an Ohio woman), "delicious scrambled eggs and Danish that came from a special bakery" (from a Pennsylvania woman), "small fresh tomatoes in season" (from an Ontario woman), and "raspberries with real cream" (from a New Mexico couple).

For guests staying longer than one night, you will need to vary your menu so that your guests don't get tired of eating the same thing all the time. A California man reports enjoying a variety of food during his extended stay at a bed and breakfast home: "Other than a nice slice of cold, fresh cantaloupe, the menu changed every day—scrambled eggs with sausage, homemade bread toasted, home-made cinnamon rolls, hot cereal." His hosts kept him quite happy with the selection.

Hot cereal is always a good option. It's inexpensive, easy to make, and great on a cold winter morning. One host registered with the Finger Lakes Bed & Breakfast Association in the Rochester, New York, area likes to serve hot oatmeal with grated apples and raisins in it. A little milk and brown sugar, "and everyone loves it," she says.

Include some regional specialties among your selections if you can. Many of your guests will be visiting your area because of its special sights, sounds, smells, and tastes. They are very interested in what it has to offer, what makes it unique. For someone who doesn't live in the South, chances are that grits exist only in the imagination. Why not let your guests sample them with the rest of their meal? And what visitor to the Southwest hasn't heard about the use of chili peppers in *everything*? Maybe they'd like to try your green chili quiche—just issue the appropriate warnings well in advance. It will surely give them something to talk about when they get back home. And there's a lot of talk about those famous Boston baked beans. Maybe a side dish at breakfast isn't a bad idea.

As you plan your menu, include only those items that you yourself enjoy eating—just in case you've overestimated the number of cantaloupes you'll be needing for this weekend's guests, or the number of banana-walnut muffins it takes to feed a family of four. And try any new recipes first yourself, before you experiment on guests at the breakfast table. And be advised to take into consideration how much you should be spending for each guest's breakfast based on your room price. According to Melodie Ebner, director of a reservation service organization in Philadelphia called Bed and Breakfast Center City, the number-one mistake that new hosts make is "spending too much money on the breakfast." If your bed and breakfast offers rooms at a low to moderate price, you should not be serving seafood soufflé with fresh crab flown in specially from the coast. You need to economize, or buying your breakfast ingredients will eat up all your profits. On the other hand, if yours can be considered luxurious accommodations, fresh crab soufflé would not be unexpected by guests who have paid a pretty penny for the privilege of staying at your B&B. Try to cost out the ingredients for preparing one serving of a full breakfast (this means dividing the cost of a dozen eggs by twelve, cutting the cost of one grapefruit in half, and so forth), and see if you can come up with a total cost per person for breakfast. The figure could vary quite a bit depending on what you serve and how wisely you shop. (You can keep costs down by buying in bulk and watching for sales.) If the figure exceeds 25 percent of a guest's share of a room's cost, you're spending too much on breakfast. And 25 percent is high; most hosts spend far less than this.

In order to save money, and to prevent breakfast from becoming a major undertaking every time you have guests, think ahead. Buy what food you can in advance, and even prepare it in advance, then freeze it. This way, you don't have to run out and buy fresh ingredients each time you're expecting guests; you can serve foods that are regional specialties but are out of season; and you can take advantage of sales and special prices on bulk quantities. Even if you've never tried to freeze anything before in your life, be assured that it is a simple process to learn and well worth the effort for what it saves you in time, trouble, and expense.

Ingredients, such as fresh fruit, can be frozen separately and kept in your freezer until you're ready to use them in a recipe. The produce should ideally be fresh and in prime condition when you acquire it; it will be only as good when it's thawed as when it went into the freezer. Fruit must be fully ripe and firm. Any that is still greenish hasn't yet reached its peak flavor and should not be used for freezing. Fruit should be frozen without hours of purchase, while it is still fresh. The longer you wait to freeze it, the more flavor it will lose.

The easiest way to freeze fruit is to "dry pack" it in plastic containers designed for the freezer. This involves sorting the fruit to discard any that are bruised or imperfect. The fruit can be left whole; no need to slice unless you want to. Wash it in ice water, but do it quickly so that the fruit does not absorb any of the water. Drain on paper towels. (Change the towels several times if need be.) Let the fruit dry; pat dry any fruit that needs it. Pour into freezer containers, leaving at least one-quarter of an inch of space between the fruit and the lid. It's advisable to use frozen fruit within three or four months, but some can be kept for up to twelve months without suffering deterioration. To thaw, place the container of frozen fruit in the refrigerator for a few hours (or overnight) before you use it. (Don't try to speed up this process by plunging the container into hot water. This will get you nothing but mush.)

You can also freeze home-made bread or muffins ahead of time. When they come out of the oven, allow them to cool, then wrap them very closely in freezer wrapping paper to keep out the air. (Ordinary waxed paper should not be substituted.) Then place in freezer. To serve, thaw first, then heat. Bread, cake, and pastries lose some of their moisture during the freezing process, so brush some water over the tops of these items before warming them in the oven. Baked breads will keep four to eight months in the freezer.

Many, many foods can be frozen successfully if you know how (onions, herbs, artichokes, salad dressings, and even butter, cheese, and eggs). Just be aware that once frozen food is thawed, it does spoil more quickly than fresh food, and it cannot be refrozen. If any of the foods you have frozen show a "freezer burn"—a dry, stringy surface—this means that the food has been improperly wrapped, allowing air to circulate. Don't use it. And the formation of large ice crystals shows that moisture has been drawn out of the food, which could cause discoloration and deterioration. The best advice if you're new at freezing foods is to try freezing and thawing—then eating—a few items yourself to be sure you've mastered the process before serving them to your guests. Learning the more complicated processes for freezing other items (or even learning how to can fruits and vegetables and make your own jams or chutney) can definitely save you money and last-minute preparations, but it can be time consuming. These activities are best left to those who think they're fun. Many hosts do, and guests love to take advantage of the results. But many don't, and there are now so many wonderful gourmet items available for purchase that no host should worry about serving store-bought items instead of something homemade.

Whatever you serve, it should be done in as attractive a way as possible. This means no jars, cans, or boxes on the table. Instead, use pretty bowls or dishes, little wicker baskets lined with colorful cloth, small ceramic or wooden boxes, or even glasses that are intended for liqueurs or wine. Lacy paper doilies on platters for serving dry foods (rolls, bread, cookies) add a special touch. Place cereals inside clear Mason jars (perhaps an assortment of small Mason jars containing individual-size portions could be arranged in a basket lined with a cloth that is color coordinated with the tablecloth). For jam and honey, place single servings in small dishes (cut glass is especially attractive). Sometimes it's possible to buy jam in small two-ounce containers. Placing an assortment of these inside a basket is a good way to give your guests a choice without having to open a number of large jars of jam.

Even the most ordinary food can be presented in an especially appealing way. Hard-boiled eggs, for example, are great to have on hand because they're nutritious, low in calories, delicious, and very easy to prepare and keep. Why not dress them up a little with a stenciled design on the shell, or one of the many types of sticky decals now available in different shapes and colors (stars, hearts, flowers)? This takes less time than dyeing the eggs (as you do at Easter), but some hosts do take the time to dye their eggs. (Decorated or dyed eggs are fun for any children who might be staying at your bed and breakfast.)

Butter is a staple at the breakfast table for rolls, toast, or muffins. Instead of just setting out a stick of butter on a dish, consider molding the butter into individual pats shaped into flowerettes, shells, or other shapes. To your guests it will look as if you've spent hours hand-sculpting the butter for them to enjoy, when actually it takes only a few minutes of your time. The mold does all the work. Different kinds of molds are available in most housewares departments or stores; if you can't find those intended just for butter, small cookie molds are fine for the job. Soften the butter at room temperature (do *not* melt it on the stove), and then press it into the molds. Refrigerate until the butter hardens inside the molds, then pop the shapes out. They will keep their form as long as they are refrigerated, but if you wish to stack one on top of the other, place squares of waxed paper in between them.

A good snack for guests in the evening is a combination platter containing cheese, crackers, and apple slices. You can create a lovely, colorful pinwheel design from the apples by using one red and one green (or more if you need it for the number of your guests). Slice the apples but do not peel. Dunk the sections into a small bowl of water into which you've squeezed about one-quarter of a lemon. (This prevents discoloration.) Then arrange the slices in alternating colors.

To serve a cantaloupe or grapefruit, instead of slicing the fruit right in half with one swipe of the knife as most of us usually do, try cutting zig-zags instead of a straight line. Each half will then have a number of turrets surrounding the edible portion of the fruit. To accomplish this, it helps if you first nick the fruit in a few places to help guide your knife as you cut your jagged line; six to eight points is a good number to create a star-like effect when you separate the halves from each other. The inside of the fruit will have ridges (you will probably have to make a few minor repairs). For a grapefruit half, remove the seeds, dribble honey over it, place a cherry in the center, and heat in the oven or broiler until hot. For a cantaloupe, scoop out the seeds and fill the cavity with blueberries, strawberries (using both creates a pleasing color combination), or black grapes.

If you enjoy baking your own bread, experiment with different shapes. Bread dough can be braided, shaped into a wreath, or even used to hand-build a snowman, a cat, a dinosaur, a guitar, even an entire tool set with hammer and nails. Use the dough as you would children's clay, shaping and poking and pinching it to create the designs you want. Then bake it. All you need is a good, basic recipe for bread (dessert breads won't hold the shapes) and your imagination. (Children especially enjoy the chance to eat a dinosaur for breakfast.)

If you wish, you can invite your guests to join you and your family for lunch or dinner, or you can offer to prepare a picnic basket for their lunch if they're going for an outing. Of course, this is an extra that is not included in the price set for bed and breakfast. Some hosts do extend this kind of invitation, and it is often most welcome. Be aware, though, that some would consider adding an extra charge for lunch or dinner "selling" food—which might bring your bed and breakfast under the scrutiny of agencies that govern the sanitation of food served in restaurants. (By offering breakfast as "complimentary," a host usually encounters no problem. After all, no one regulates how you prepare and serve a meal in your own home—on a *gratis* basis—to friends, family, or business associates.) Of course, a bed and breakfast in a private home is *not* a restaurant, but just what it is has yet to be agreed upon by agencies invested with the responsibility of looking out for the consumer. Sometimes there is confusion, which grows when a host starts offering lunches and dinners—and attaching prices to them. So proceed with caution if you wish to offer more than the "free" breakfast; talk first with other bed and breakfast hosts and managers of reservation service organizations in your area who might have some experience with this issue. If you plan to open a full-time inn, where a restaurant is part of your operation, it's a different story altogether. Here, there is no question that your "restaurant" is indeed a restaurant; you will, of course, have to comply with any regulations governing such commercial enterprises.

Where alcohol is concerned, there is no confusion. No one can sell alcoholic beverages without first obtaining a license to do so. Because of this, bed and breakfast hosts simply do not sell liquor to their guests. Some offer a complimentary drink to their guests upon arrival or in the evening before bed. Others allow guests to bring in their own liquor if they wish; ice and mixers can be provided by the host. Be aware that offering or permitting alcohol could affect insurance coverage for your B&B, as it is considered an additional risk.

Especially for children

Creamed eggs are yucky. So are fried tomatoes, a Brie and spinach omelet, and salmon roulade. Ask any five-year-old. If you're going to be hosting children at your bed and breakfast, you've got to think about what to serve them as a breakfast that they will actually agree to eat. As a group, children are just not very adventurous when it comes to food. It seems as if somewhere along the line, all of the children under twelve had a meeting and decided not to eat anything that they had not already tried. The gourmet items that their parents love will most likely remain untouched on the plates of your young visitors.

When the parents are making the reservation with you, ask what their children like to eat. "I have Cheerios. Will they like that? Or will they eat scrambled eggs and toast?" If the child is a fussy eater, the parents can make a few suggestions: "He eats Wheaties, loves raisin toast, and adores pancakes." An advance tip like this can help you plan the menu for the whole family: Go with the creamed eggs and fried tomatoes for the adults, but get a box of Wheaties next time you're at the supermarket; plan to serve raisin toast (and a lot of it) with the quiche; or make pancakes for everyone.

If you don't have the occasion to question the parent about a child's usual diet, you can't go wrong by stocking up on small individual packages of assorted cereals. There's bound to be something in the snack-pack that the child likes, and the other boxes will keep until your next young visitors arrive. Try to stay away from those cereals that are coated with sugar or chocolate, as many parents can be just as fussy about the nutrition value of what their children eat.

Fresh fruit is also a good bet for young people—bananas, apples, oranges. Many children also enjoy eating hard-boiled eggs (especially if they're decorated with decals or stencils or are dyed). And the old standby—peanut butter and jelly sandwiches—can often get a fussy but hungry child through breakfast. Indeed, it's very hard to predict what children of any age will be willing to eat at the breakfast table. All you can do is try. Who knows? They might even eat the creamed eggs.

9
The Business of B&B

Some hosts view their bed and breakfast activities as a hobby. They accommodate only a small number of visitors each year and like it that way, despite the fact that the income from their B&B effort is minimal. They keep a low profile in the community by not advertising openly; rather, they work only through a reservation service organization, which safeguards their personal privacy. Other hosts look at their bed and breakfast activities as a business venture. They go public with advertising campaigns, take out memberships in community organizations, and work to develop a home-based, income-producing business. (Some of the more ambitious bed and breakfast hosts then decide to go on to the next step, opening an inn, which moves them into the realm of a commercial enterprise.)

When it comes to legal matters, what's important is not so much how you view your B&B activities, but how they are viewed by the agencies invested with the responsibilities of regulating small businesses or protecting the health and welfare of the general public. Your level of hosting is just one consideration that may come under the scrutiny of federal, state, or local agencies that take an interest in your bed and breakfast. Because bed and breakfast is a relatively new concept in this part of the world, be advised that you may encounter confusion or contradiction when dealing with representatives of different regulating agencies. Therefore, it's advisable to be as well informed as possible before you open your B&B.

Following is a discussion of some of the main aspects of the business of bed and breakfast that every host must be concerned with—zoning laws, insurance coverage, health and safety, taxes, and record keeping. The information and suggestions given here are intended as background for the individual bed and breakfast host. It is no substitute for the professional advice of an attorney or an accountant, and it cannot reflect the differences in regulations from community to community or new developments in the bed and breakfast industry as a whole that take place after the publication of this book. Each host has to take personal responsibility for gathering the information that pertains to his or her own bed and breakfast activities.

If you run into problems, free counseling about business matters is available from the Small Business Administration (SBA) office in your area, or its affiliate called SCORE (Service Corps of Retired Executives). In addition, the SBA and the Internal Revenue Service both publish informative pamphlets dealing with a variety of aspects of small-business management. And don't overlook one of the best sources of information about operating a bed and breakfast home in your particular locality—the local reservation service organization. If you choose to list your home with an RSO, that organization can be enormously valuable in helping you set up your B&B in compliance with established guidelines.

If you still feel like you're operating in the dark, you might find it helpful to obtain the B&B Legislation Kit compiled by the American Bed & Breakfast Association (16 Village Green, Crofton, Maryland 21114, phone 301-261-0180). The kit includes over 200 pages of actual case studies and regulations that have been enacted throughout the U.S.

So do your homework. Explore regulations that could apply to your bed and breakfast activities, get advice if you need it, and take steps to comply where necessary. Understand what your B&B is, and what it is not: Be ready to explain the differences if the occasion arises that your B&B is mistakenly classified as an inn, a hotel, or a restaurant! It will take time for regulating agencies to catch up with the bed and breakfast movement, so it's to your advantage to be armed with as much information as you possibly can as the process continues.

Zoning

Back in 1916, the first zoning regulations were enacted in this country as a way to plan the growth and development of neighborhoods. Because of zoning, you won't see a shoe factory opening across the street from you, or a large luxury hotel going up next door. Simply, the idea was that businesses and residences should not mix; they needed separate "zones" within a community in order to safeguard the quality of life for the people living there. The early zoning codes did not clearly address the conflicting idea of a home-based business—a person working out of a residence. Home-based businesses in some areas were prohibited by law, largely because of efforts to do away with "sweat shops" where working conditions were poor, wages were exceedingly low, and young children far below working age were employed.

Such regulations were intended to protect people from exploitation in the work place and to improve living conditions in general, but they were adopted before the relatively new concept of bed and breakfast took hold in this country. A B&B is not a factory, or a hotel, or a sweat shop. But what is it? The fact that there is no clear-cut definition or precedent on the books has caused confusion in more than one community. Too often, local zoning board officials mistakenly apply existing regulations to bed and breakfast, regardless of the fact that B&B does not fit neatly into categories that have already been defined. In some communities, however, zoning codes have been updated to allow for the operation of bed and breakfast homes. (Norma and Bill Grovermann, owners of the Prince George Inn B&B in Annapolis, Maryland, report that they even worked with the mayor to include bed and breakfast in that city's zoning code.) In many more communities, the issue has not yet been addressed at all on the official level.

Because zoning boards make their decisions independently of one another, a favorable resolution in one city or county unfortunately does not mean a favorable resolution in another, even within the same state. Still, zoning boards will at times look to one another for guidance, so a collective body of favorable zoning rulings does work to the advantage of the bed and breakfast industry as a whole. For example, it is expected that a 1983 New York court ruling that defined bed and breakfast as a "customary home occupation" will be helpful in clarifying local zoning laws within that state—and perhaps other states as well—for years to come. According to a report on bed and breakfast issued by the New York State Sea Grant Extension Program, "Customary home occupations typically are exempted from certain residential zone limitations." (*Considerations in Starting a Bed and Breakfast Business* is available for 75 cents from New York Sea Grant Extension Program, Fernow Hall, Cornell University, Ithaca, New York 14853.) There is talk of a national study, but until the time this is undertaken and recommendations made by the American Planning Association for uniform treatment of bed and breakfast homes across the country, decisions will continue to be made—sometimes at variance with one another—by local zoning boards.

Anyone intending to open a bed and breakfast home should be aware of what the zoning regulations are in his or her community before proceeding. (If you're looking to purchase a house specifically for the purpose of opening a B&B, make sure you check out zoning codes *before* you buy.) The best advice is to explore regulations cautiously, gathering as much information as you can from other sources before you have direct contact with anyone at the zoning board. (A premature contact could force a decision that reflects local officials' unfamiliarity with bed and breakfast.) A good first step is to talk to other bed and breakfast hosts in your immediate neighborhood and the manager of any local reservation service organization. Also get in touch with any others who run home-based businesses in your area—hairdressers, accountants, graphic designers, tailors. Their experience with local ordinances will help you get a perspective on the situation.

It's possible that you will need to obtain a variance or go before a zoning board hearing. The board will be interested in how much hosting you plan to do and whether the activity will disturb the neighborhood in any way—such as causing noise or parking problems. Be ready to distinguish your B&B from a "rooming house" that accommodates "tenants," as there may be a precedent excluding boarding houses, inns, hotels, or motels from residential areas. A bed and breakfast home that accommodates occasional guests, displays no signs, and in no way diminishes the quality of life enjoyed by the residents is very different from any of these commercial establishments. Eventually, this fact will become common knowledge. In time, confusion will be replaced by recognition of bed and breakfast for what it is and support for the contribution B&B can make to a community.

Insurance

As a bed and breakfast host, you are of course concerned about the safety and well-being of your guests, just as you are about that of your family, your property, and yourself. A host's concerns about possible fire, theft, personal injury, or property damage should take two forms—prevention and insurance.

As a host, you have to be keenly alert to possible hazards and take whatever precautions necessary: Remove throw rugs that don't have a nonskid backing; put up gates at the top and bottom of staircases if you plan to host children; restrict the use of your swimming pool to daylight hours; install grab bars for support at the bathtub and in the shower; require guests wishing to make use of your sailboat, weight-lifting equipment, or toboggan to sign a liability disclaimer; install smoke alarms and provide fire extinguishers in strategic places; install sprinklers if your house is three or more stories; require guests traveling with a pet to sign a statement of liability in the event that the animal causes damage; install a burglar alarm and a double-lock system for front and back doors. To be on the safe side, you might want to serve nonalcoholic drinks only. Serving alcohol could also affect your eligibility for insurance coverage, as it is considered an additional risk. For each host, there is a unique set of circumstances that could require other preventative measures as well. (See the next section, "Safety Precautions.")

Although you may already carry some form of homeowner's insurance, do not assume that your current policy automatically covers your bed and breakfast activities. It is advisable to contact your insurance agent before opening your home for B&B to discuss, first, exactly what your policy does cover as far as your bed and breakfast is concerned and, second, additional insurance if necessary.

It is not unusual for a host to find that his or her insurance agent has no experience with bed and breakfast. Be ready to explain the nature of what you plan to do, as well as the level of hosting you realistically expect. If you estimate that you will accommodate only an occasional guest, it's possible that your current homeowner's policy could cover you as is, but have your insurance agent confirm that this is the case. Ask for the confirmation *in writing*, just in case the occasion does arise in the future when you need to rely on the agent's favorable interpretation of your existing policy. If you expect that you will be hosting a considerable number of guests—or plan to actively court the business of individuals with physical disabilities, guests with children, or guests with pets—you should discuss the acquisition of coverage beyond what your homeowner's policy provides.

If your regular insurance agent is not helpful to you in securing the extra liability, fire, or theft coverage that you want (and that your attorney recommends), talk to another agent. This is new ground for most insurance agents and they are cautious, sometimes to the point of not being helpful at all. Some hosts have found it necessary to go to more than one agent before they were able to obtain the kind of insurance they wanted to supplement their existing homeowner's policy. Other hosts have resorted to purchasing a commercial insurance package covering the items they were most concerned about.

Be sure to check your automobile insurance coverage as well during this process. Many hosts will use their own vehicles to transport their guests to and from the airport, train station, or bus station or will offer a ride at other times if it is convenient (with or without a fee attached to the service). If you plan to offer this amenity to your guests, find out to what extent your current policy covers passengers, and if that coverage extends to those who have a business connection to you, or who pay a fee for transportation to you. You might have to make either adjustments in your policy or adjustments in the transportation services you provide for your guests.

If you join the *Tourist House Association of America*, or list your B&B with a reservation service organization affiliated with either The National Network or Bed & Breakfast Reservation Services World-Wide, you are eligible to obtain general liability insurance. At this writing, all three organizations offer basically the same insurance package, through the same agent, for owner-occupied bed and breakfast homes. In addition, there are two insurance agencies operating on a national level that specialize in bed and breakfast coverage. Bed & Breakfast Insurance Services is operated by Michael Erlin, a former innkeeper, for bed and breakfast homes of three or more rooms. (Bed & Breakfast Insurance Services, 211 Woodward Avenue, Sausalito, California 94965, phone 800–442–8844 or 415–332–7147). Arndt McBee Insurance Agency has no restriction on the number of guest rooms in a bed and breakfast home or inn, so even if you plan to use only one room for B&B, you can still obtain insurance coverage. (Arndt McBee Insurance Agency, Inc., 824 North Queen Street, Martinsburg, West Virginia 25401, phone 800–825–4667 or 304–263–6906).

Safety precautions

When it comes to the safety and well-being of your guests, let common sense be your guide. Of course, you have already taken measures for your health and safety and that of your family, but take the time to check the following recommendations to see if there is anything else that should be done before you open your bed and breakfast. Make it a priority to find out about regulations that may apply to your bed-and-breakfast operation. (In a recent nationwide survey, 64 percent of the bed and breakfasts contacted reported that they are regularly inspected by state or local officials.)

Fire prevention and early detection should be a major concern. Peg Tierney, owner of a reservation service organization called Bed & Breakfast of Maine, advises hosts to have smoke alarms and fire extinguishers on each floor of the house; to have one of each in every guest bedroom is not too many. As this book goes to print, there is national legislation pending that, if passed, would make sprinklers mandatory for bed and breakfast homes of three or more stories. Easy exit to outside from every guest bedroom is also essential. Gary Winget of the Bed & Breakfast Registry in Minnesota will not accept hosts with basement or third-floor guest rooms unless there are approved fire exits. One Philadelphia host reports that she purchased a fire ladder to keep inside one guest bedroom located on the second floor. The owner of an RSO in Tempe, Arizona, called Mi Casa–Su Casa tells hosts to make sure that all windows can be opened to allow escape or rescue in the event of fire. In general, a bed and breakfast home should conform to local and state fire codes.

Floranne McCraith, the manager of Leatherstocking Bed & Breakfast, an RSO in New York, advises her hosts to prohibit guests from smoking in the bedrooms. (Some hosts prohibit smoking in their homes altogether because of the fire hazard.) And although it's wonderful to be able to provide guests with the amenity of a fireplace in their bedroom, be sure to explain how to use it properly and how to extinguish the fire completely. Peg Tierney recommends that hosts conduct a house check in common rooms before retiring to check fireplace embers and cigarettes in ashtrays, if you do allow smoking.

To safeguard against accidental injury, Arline Kardasis of Bed & Breakfast Associates Bay Colony, an RSO in Boston, instructs hosts listed with that agency to remove obstacles from hallways and stairways so that no one can trip over them. The home in general should be in good repair to provide a safe environment, say the owners of Bed & Breakfast of Rhode Island—"no broken steps, no faulty wiring."

The Bed & Breakfast Registry recommends that handrails be placed on all stairways. Eye Openers Bed & Breakfast in Altadena, California, requires its hosts to tack securely all carpeting and rugs. (Slippery throw rugs should be removed altogether.) If children will be visiting your bed and breakfast, it's a good idea to install gates across open stairways, says Susan Morris, owner of Southern Comfort Bed & Breakfast.

The bathroom can be made safer to guard against falls by installing grab bars on the tub and shower, according to the owner of RMF Bed & Breakfast in Atlanta. The managers of Be Our Guest, an RSO in Plymouth, Massachusetts, tell their hosts to put nonskid strips in the bathtub.

Be aware of possible hazards out of doors. "In wintertime, keep walks and stairs clear of ice and snow," says Margot French, owner of Folkstone Bed & Breakfast in Massachusetts. The owner of Kingston Area Bed & Breakfast recommends a hand railing on steps leading to the front and back doors, and a railing around porches. "We have a huge deck on the ocean side and have just had a new, safe railing installed," say Robbie and Don Smith, owners of Spindrift Bed & Breakfast in Bandon, Oregon.

Good lighting out of doors is important for your guests' safety. The owner of Pittsburgh Bed & Breakfast suggests that driveways be lit. The owners of Ohio Valley Bed & Breakfast tell hosts to make sure that the parking area where guests leave their cars is secure and well lit. If guests are out at night, the porch light should be left on until their return. One Boston B&B owner installed a photoelectric floodlight that comes on whenever movement is detected outside of the house.

Good lighting inside the house is especially important because your guests are unfamiliar with the layout of your home. At night, they can become disoriented easily. It's advisable to have a night light on in the hallway for the entire night. You might even want to make a night light available to guests to use inside their bedroom if they wish. Make sure that there is a lamp or other light switch right next to the bed. "A good safety item that happens to be cheap to operate—only pennies a month—is the little two-pronged low-wattage night light. We've had some for fifteen years, and they are a must for people stumbling around in the night trying to locate a bathroom in a strange house," report the managers of Be Our Guest.

Be sure that you have good, solid locks on exterior doors, ground-floor windows, and bedroom doors. The owner of Mi Casa–Su Casa recommends to her hosts who happen to have sliding glass doors that they use metal screw pins or key-controlled window locking devices as a burglary prevention.

New hosts always wonder whether it is safe to give a house key to guests. Although bed and breakfast guests do seem to be cut from the best cloth, and the screening procedure should have eliminated any prospective guests who are not open about who they are and what they do, it's always best to take normal precautions. It is not recommended that you give a house key to guests. Try, as much as possible, to arrange your schedule around their comings and goings. But when this is not possible, you might decide that lending a house key is necessary. Use your good judgment about this. Some hosts have a double-lock on exterior doors, then they lend guests the key to only one of the locks, and collect it immediately after the schedule conflict is over. Bed & Breakfast of Rhode Island recommends that any key lent to guests be stamped or tagged "Do Not Duplicate." A locksmith will think twice about making a copy if asked.

Depending on the layout and amenities of your home, you might need to institute other safety measures. If you have a swimming pool, for example, you might want to enforce a rule prohibiting swimming after dark. Susan Morris, owner of Southern Comfort Bed & Breakfast, recommends that hosts who have pools ask guests to sign a release if they wish to use it. If children will be visiting your B&B, there must be an enclosure around the pool to prevent them from wandering up to the edge. If you don't have such an enclosure, you should restrict the children you accept at your B&B to twelve years of age or older. One host who lives near a river used to supply a raft for guests to use but discontinued this amenity upon the advice of her insurance agent. Hosts who accept young children need to be especially aware of possible hazards. Besides gates across the stairways, there should be locks on lower cabinets and safety plugs in electrical outlets.

If you serve only a complimentary breakfast and snacks to your guests, you must meet the following basic guidelines for the health and safety. All food and drink must be stored and handled in such a manner as to prevent contamination. Sanitary facilities must meet local code. And the water supply must be from an approved source. "A bed and breakfast operation currently is not considered a restaurant, and a commercial kitchen is not required," concluded a study conducted by the New York Sea Grant Extension Program at Cornell University regarding considerations in starting a bed and breakfast business. This is generally true from locality to locality, but there has been sporadic confusion in certain areas about whether the "commercial" guidelines for the health and safety of customers in a restaurant should be applied to bed and breakfast homes. One Washington State host tells the horror story of being required to install a dishwasher that cost $10,000 because that's what the local restaurant code called for. In some cases, the confusion resulted when hosts offered lunches or dinners for an extra fee—that is, they were "selling" food. (Breakfast, on the other hand, is "free"—included in the price of the room.) Check with your local reservation service organization to find out if there has been any confusion about this issue in your area.

A host must also be prepared to deal with any medical emergency that arises. Keep a first-aid kit on hand, plus some common medicines for reducing fever. (It's best not to leave medicines in the cabinet in the guest bathroom, however, except perhaps for a few low-strength tablets designed to relieve symptoms of colds or flu. Drugstores stock small packets of such medications.) It's good practice to get the name of a close relative or friend during the screening process or upon a guest's arrival. "We obtain emergency numbers and names for guests when making reservations," say the owners of Bed & Breakfast Atlanta.

Near the telephone, keep a card that contains a listing of emergency numbers: those of the fire department, the police department, the nearest hospital, a local physician, ambulance, the poison control center. In the event that an emergency does arise, you or your guests will be able to move into action as quickly as possible.

Taxes

Before you open a bed and breakfast in your home, make it your business to educate yourself thoroughly about the tax laws that would apply to your operation. A heart-to-heart talk with an accountant or a representative of the Internal Revenue Service (or both) during the early planning stages will help you understand what your legal responsibilities are. And once you know what your obligations are, and the options available to you, you will be in a better position to devise an intelligent business plan for the start-up and growth of your bed and breakfast operation over its first three to five years. This is true even if you expect your venture to start small, and perhaps stay small for some time. You can make tax laws work to your advantage if you have good counsel. Make sure you get it.

Following is a discussion of some of the main concerns that you will have as a "sole proprietor" of a bed and breakfast operated out of your own home. Note that tax laws have been known to change from year to year, and they sometimes differ from state to state. Because of this, the information given here is intended as background only, designed to familiarize you with the basics. One of your responsibilities as a bed and breakfast host is to identify the tax laws that do apply to your particular set of circumstances, and then take the steps necessary to comply with reporting requirements and payment of any taxes due.

Running a bed and breakfast out of your own home is considered a "sole proprietorship" for federal tax purposes. Earned income from your B&B activities is reported on Schedule C, which is filed in addition to the usual Form 1040 if you have taxable income from another source as well. Schedule C is the place to report the total income you received from

B&B (the "gross income") and deductions for the expenses you've paid for your B&B operations. (When you subtract the total amount for expenses from the gross income, the result is your "net income" or the taxable portion of your income from B&B.)

There are guidelines for determining legitimate business expenses. All the expenses that you claim must have been incurred in connection with your business (that is, they were not personal expenses—such as the purchase of a hot tub that is not intended for guests' use). The expenses must also be ordinary and necessary for the business. (For example, printing brochures to advertise your B&B is a very common, "ordinary" thing to do—but taking a round-the-world trip to distribute them could be viewed with a little suspicion.) And finally, the amount declared for any expense must be reasonable. (Five dollars spent on the economy size of laundry detergent is "reasonable," but $5,000 spent on a hammer might come under scrutiny.) Typical deductible business expenses for your B&B operation are those for:

Business cards
Brochures
Advertising
Accounting fees
Commission to RSO
Membership dues to chamber of commerce
Laundry
Ledgers
Business insurance
A course in bookkeeping
Magazines/newspapers
Postage
Food
Coffee
Soap
Facial tissue
This book

Items that will have long-term use over several years' time or more cannot be immediately written off for the full amount that they cost; they must be depreciated for a percentage of their cost over a period of time. The amount is calculated and reported on Form 4562. Typical expenditures that can be depreciated are those for:

Furniture
Air conditioner for guest room
Fixtures
Typewriter
Computer
Major repairs

Expenditures that are partly for bed and breakfast and partly personal can be prorated so that the business portion is either deducted as a business expense or depreciated. Business use of your family car is one of these. So is the portion of your home that is used exclusively and regularly for bed and breakfast. (Note that in terms of taxes, the sale of a home that has been used for a business is more complicated than the sale of a residence only. If you see a possible sale of your B&B home in the future, be sure to discuss with your accountant the best way to fulfill your tax obligations with this in mind.)

If you make a net income of more than $400 from your bed and breakfast, then you must also file a self-employment tax on Form SE. This is Social Security tax for people who are self-employed. The self-employed must also take the initiative to pay quarterly taxes based on income they expect to earn in the coming year, as no employer is withholding part of their earnings for this purpose. IRS Estimated Personal Tax Form 1040ES is used for these quarterly payments.

Check the tax laws of your particular state carefully to determine whether or not your state requires some form of income tax on home-based businesses. (Some do not.) If yours does have a reporting procedure that you must follow, do not assume that the rules are the same as those for federal income tax. In most states they are similar to an extent, but usually with some exceptions. Some states are satisfied with a photocopy of the federal Schedule C, but others have their own separate set of calculations that must be completed according to a separate set of rules. And be aware that some states have what's called a "State Gross Receipts Tax" that is levied in addition to regular income tax; find out if your state is among these. Some states also require a room occupancy excise tax for bed and breakfast establishments operating above a minimum number of rooms; find out if your B&B falls into the taxable category.

Any sales tax due is also collected by the state. Sales-tax laws differ from state to state. In some states, so far, sales tax is not collected for bed and breakfast activities in one's home. To find out if you should be paying sales tax for B&B, or for items that you sell as a sideline to your B&B operation (such as quilts or other arts and crafts), contact the state department of taxation. Be prepared to meet with some confusion; some states have established definite policies about sales tax where bed and breakfast is concerned, but many more have not. If you're given a decision, ask for it in writing so that there is no confusion later on. If you are required to collect, and remit, sales tax, find out what percentage your state requires, add the tax to each guest's bill, and pay the tax due according to the schedule set up by the state (usually four times a year).

If you hire anyone to help you run your bed and breakfast (for example, someone to clean on a regular basis or do secretarial work), you are also responsible for unemployment and Social Security taxes on employees.

As resources, contact your local IRS office for free copies of the following helpful publications: *Tax Guide for Small Businesses* (#334), *Business Use of Your Home* (#587), *Self-Employment Tax* (#533), Form 4562 and Instructions, *Information for Business Taxpayers* (#583), and *Your Federal Income Tax* (#17).

In addition, the U.S. Small Business Administration provides (for fifty cents apiece) the following pamphlets: *Steps in Meeting Your Tax Obligations* (MA 1.013) and *Getting the Facts for Income Tax Reporting* (MA 1.014). Contact your local SBA office for copies or write to: U.S. Small Business Administration, P.O. Box 30, Denver, Colorado 80201–0030.

Don't overlook the help that is available for your local reservation service organization. The RSO manager is familiar with the tax laws as applied in your locality and can most likely be counted on for a few pointers if you are listed with the agency. In some cases, the RSO takes responsibility for collecting sales tax whenever reservations are placed through the agency. (This relieves the host of the sales tax worry as long as guests are accepted *only* through the RSO.) Other RSOs leave the sales tax collection to individual hosts.

There are some RSOs that provide more than advice to their hosts when tax time rolls around. "At the end of each year we send hosts an accounting of all the guests that they have had. We do not help them with the actual tax preparation, but we do suggest to them what can and can't be considered a deduction, such as free room nights given as promotion, cleaning supplies, etcetera," says Rick Madden, former manager of Bed & Breakfast Colorado. Gary Winget of the Bed & Breakfast Registry, a national RSO based in St. Paul, Minnesota, says that this agency "offers an easy-to-use record-keeping system that is maintained on the host's check register and provides monthly and year-to-date income and expense computer printouts. As a result, the host has current financial information for management of his or her operations and the documentation needed to easily complete all tax forms."

Keeping records

As a way to advise prospective hosts about the realities of running a bed and breakfast, managers of reservation service organizations across North America were asked to identify the biggest mistake made by new B&B hosts. Nancy Jenkins, former manager of the Bed & Breakfast Exchange in St. Helena, California, said this: "Not being well enough prepared for the bookkeeping and accounting aspects of the business." Too many new hosts tend to indulge solely in the fun part of hosting—meeting guests and making their stay a wonderful experience. (After all, that's why they got involved with B&B in the first place.) But they pay too little attention to their finances, so when it's time to give Uncle Sam some facts and figures it's nearly an impossible task to recreate an entire year of receipts and disbursements and to produce records that were never kept.

No matter how much, or how little, hosting you plan to do, it is absolutely essential that you keep accurate records of your activities. First of all, your bed and breakfast income is subject to taxes. (See the section on taxes in this chapter.) You need good records in order to determine how much you do or do not owe and to substantiate your figures to the satisfaction of the federal or the state government, or both. Just as important, you need to give yourself the benefit of understanding your own business and planning for its future. Are you making or losing money? Has the volume of guests increased or decreased over the past year, compared with the year before? Where do you want your bed and breakfast operation to be a year from now? Three years from now? Five years? If you want growth, you have to plan for it. To devise an intelligent business plan, you need a way to assess where you are now, how your situation compares with those of previous years, and what it will take to reach your goals. Good records are the key.

The first step in setting up a record-keeping system should come before you ever start hosting. Examine your home in terms of its readiness to provide all of the basics necessary to accommodate bed and breakfast guests. Will you have to make some changes or improvements before you can accept guests? (Refer to the checklists for bedroom and bathroom basics in chapter 3.) To get your home ready, you will most likely have some "start-up" expenses. Make a list of items you will have to buy and renovations you will have to make, along with approximate costs. The following list includes some typical examples of start-up expenses that some new hosts find necessary:

> I recently renovated my bathroom, which was in poor shape; at least I thought so," says the owner of RMF Bed & Breakfast in Atlanta, Georgia. "I am very proud of it and for a while I was showing it to everyone. One of my guests, who was a repeat guest from before the renovation, said, when shown the room, 'It's very nice. It was okay before, too.' At first I was a bit disappointed, but upon reflection I felt very good. Perhaps the defects of the rest of my home, like the bathroom, aren't so apparent to others. It may be that I am more disturbed than anyone else by the imperfections."

New mattress
New sheets
New pillows
New towels
Extra towel racks
Brochures
Shampooing rugs
Refinishing bedside table
Painting bathroom
Insurance
Legal advice
Smoke detectors
Membership fee for RSO
Membership fee in B&B association
Ice bucket
Serving tray
Installing railing around porch
Air conditioner
Repairing broken step
New locks
Soap dishes
Night lights
Clock for guest room

Once you've totaled the estimated costs for all of the items you would like to buy and improvements you would like to make, go back over the list and see if there's anything that can be omitted as not absolutely essential. Heed the advice of Carolyn Morrow, owner of Leftwich House, a bed and breakfast in Graham, North Carolina: "Spend as little as possible. You'll need capital until your business is established." You should be ready to make necessary expenditures for your guests' comfort, but you must know where to draw the line. (A new shade for the lamp in the guest room might be nice, but will the old one do for a while?) Trim your start-up costs as much as you reasonably can without sacrificing the quality of the accommodations your B&B offers.

After determining what you need to open your home for bed and breakfast, and figuring a total amount for them, then consider what your ongoing expenses would be for day-to-day operation of your B&B. Such expenses might include:

- Food
- Beverages
- Coffee filters
- Hand/face soap
- Sample sizes of lotion/shampoo
- Laundry
- Use of automobile (gas and mileage)
- Facial/toilet tissue
- Stamps
- Envelopes
- Telephone calls
- Electricity
- Heat
- Cleaning help
- Cleaning supplies

At first, it's difficult to come up with a daily, weekly, or "per guest" figure on operational expenses. Once you've hosted for a while, you're in a much better position to predict how many boxes of facial tissue or cans of cleanser you will go through in a typical year. Having this information can certainly help you budget for the long term. But for now, concentrate on making as complete a list of operational expenses as possible so that you can plan to document them in your records.

When it comes to setting up a record-keeping system for your bed and breakfast, there's only one rule to follow: Choose a system that you understand thoroughly and control completely. Basically, your job is to keep track of what's coming in (receipts) and what's going out (disbursements). There are a number of methods designed to help you fulfill these two functions, from a simple ledger to a sophisticated software package. If you are a whiz at your PC, then computerizing your records is probably the best system for you. But if you start to nod off whenever conversation turns to floppy discs and megabytes, you should not try to use a computer that you know in your heart you don't want and will probably never understand. Even if your record-keeping system consists of nothing more than a series of handwritten notes on recipe cards filed by month, this is all you need as long as you have the information you want at your fingertips. So look at the options available and then decide what works best for you.

Keeping a guest register is advisable as a record-keeping tool. This is a large ledger type of book in which your guests sign in upon arrival with their name, address, phone number, how many nights they plan to stay, and dates of the visit. A guest register is a convenient way to keep track of how many guests you accommodate over a period of time, and how many nights your rooms are booked per month or per year. The contents can be used to identify the extent of your best "seasons" out of the year (when large numbers of guests visit because of the fall foliage, skiing, sunning, cherry blossom time, or tulips in flower, for examples). The register can show you when you should go easy on the advertising because you'll already be operating at capacity and won't be able to accommodate any more guests anyway, and when you should do some creative marketing to bring guests to your door in the off-season. (How about a "How-to-make-a-quilt Weekend featuring Bed and Breakfast"?) You can purchase an attractive ledger for use as a guest register in most stationery stores.

In addition to the guest register (which supplies you with a valuable chronological reference), you should keep an information record for each guest who visits your home, filed alphabetically by the guests' last names. (Start a new file each year so that if you find it necessary to undertake a year-by-year review, or isolate just one year in particular, it will be an easy matter.) The information can be computerized, but it can be just as easily recorded on sturdy 4″ × 6″ or 5″ × 8″ cards, whichever you prefer.

The information record should include the guest's name, address, and telephone number, along with the dates of arrival and departure, total number of nights stayed, number of people in the party (either write down all the names on the same card, or make separate cards for each person, if you prefer), which room or rooms were occupied, city/state taxes collected, and total amount paid for B&B. Some hosts also like to record the license number and make of a guest's vehicle, plus personal notes that will help jog their memories later when it's time to send follow-up notes to former guests (such as a guest's interest in stamp collecting, or the date of someone's birthday or anniversary). Also write down how the guest heard about your bed and breakfast; a review of the sources at the end of every year can help you identify the advertising strategies that are working and those that aren't.

According to Liza Roman, the owner of a Boston-based bookkeeping firm called Roman Numerals that services some bed and breakfast clients in the area, one of the best aids available for keeping track of all funds that go in and out of your B&B operation is a checking account that you set up separately from your personal account. Of course it isn't mandatory to do this, but it's advisable because the checkbook provides clear documentation of how much money you handle for your B&B during any month or any year. (Trying to untangle this information from your personal account can be quite a chore.)

The best type of checkbook to use is the ledger style, which provides space for you to make clarifying notes for all transactions. Some of these checkbooks come with stubs or carbon copies for your easy reference. The more documentation you have for money coming in and going out, the better off you'll be at tax time.

In addition to the checkbook, you will need to keep a "cash receipts journal" and a "cash disbursements journal." (Journals for these purposes can be purchased at office-supply stores.) In the receipts journal, keep a record of all the money coming in. Each deposit in your B&B checking account will also be recorded here. In the disbursements journal, keep a record of all the money going out. For this, it's best to establish in advance certain categories for expenditures and list these in separate columns—such as those for office supplies, laundry, food/beverages, membership dues, telephone, postage, outside labor, gas and mileage, and commission to RSO. (Some hosts elect to keep just *one* journal and use it for both receipts and disbursements. Because most—or all—of the income that bed and breakfast hosts receive comes from one source, paying guests, one column can be set aside for this.)

For each disbursement, you should have a receipt. To keep receipts, a simple but effective method is to buy twelve large manila envelopes at the beginning of each year and label them by month. Place all the receipts you collect for a particular month in the appropriate envelope. It's very helpful to write on the back of each receipt what the expenditure was for—envelopes, stamps, laundry services. When it comes time to reconcile your receipts with your entries, the process is much easier. Keep receipts for *everything*, no matter how small the amount spent.

In addition to the receipts and disbursements journals, it's a good idea to keep a personal log, almost like a diary, of your day-to-day bed and breakfast activities. An appointment calendar that provides lots of space for notes will do nicely. Here, record what you do that does not show up in the other two journals: "Cleaned guest room, made breakfast for guests, took them to airport (12 miles round-trip), and did laundry." This personal log can help you substantiate what your bed and breakfast activities involve if the occasion ever arises. (Some hosts have found it necessary to prove to local authorities how a B&B differs from a strict rent situation.) It will also provide a basis for determining a deduction for the business use of your car.

The final recommendation for keeping good records is that you establish a petty cash fund for your B&B operation. It's wise to pay for everything you can from your B&B checking account (instead of by cash, by personal check, or by credit card) so that you'll have that additional documentation in the checking account ledger, plus cancelled checks. But there are some small expenditures for which you can't realistically write a check. A petty cash fund can supply you with the small amounts of cash that you need, in exchange for voucher slips filled out every time you use some of the money. (Voucher slips can be bought in office-supply stores.) Vouchers and receipts can be used for deductions at tax time.

If the idea of setting up a record-keeping system by yourself still seems overwhelming, there are alternatives. One is to consult a bookkeeper or an accountant to help, or ask for advice from your local Small Business Administration office. Or you might want to check into an organizing system called the "Ultramanager" that was designed for use by bed and breakfast hosts. (For information on this product, write to B&B Enterprises, P.O. Box 29522, St. Helena, California 94574.) You could also consult or hire a part-time bookkeeper to take care of your records for you (the expense is tax-deductible) or look into internship programs at local colleges. Schools with programs in accounting or business often seek out internship opportunities for their students; the sponsor pays little or nothing for the service. The choice is up to you. The important thing is that one way or the other, the records that you need must be kept accurately.

Appendix I:
The Helping Hands Network

KEY

H Will be happy to answer questions from aspiring hosts about B&B hosting.

H Will be happy to receive brochures or business cards from B&Bs across the country to make available to guests in exchange for the same service from other "Helping Hands."

Alaska
Jean Parsons
Accommodations Alaska Style
Stay With A Friend
3605 Arctic Boulevard, Suite 173
Anchorage 99503
(907) 344-4006
H *H*

Arizona
Marjorie Ann Lindmark
Bed 'n' Breakfast in Phoenix
5995 East Orange Blossom Lane
Phoenix 85018
(602) 994-3759
H *H*

Arkansas
Barbara Gavron
Singleton House
11 Singleton
Eureka Springs 72632
(501) 253-9111
H *H*

California
Bob and Hattie Michalis
Gull House
P.O. Box 1381
Avalon 90704
(213) 510-2547
H *H*

B&G's B&B
12357 Via Cabezon
San Diego 92129
(619) 484–0143

Theresa Wigginton
Madison Street Inn
A Victorian Bed and Breakfast Inn
1390 Madison Street
Santa Clara 95050
(408) 249–5541

Carolyn and Bill Canfield
Ocean View House
P.O. Box 20065
Santa Barbara 93102
(805) 966–6659

Bob and Sandy Runkle
Friends We Haven't Met
10071 Starbright Circle
Westminster 92683
(714) 531–4269

Georgia
RMF Bed & Breakfast
1310 Iverson Street, N.E.
Atlanta 30307
(404) 525–5712

Indiana
Paul and Ruth Miller
Green Meadow Ranch
Route 2, Box 592
Shipshewana 46565
(219) 768–4221

Iowa
Mary Nichols
Hannah Marie Country Inn
RR 1, Highway 71 South
Spender 51301

Kentucky
Ronna Lee Hunter
Bowling Green Bed & Breakfast
659 East 14th Avenue
Bowling Green 42101
(502) 781–3861

Maine
Hannah and Dan Rothermel
Hannah's Loft Bed & Bread
Chases Pond Road
RR 2, Box 117
York 03909
(207) 363–7244

Prentice Strong Jr.
Penury Hall
Main Street
Southwest Harbor 04679
(207) 244–7102

Wild Rose of York
78 Long Sands Road
York 03909
(207) 363–2532

Maryland
Norma and Bill Grovermann
Prince George Inn B&B
232 Prince George Street
Annapolis 21401
(301) 263-6418

Betsy Grater
Betsy's Bed & Breakfast
1428 Park Avenue
Baltimore 21217
(301) 225-0001

Massachusetts
Carolyn and Jack O'Toole
The Captain Samuel Eddy House
609 Oxford Street South
Auburn 01504
(508) 832-5282 or 832-3149

Margot French
Folkstone Bed & Breakfast
P.O. Box 931
Boylston 01505
(508) 869-2687

Jeanne D. Gilbert
Gilbert's Bed & Breakfast
30 Spring Street
Rehoboth 02769
(508) 252-6416

Michigan
The Parsonage 1915
6 East 24th Street
Holland 49423
(517) 396-1316

Missouri
Krista and Jorgen Wibskov
Lamplight Inn B&B Guesthouse
207 East School Street
Bonne Terre 63628
(314) 358-4222

Anchor Hill Lodge
Route 1, Box 750
Rogersville 65742
(417) 753-2930

Caroyl's B&B
9906 N.W. 75th Terrace
Kansas City 64152
(816) 587-8969

New Hampshire
Linda and David Nichols
Hidden Brooks Bed & Breakfast
Box 402
Dublin 03444
(603) 563-8452

Sandra J. Conley and
Martin Kelly
Applebrook
Route 115A
P.O. Box 178
Jefferson 03583
(603) 586-7713

Bob and Linda Dahlberg
Victorian Harvest Inn
Locust Lane, Box 1763
North Conway 03860
(603) 356-3548
H *H*

New Jersey

Cecelia and Pat Swezeny
Cozy Acres B&B
230 Ivins Avenue
McKee City 08232
(609) 646-3371
H

Eileen Rodan and Wish Zorawski
Cape Associates
Box 118
340 47th Place
Sea Isle City 08243
(609) 263-8700
H *H*

New Mexico

Phil and Joan Blood
Chinguague Compound
Post Office Box 1118
San Juan Pueblo 87566
(505) 852-2194
H *H*

New York

Donna Tanney
Gates Hill Homestead
Dugway Road
Brookfield 13314
(315) 899-5837
H *H*

Joan Ballinger
The Eastwood House
45 South Main Street (Route 39)
Castile 14427
(716) 493-2335
H *H*

Rae and Gene Vandenbord
Silver Maples Bed and Breakfast
Scotch Mountain Road
DeLancey 13752
(607) 746-3516
H *H*

Edith van Horne
Historian Bed & Breakfast
Route 5, Box 224
Nelliston 13410
(518) 993-2233
H

Cynthia and Charles Whited
Strawberry Castle
1883 Penfield Road
Penfield 14526
(716) 385-3266
H *H*

Mary E. Decker
Corner House
110 East Market Street
Rhinebeck 12572
(914) 876-4758
H *H*

Lona and George Smith
Summerwood
72 East Main Street
Richfield Springs 13439
(315) 858-2024
H *H*

Elaine N. Samuels
Ivy Chimney
143 Didama Street
Syracuse 13224
(315) 446–4199

Stanley and Carol Sambora
Bed & Breakfast of Waterville
211 White Street
Waterville 13480
(315) 841–8295

Seafield House
Two Seafield Lane
Westhampton Beach 11978
(516) 288–1559

North Carolina
Maureen Titlow
4023 Randolph Road
Charlotte 28211
(704) 364–4760

Carolyn L. Morrow
Leftwich House
215 East Harden Street
Graham 27253
(919) 226–5978

Ohio
Donna Lendrum
The Beach House
213 Kiwanis Avenue
Huron 44839
(419) 433–5839

Patricia Boetteher
3 B's Bed & Breakfast
103 Race Street
Spring Valley 45370
(513) 862–4241

Oregon
Alyce Levy
Royal Carter House
514 Siskiyou Boulevard
Ashland 97520
(503) 482–5623

Isabel Wheeler
Wheeler's Bed & Breakfast
Post Office Box 8201
Coburg 97401
(503) 344–1366

Betty Gallucci
P.O. Box 1303
Lake Oswego 97034
(503) 636–6933

Pennsylvania
Charlotte Kanofsky
Mrs. K's Bed & Breakfast
404 Ridge Avenue
Kennett Square 19348
(215) 444–5559

Meadow Spring Farm
301 East Street Road (Route 926)
Kennett Square 19348
(215) 444–3903

Mr. and Mrs. Charles Groff
Sycamore Haven Farm
35 South Kinzer Road
Kinzers 17535
(717) 442–4901

Meadowview Guest House
2169 New Holland Pike
Lancaster 17601
(717) 299–4017

Arlene Hershey
Box 93, Route 896
Lincoln University 19352
(215) 932–9257

Elsa Dimick
Longswamp Bed and Breakfast
R.D. 2, Box 26
Mertztown 19539
(215) 682–6197

Marjorie Amrom
Trade Winds
943 Lombard Street
Philadelphia 19147
(215) 592–8644

Catherine C. Hatala
1513 Rodman Street
Philadelphia 19146
(215) 735–0370

Jane Spivack
2221 Delancey Place
Philadelphia 19103
(512) 545–1980

Sandra and Gary McKnight
Applebutter Inn
152 Applewood Lane
Slippery Rock 16057
(412) 794–1844

Ursula A. Gusse
Mrs. G's Bed and Breakfast
256 West Ridge Avenue
State College 16803
(814) 283–0733

Rhode Island

Jeanne Lewis
Fairfield-By-The-Sea
527 Green Hill Beach Road
Green Hill 02879
(401) 789–4717

Mildred Snee
The House of Snee
191 Ocean Road
Narragansett 02882
(401) 783–9494

Amy Weintraub and Edwina Sebest
Brinley Victorian Inn
23 Brinley Street
Newport 02840
(401) 849–7645

Ellen L. Madison
Woody Hill Guest House B&B
R.R. 3, Box 676 E
Woody Hill Road
Westerly 02891
(401) 322-0452
H 𝓗

South Carolina
Mary Shaw
The Shaw House
8 Cypress Court
Georgetown 29440
(803) 546-9663
H 𝓗

South Dakota
Glenn and Joy Hagen
Lakeside Farm
R.R. 2, Box 52
Webster 57274
(605) 486-4430
H 𝓗

Tennessee
George and Barbara Painter
Turkey Nest Rest
108 Benson Lane
Gatlinburg 37738
(615) 436-5124
H 𝓗

Vermont
Blue Wax Farm
Route 1, Box 63
East Burke 05832
(802) 626-5542
H 𝓗

Lincoln Alden
Watercourse Way B&B
Route 132
South Strafford 05070
(802) 765-4314
H 𝓗

Pat and Paul Hunt
Hunts' Hideaway
R.R. 1
West Charleston 05872
(802) 895-4432
H 𝓗

Virginia
Rita Duncan
Blue Ridge B&B, Rocks & Rills
Route 2, Box 3895
Berryville 22611
(703) 955-1246
H 𝓗

Roy E. Mixon
Rockland Farm Retreat
Route 1, Box 1120
Bumpass 23024
(703) 895-5098
H 𝓗

Camille Harris
The Foster-Harris House
P.O. Box 333
Washington 22747
(703) 675-3757
H 𝓗

Washington
Jody Weaver
Hanson House Bed & Breakfast
1526 Palm Avenue SW
Seattle 98116
(206) 937-4157
H 𝓗

West Virginia

Hazel Hudock
Prospect Hill B&B
P.O. Box 135
Gerrardstown 25420
(304) 229-3346

Ernest and Edna Shipe
Valley View Farm
Route 1, Box 467
Mathias 26812
(304) 897-5229

Lisa Hileman
Countryside
Summit Point 25446
(304) 725-2614

Jamaica

Sydney and Rachel Munroe
Spring Garden Bed & Breakfast
c/o Ketto P.A.
Westmoreland, Jamaica
West Indies
(809) 957-4323

Appendix II: Reservation Service Organizations in North America

KEY

C The reservation service organization has contributed information for this book.

\+ The reservation service organization represents hosts in more than one state or region. (Note: When seeking out RSOs that accept host homes in your area, check your home state *and* neighboring states as well.)

National Reservation Service Organizations

Bed and Breakfast Service (BABS)
P.O. Box 5025
Bellingham, Washington 98227
(206) 733-8642
C +
National.
Contact: Dolores and George Herrmann.

Bed & Breakfast Registry
P.O. Box 8174
St. Paul, Minnesota 55108
(612) 646-4238
C +
National plus Canada and Mexico.
Contact: Gary and Mary Winget.

Reservation Service Organizations by State

Alabama

Bed & Breakfast Birmingham
P.O. Box 43190
Birmingham 35243
(205) 967-3859
Greater Birmingham.
Contact: Debbie Battles.

Bed & Breakfast Montgomery
P.O. Box 886

Milbrook 36054
(205) 285–5421
Montgomery area.
Contact: Helen Maier.

Alaska

Accommodations Alaska Style/Stay With A Friend
3605 Arctic Boulevard, Box 173
Anchorage 99503
(907) 344–4006
C
Anchorage and area.
Contact: Jean Parsons.

Alaska Bed and Breakfast
P.O. Box 1321
Juneau 99802
(907) 586–2959
Statewide.
Contact: Muriel Elder.

Alaska Private Lodgings
1236 West 10th Avenue
Anchorage 99501
(907) 258–1717
Anchorage and area.
Contact: Mary Reardon.

Fairbanks Bed & Breakfast
Box 74573
Fairbanks 99707
(907) 452–4967
Fairbanks area.
Contact: Barb and Greg Neubauer.

Arizona

Bed & Breakfast in Arizona
P.O. Box 8628
Scottsdale 85252
(602) 995–2831
+
Statewide.
Contact: Trisha Wills and Tom Thomas.

Mi Casa–Su Casa Bed & Breakfast
P.O. Box 950
Tempe 85281
(602) 990–0682
C +
Statewide, plus Utah, California, New Mexico, and Nevada.
Contact: Ruth Young.

Bed and Breakfast Scottsdale and The West
P.O. Box 3999
Prescott 86302–3999
(602) 776–1102
+
Scottsdale area plus New Mexico.
Contact: Joyce and George Thomson.

Old Pueblo Homestays
P.O. Box 13603
Tucson 85732
(602) 790–2399
Tucson.
Contact: Rena Kiekebusch and Dorna Nelson.

Arkansas

Arkansas and Ozarks Bed & Breakfast
White River Landing, Inc.
Route 1, Box 38
Calico Rock 72519
(501) 297–8764
Arkansas and Ozarks.
Contact: Carolyn S. Eck.

California

Bed & Breakfast International
1181 B Solano Avenue
Albany 94706
(415) 525–4569
C
Northern California.
Contact: Jean Brown.

Digs West
8191 Crowley Circle
Buena Park 90621
(714) 739–1669
Southern California.
Contact: Jean Horn.

Hospitality Plus
P.O. Box 388
San Juan Capistrano 92693
(714) 496–7050
San Juan Capistrano.
Contact: Deborah Sakach.

House Guests USA
P.O. Box 1185
Huntington Beach 92647
(714) 891–3736
Greater Los Angeles and Orange County.
Contact: Layne Neugart.

American Family Inn/Bed & Breakfast San Francisco
P.O. Box 349
San Francisco 94101
(415) 931–3083
C
Greater San Francisco wine & gold country, Monterey, Carmel.
Contact: Richard & Susan Kreibich.

Bed & Breakfast of Southern California
1943 Sunny Crest Drive, Suite 304
Fullerton 92635
(714) 738–8361
Southern California.
Contact: Joyce Garrison.

California Houseguests, International, Inc.
18653 Ventura Boulevard, #190 B
Tarzana 91356
(818) 344–7878
Statewide.
Contact: Trudi Alexy.

Co-Host, America's Bed & Breakfast
P.O. Box 9302
Whittier 90608
(213) 699–8427
Southern California.
Contact: Coleen Davis.

Eye Openers Bed & Breakfast Reservations
P.O. Box 694
Altadena 91001
(213) 684–4428 or (818) 797–2055
C
Statewide.
Contact: Ruth Judkins.

Bed & Breakfast Exchange
1458 Lincoln Avenue #3
Calistoga 94515
(707) 942–5900
C
Napa and Sonoma Counties plus Gold Country and San Francisco.
Contact: Larry Paladini.

Bed and Breakfast of Los Angeles
32074 Waterside Lane
Westlake Village 91361
(818) 889–8870 or 7325
C
Southern California.
Contact: Angie Kobabe and Peg Marshall.

Napa Valley Finest Lodgings
1834 First Street
Napa 94559
(707) 224–4667
C
Napa Valley plus Sonoma.
Contact: Pat Wattenburger.

Carolyn's Bed & Breakfast Homes in San Diego
416 Third Avenue, #25
Chula Vista 92010
(619) 422–7009
C

San Diego area.
Contact: Barbara Schubert.

Rent A Room International—Bed and Breakfast
11531 Varna Street
Garden Grove 92640
(714) 638-1406
Statewide.
Contact: Esther MacLachlan.

Wine Country Bed and Breakfast
P.O. Box 3211
Santa Rosa 95403
(707) 578-1661
Northern California.
Contact: Helga Poulsen.

Colorado

Bed & Breakfast Colorado
P.O. Box 12206
Boulder 80303
(303) 494-4994 and (800) 373-4995
C
Statewide.
Contact: Kate and Jim Carey.

Bed & Breakfast Rocky Mountains
P.O. Box 804
Colorado Springs 80901
(719) 630-3433
C +
Statewide plus New Mexico and Utah.
Contact: Kate Winters.

Bed & Breakfast Vail/Ski Areas
P.O. Box 491
Vail 81658
(303) 949-1212
Ski areas.
Contact: Kathy Fagan.

Connecticut

Nutmeg Bed & Breakfast
P.O. Box 1117
West Hartford 06107
(203) 236-6698
C
Statewide.
Contact: Michelle Souza.

Bed and Breakfast, Ltd.
P.O. Box 216
New Haven 06513
(203) 469-3260
C
Statewide.
Contact: Jack Argenio.

Covered Bridge Bed and Breakfast
P.O. Box 447
Norfolk 06058
(203) 542-5594
C +
Southwestern New England.
Contact: Diane Tremblay.

Delaware

Bed & Breakfast of Delaware
Box 177, 3650 Silverside Road
Wilmington 19810
(302) 479-9500 or 478-1437
+
Statewide plus Maryland and Pennsylvania.
Contact: Mildred Alford.

District of Columbia

Bed 'n' Breakfast, Ltd., of Washington, D.C.
P.O. Box 12011
Washington, D.C. 20005
(202) 328-3510
C +
D.C. area plus Maryland and Virginia.
Contact: Jackie Reed.

The Bed & Breakfast League, Ltd./Sweet Dreams and Toast
3639 Van Ness Street, NW

P.O. Box 9490
Washington, D.C. 20008
(202) 363-7767
C +
Statewide.
Contact: Millie Groobey.

Florida

Bed & Breakfast Co.—Tropical Florida
P.O. Box 262
South Miami 33243
(305) 661-3270
C
Tropical Florida plus Nassau and Puerto Rico.
Contact: Marcella Schaible.

Florida Suncoast Bed and Breakfast
119 Rosewood Drive
Palm Harbor 33563
(813) 784-5118
West coast of Florida.
Contact: Carol Hart.

A&A Bed & Breakfast of Florida, Inc.
P.O. Box 1316
Winter Park 32790
(407) 628-3233
Orlando area and Central Florida.
Contact: Brunhilde Fehner.

B&B Suncoast Accommodations
8690 Gulf Boulevard
St. Pete Beach 33706
(813) 360-1753
C
West coast of Florida.
Contact: Danie Bernard.

Bed & Breakfast, Inc., of the Florida Keys
5 Man-O-War Drive
Marathon 33050
(305) 743-4118
August and September in New Jersey.
(201) 223-5979
C
Keys and east coast of Florida.
Contact: Joan Hopp.

B&B Reservations of Orlando
8205 Banyan Boulevard
Orlando 32819
(407) 352-9157
Orlando and central Florida.
Contact: Bobbie Jean Havlish.

Georgia

Bed & Breakfast Atlanta
1801 Piedmont Avenue, #208
Atlanta 30324
(404) 875-0525 or 875-9672
C
Atlanta and selected sites around Georgia.
Contact: Paula Gris and Madalyn Eplan.

Atlanta Hospitality
2472 Lauderdale Drive NE
Atlanta 30345
(404) 493-1930
+
Atlanta; Brooklyn, New York; and Boston, Massachusetts
Contact: Erna Bryant, Candee Evans.

Bed & Breakfast Hideaway Homes
P.O. Box 300
Blue Ridge 30513
(404) 632-2411
+
Northern Georgia plus eastern Tennessee and western North Carolina.
Contact: Betty Jackson.

Quail Country Bed & Breakfast, Ltd.
1104 Old Monticello Road
Thomasville 31792
(912) 226-6882

Thomasville area.
Contact: Mercer Watt and Kathy Lanigan.

Hawaii

Bed & Breakfast Hawaii
Box 449
Kapaa 96746
(808) 822-7771
Statewide.
Contact: Evie Warner and Al Davis.

Bed & Breakfast Honolulu
3242 Kaohinani Drive
Honolulu 96817
(808) 595-7533 or (800) 288-4666 (from Continental U.S.)
Statewide, all islands.
Contact: Gene Bridges.

Pacific-Hawaii Bed & Breakfast
19 Kai Nani Place
Kailua, Oahu 96734
(808) 262-6026
Statewide—Oahu, Maui, Kauai, Island of Hawaii.
Contact: Doris Epp.

Bed and Breakfast Maui Style
P.O. Box 886
Kihei 96753
(808) 879-7865
Maui.
Contact: Jeanne Rominger.

Idaho

Bed & Breakfast Travel Connections
5805 Pine Grove Drive
Coeur d'Alene 83814
(208) 765-9090
+
Statewide plus Montana, Washington, and Canada.
Contact: Barbara Hampton.

Bed & Breakfast of Idaho
109 West Idaho Street
Boise 83702
(208) 342-8066 or 336-5174
Boise and statewide.
Contact: Tom and Phyllis Lupher.

Illinois

Bed & Breakfast/Chicago, Inc.
Box 14088
Chicago 60614
(312) 951-0085
Chicago area.
Contact: Mary Shaw.

Prairie Hospitality, Inc.
P.O. Box 3035
Oak Park 60303
(312) 386-8620
Statewide.
Contact: Judith Newitt.

Indiana

Bed & Breakfast/Indiana, Inc.
P.O. Box 481
Nashville 47448-0481
(812) 988-0733
Statewide.
Contact: Marcia P. Wray

Indiana Amish Country Bed & Breakfast
1600 West Market Street
Nappanee 46550
(219) 773-4188
Elkart County.
Contact: Sonya L. Harman.

Iowa

Bed & Breakfast Iowa, Ltd.
P.O. Box 430
Preston 52069
(319) 689-4222
+
Statewide and Beresford, South Dakota.
Contact: Wilma Bloom.

Kansas

Bed & Breakfast Kansas City
P.O. Box 14781
Lenexa 66215
(913) 888-3636
+
Statewide plus Missouri.
Contact: Edwina Monroe.

Kentucky

Ohio Valley Bed & Breakfast
6876 Taylor Mill Road
Independence 41051
(606) 356-7865
C +
Statewide plus Ohio and Indiana.
Contact: Nancy Cully.

Bluegrass Bed & Breakfast
Route 1, Box 263
Versailles 40383
(606) 873-3208
C
Lexington and central Kentucky.
Contact: Betsy Pratt.

Kentucky Homes Bed and Breakfast
1431 Saint James Court
Louisville 40208
(502) 635-7341
+
Statewide plus Indiana and Tennessee.
Contact: Lillian Marshall.

Louisiana

New Orleans Bed and Breakfast
Box 8163
New Orleans 70182
(504) 822-5038 or 5046
C
New Orleans.
Contact: Sarah-Margaret Brown.

Bed & Breakfast, Inc.
1360 Moss Street
Box 52257
New Orleans 70152-2257
(504) 525-4640
+
New Orleans plus Barbados.
Contact: Hazell Boyce.

Southern Comfort Bed & Breakfast Reservation Service
2856 Hundred Oaks
Baton Rouge 70808
(504) 346-1928
C +
Statewide plus Mississippi, New Mexico, and Acapulco.
Contact: Susan Morris and Helen Heath.

Maine

Bed & Breakfast Down East, Ltd.
Box 547
Eastbrook 04634
(207) 565-3517
C
Statewide.
Contact: Sally Godfrey.

Bed & Breakfast of Maine
32 Colonial Village
Falmouth 04105
(207) 781-4528
C
Statewide.
Contact: Peg Tierney.

Maryland

Amanda's Bed and Breakfast Reservation Service
1428 Park Avenue
Baltimore 21217-4230
(301) 225-0001
+
Statewide plus Virginia, Pennsylvania, Delaware, District of Columbia, and West Virginia.
Contact: Betsy Grater.

The Traveller in Maryland
P.O. Box 2277
Annapolis 21404
(301) 269–6232 or 261–2233
Statewide.
Contact: Cecily Sharp-Whitehill.

Massachusetts

Bed & Breakfast Associates
Bay Colony, Ltd.
Box 57166
Babson Park Branch
Boston 02156–0166
(617) 449–5302
C
Eastern Massachusetts.
Contact: Arline Kardasis and Marilyn Mitchell.

Bed and Breakfast Brookline/Boston
Box 732
Brookline 02146
(617) 277–2292 or 884–7748
C
Brookline, Boston area, Cape Cod, and Nantucket.
Contact: Anne Diamond and Colleen Hartford.

House Guests of Cape Cod
Box 1881
Orleans 02653
(508) 896–7053
Cape Cod plus Nantucket and Martha's Vineyard.
Contact: Charles DiCesare and Richard Griffin.

Bed & Breakfast Cape Cod
P.O. Box 341
West Hyannisport 02672
(508) 775–2772
C
Cape Cod.
Contact: Clark Diehl.

Berkshire Bed & Breakfast Homes
106 South Street
P.O. Box 211
Williamsburg 01096
(413) 268–7244
+
Western Massachusetts plus New York.
Contact: Eleanor Hebert.

Bed & Breakfast Marblehead & North Shore
P.O. Box 172
Beverly 01915
(508) 921–1336
C +
North Shore area plus Vermont and New Hampshire.
Contact: Helena Champion.

Bed & Breakfast Agency of Boston
47 Commercial Wharf
Boston 02110
(617) 720–3540
Downtown Boston.
Contact: Ferne Mintz.

Orleans Bed & Breakfast Associates
P.O. Box 1312
Orleans 02653
(508) 255–3824
C
Harwich to Truro on Cape Cod.
Contact: Mary Chapman.

Host Homes of Boston
P.O. Box 117 Waban Branch
Boston 02168
(617) 244–1308
Boston, Brookline, and Newton.
Contact: Marcia Whittington.

Pineapple Hospitality, Inc.
47 North 2nd Street, #3A
New Bedford 02744

(508) 997-9952
C +
New England.
Contact: Judy Mulford.

Bed and Breakfast Cambridge and Greater Boston;
Bed and Breakfast in Minuteman Country
P.O. Box 665
Cambridge 02140
(617) 576-1492
Cambridge and Boston area plus Lexington, Bedford, and Route 128 area.
Contact: Pam and Tally Carruthers.

Be Our Guest Bed & Breakfast, Ltd.
P.O. Box 1333
Plymouth 02360
(508) 837-9867
C
Plymouth and area.
Contact: Mary Gill.

Folkstone Bed & Breakfast
P.O. Box 931
Boylston 01505
(508) 869-2687
C
Central Massachusetts.
Contact: Margot French.

Greater Boston Hospitality
Box 1142
Brookline 02146
(617) 277-5430
C
Greater Boston.
Contact: Lauren Simonelli and Kelly Simpson.

Greater Springfield Bed & Breakfast
25 Bellevue Avenue
Springfield 01108
(413) 739-7400
Greater Springfield.
Contact: Linda McCarthy.

Nantucket Accommodations
P.O. Box 217
Nantucket 02554
(508) 228-9559
Nantucket.
Contact: Don Polvere.

New England Bed & Breakfast
1045 Centre Street
Newton Centre 02159
(617) 244-2112 or 498-9819
+
Massachusetts and New England area.
Contact: John Gardiner.

The Bed & Breakfast Folks
48 Springs Road
Bedford 01730
(617) 275-9025
North and west of Boston.
Contact: Phyllis Phillips.

Around Plymouth Bay
P.O. Box 6211
Plymouth 02360
(508) 747-5075
Plymouth and Cape Cod area.
Contact: Gail Tufts and Ann Kopke.

Michigan

Bed & Breakfast in Michigan
Box 1731
Dearborn 48121
(313) 561-6041
Statewide.
Contact: Diane Shields.

Frankenmuth Area Bed & Breakfast
337 Trinklein Street
Frankenmuth 48734
(517) 652-8897 or 6747

Frankenmuth and area.
Contact: Beverley Bender and Doris Schmitzer.

Mississippi
Lincoln, Ltd., Bed and Breakfast
Box 3479
Meridian 39303
(601) 482-5483
+
Mississippi plus eastern Louisiana, western Alabama, and southeastern Tennessee.
Contact: Barbara Hall.

Missouri
Bed & Breakfast of St. Louis/River Country of Missouri & Illinois, Inc.
1 Grandview Heights
St. Louis 63131
(314) 965-4328
+
Statewide plus southern Illinois.
Contact: Mike Warner.

Bed & Breakfast Kansas City
P.O. Box 14781
Lenexa 66215
(913) 888-3636
+
Missouri plus Kansas.
Contact: Edwina Monroe

Ozark Mountain Country Bed & Breakfast
Box 295
Branson 65616
(417) 334-4720 or 5077
+
Southwestern Missouri and northwestern Arkansas.
Contact: Kay Cameron.

Montana
Bed & Breakfast Western Adventure
P.O. Box 20972
Billings 59104
(406) 259-7993
+
Montana plus Wyoming.
Contact: Paula Deigert.

Western Bed & Breakfast Hosts
P.O. Box 322
Kalispell 59901
(406) 257-4476
Contact: Sylva B. Jones.

Nebraska
Bed & Breakfast of the Great Plains
P.O. Box 2333
Lincoln 68502
(402) 423-3480
Contact: Rose Ann Foster.

New Hampshire
New Hampshire Bed & Breakfast
RFD 3, Box 53
Laconia 03246
(603) 279-8348
New Hampshire.
Contact: Martha Dorais.

New Jersey
Bed & Breakfast of New Jersey
Suite 132, 103 Godwin Avenue
Midland Park 07432
(201) 444-7409
Statewide.
Contact: Aster Mould.

Bed & Breakfast of Northern New Jersey
11 Sunset Trail
Denville 07834
(201) 625-5129
Northern New Jersey.
Contact: Alex Bergins.

New Mexico
Bed & Breakfast of Santa Fe

625 Don Felix
Santa Fe 87601
(505) 982–3332
Santa Fe and statewide.
Contact: Gloria Bennett.

Taos Home Bed and Breakfast
P.O. Box 177
Taos 87571
(505) 758–0287
Taos.
Contact: Mari Ulmer.

New York

A Reasonable Alternative
117 Spring Street
Port Jefferson 11777
(516) 928–4034
Long Island, Westchester counties.
Contact: Kathleen Dexter.

The American Country Collection of Bed & Breakfast
984 Gloucester Place
Schenectady 12309
(518) 370–4948
+
Northeastern New York plus Vermont and western Massachusetts.
Contact: Beverly Walsh.

Leatherstocking Bed & Breakfast
389 Brockway Road
Frankfurt 13340
(315) 733–0040
C
Central New York.
Contact: Floranne McCraith.

Urban Ventures
Box 426
New York 10024
(212) 594–5650
C
New York City.
Contact: Mary McAuley.

At Home in New York
P.O. Box 407
New York 10185
(212) 956–3125
Manhattan, Brooklyn, Queens, and Staten Island.
Contact: Lois Rooks.

Bed & Breakfast of Long Island
P.O. Box 392
Old Westbury 11568
(516) 334–6231
Long Island.
Contact: Naomi Kavee.

Abode Bed & Breakfast
P.O. Box 20022
New York 10028
(212) 472–2000
New York City and Brooklyn Heights.
Contact: Shelli Leifer.

Rainbow Hospitality Bed & Breakfast
758 Richmond Avenue
Buffalo 14222
(716) 283–4794 or 773–1814
+
Western New York State and southern Ontario, Canada.
Contact: Cheryl Beggie and Georgia Brannin.

Blue Heron Bed & Breakfast Reservation Service
384 Pleasant Valley Road
Groton 13073
(607) 898–3814
New York.
Contact: Susan E. Camin.

Bed & Breakfast U.S.A., Ltd.
P.O. Box 606
Croton-on-Hudson 10520
(914) 271–6228
+

Statewide plus Massachusetts, Pennsylvania, District of Columbia, and Florida.
Contact: Barbara Notarius.

B&B Network of New York
134 West 32nd Street, Suite 602
New York 10001
(212) 645–8134
New York.
Contact: Leslie Goldberg.

B&B USA
5 Grand View Avenue
Troy 12180
(518) 273–1851
Eastern New York State plus Connecticut and Massachusetts.
Contact: Doris Tomer.

Bed & Breakfast Referral of the Greater Syracuse Area
143 Didama Street
Syracuse 13224
(315) 446–4199
C
Greater Syracuse plus Finger Lakes and Cazenovia.
Contact: Elaine Samuels.

Bed & Breakfast Rochester
Box 444
Fairport 14450
(716) 223–8877
C
Rochester area.
Contact: Beth Kinsman.

Cherry Valley Ventures, a Bed and Breakfast System
6119 Cherry Valley Turnpike
Lafayette 13084
(315) 677–9723
C
Statewide.
Contact: Gloria Pallone.

City Lights Bed & Breakfast, Ltd.
P.O. Box 20355, Cherokee Station
New York 10028
(212) 877–3235
C
New York City.
Contact: Dee Staff.

North Carolina

Bed & Breakfast in the Albemarle
P.O. Box 248
Everetts 27825
(919) 792–4584
Northeastern North Carolina.
Contact: Dorothy Williford.

North Dakota

The Old West B&B
Box 211
Regent 58650
(701) 563–4542
+
Statewide plus South Dakota and Montana.
Contact: Marlys Prince.

Ohio

Buckeye Bed & Breakfast
P.O. Box 130
Powell 43065
(614) 548–4555
Ohio.
Contact: Don Hollenback.

Columbus Bed & Breakfast
769 South Third Street
Columbus 43206
(614) 443–3680
C
German Village.
Contact: Howard Burns.

Private Lodgings
P.O. Box 18590
Cleveland 44118
(216) 321–3213

Greater Cleveland and suburbs.
Contact: Jane McCarroll.

Oregon

Bed & Breakfast Accommodations Oregon—Plus
5733 Southwest Dickinson Street
Portland 97219
(503) 245–0642
+
Oregon, Washington, and California.
Contact: Marcelle Tebo.

Northwest Bed & Breakfast
610 Southwest Broadway, Suite 609
Portland 97205
(503) 243–7616
C +
Pacific Northwest plus Canada and Hawaii.
Contact: Laine Friedman.

Pennsylvania

Bed & Breakfast of Philadelphia
Box 630
Chester Springs 19425
(215) 827–9650
+
Philadelphia and suburbs plus nearby New Jersey and Delaware.
Contact: Betsy Augustine.

Hershey Bed & Breakfast
P.O. Box 208
Hershey 17033
(717) 533–2928
Southeastern Pennsylvania.
Contact: Renee Deutel.

Bed & Breakfast of Valley Forge
P.O. Box 562
Valley Forge 19481
(215) 783–7838
Valley Forge and Philadelphia.
Contact: Carolyn J. Williams.

Pittsburgh Bed & Breakfast
2190 Ben Franklin Drive
Pittsburgh 15237
(412) 367–8080
C
Southwestern Pennsylvania.
Contact: Judy Antico.

Bed & Breakfast Connections
P.O. Box 21
Devon 19333
(215) 687–3565
Philadelphia, Center City, Mainline, and suburbs.
Contact: Anne Goodman.

Bed & Breakfast of Southeast Pennsylvania
146 West Philadelphia Avenue
Boyertown 19512
(215) 367–4688
C
Southeast.
Contact: Patricia Fedor and Ruth Morrison.

Guesthouses
RD 9
West Chester 19380
(215) 692–4575
+
Pennsylvania plus Delaware, New Jersey, and Maryland.
Contact: Janice Archibald.

Bed & Breakfast Center City
1804 Pine Street
Philadelphia 19103
(215) 735–1137
C
Philadelphia area.
Contact: Melodie Ebner.

Bed & Breakfast of Chester County
P.O. Box 825
Kennett Square 19348

(215) 444-1367
C +
Chester County and area plus Delaware.
Contact: Doris Passante.

Bed & Breakfast of Lancaster County
P.O. Box 19
Mountville 17554
(717) 285-5956
Lancaster County.
Contact: Pat Reno.

Rest & Repast Bed & Breakfast Service
P.O. Box 126
Pine Grove Mills 16868
(814) 238-1484
C
Central Pennsylvania.
Contact: Linda Feltman and Brent Peters.

Rhode Island

Bed & Breakfast of Rhode Island
38 Bellevue Avenue, Suite E
P.O. Box 3291
Newport 02840
(401) 849-1298
C +
Statewide plus Massachusetts and Connecticut.
Contact: Joy Meiser and Ken Mendis.

Anna's Victorian Connection
5 Fowler Avenue
Newport 02840
(401) 849-2489
Statewide.
Contact: Susan White.

Castle Keep Bed and Breakfast Registry
44 Everett Street
Newport 02840
(401) 846-0362
Rhode Island.
Contact: Dorothy Ranhofer and Audrey Grimes.

South Carolina

Historic Charleston Bed & Breakfast
43 Legare Street
Charleston 29401
(803) 722-6606
C
Charleston.
Contact: Charlotte Fairey.

Charleston Society Bed & Breakfast
84 Murray Boulevard
Charleston 29401
(803) 723-4948
Historical area of Charleston.
Contact: Eleanor Rogers.

South Dakota

South Dakota Bed & Breakfast
P.O. Box 90137
Sioux Falls 57105
(605) 528-6571
Statewide.
Contact: Kathy Hales and Karen Olson.

Tennessee

Host Homes of Tennessee
P.O. Box 110227
Nashville 37222-0227
(615) 331-5244
C
Statewide plus Kentucky, Mississippi, and Georgia.
Contact: Fredda Odom.

Texas

Bed & Breakfast Texas Style, Inc.
4224 West Red Bird Lane
Dallas 75237
(214) 298-8586
C +

Texas plus Oklahoma, Mississippi, Georgia, and London.
Contact: Ruth Wilson.

King William Bed & Breakfast Registry
201 East Rische
San Antonio 78204
(512) 227-1190
San Antonio and New Braunfels.
Contact: Frances Bouchat.

Bed and Breakfast Hosts of San Antonio
166 Rockhill
San Antonio 78209
(512) 824-8036
San Antonio and area.
Contact: Lavern and Vicky Campbell.

Bed and Breakfast of Fredericksburg
102 South Cherry
Fredericksburg 78624
(512) 997-4712
Fredericksburg area.
Contact: Kathy Kopp.

Bed and Breakfast Society of Texas
921 Heights Boulevard
Houston 77008
(713) 868-4654
C
Houston and state.
Contact: Marguerite Swanson.

Gastehaus Schmidt
501 West Main
Fredericksburg 78624
(512) 997-5612
Fredericksburg and area.
Contact: Dr. Charles and Loretta Schmidt.

Sand Dollar Hospitality Bed and Breakfast
3605 Mendenhall
Corpus Christi 78415
(512) 853-1222
Corpus Christi area and Rockport.
Contact: Pat Hirshbrunner.

Vermont

Vermont Bed & Breakfast Reservation Service
P.O. Box One
East Fairfield 05448
(802) 827-3827
Statewide and New England.
Contact: Jane and Karl Zurn.

American Bed & Breakfast of New England
P.O. Box 983
St. Albans 05478
(802) 524-4731
C +
New England plus New York State.
Contact: Bob Precoda.

Virginia

Bensonhouse
2036 Monument Avenue
Richmond 23220
(804) 648-7560
Richmond plus Williamsburg, Fredericksburg, and Northern Virginia; specializing in corporate relocation.
Contact: Lyn Benson.

Guesthouses Bed & Breakfast, Inc.
P.O. Box 5737
Charlottesville 22905
(804) 979-7264
Charlottesville plus Albemarle City and Luray.
Contact: Mary Hill Caperton.

Rockbridge Reservations
Sleepy Hollow
Brownsburg 24415
(703) 348-5698
South central Virginia.
Contact: Elizabeth B. Anderson.

Sojourners Bed & Breakfast
P.O. Box 3587
Lynchburg 24503
(804) 384–1655
Lynchburg and central Virginia.
Contact: Ann and Clyde McAlister.

Blue Ridge Bed & Breakfast
Rocks & Rills
Route 2, Box 3895
Berryville 22611
(703) 955–1246
C +
Virginia plus West Virginia, Maryland, and Pennsylvania.
Contact: Rita Duncan.

Shenandoah Valley Bed & Breakfast Reservations
P.O. Box 305
Broadway 22815
(703) 896–9702
Shenandoah Valley.
Contact: John and Nancy Stewart.

Bed & Breakfast of Tidewater Virginia
P.O. Box 3343
Norfolk 23514
(804) 627–1983 or 9409
C
Norfolk and area.
Contact: Ashby Willcox and Susan Hubbard.

Princely Bed and Breakfast, Ltd.
819 Prince Street
Alexandria 22314
(703) 683–2159
Alexandria.
Contact: E. J. Mansmann.

Washington

Pacific Bed & Breakfast Agency
701 NW 60th Street
Seattle 98107
(206) 784–0539
C +
Statewide plus Oregon and British Columbia.
Contact: Irmgard Castleberry.

Travellers' Bed & Breakfast
P.O. Box 492
Mercer Island 98040
(206) 232–2345
+
Statewide plus Idaho, northern Oregon, and British Columbia.
Contact: Jean Knight.

Wisconsin

Wisconsin Southern Lakes Bed & Breakfast Reservation Service
P.O. Box 322
Fontana-On-Geneva Lake 53125
(414) 275–2266
Southern Lakes area.
Contact: Suzanne Brooks.

Bed & Breakfast Guest Homes
RR 2
Algoma 54201
(414) 743–9742
C
Statewide.
Contact: Eileen Wood.

Jamaica

Jamaica Travel Guide Centre
Bed & Breakfast Service
P.O. Box 55, Morant Bay Post Office
St. Thomas
Jamaica, West Indies
(809) 982–2548
Contact: Joe Corniffe.

Canadian Reservation Service Organizations

All Seasons Bed & Breakfast Agency
Box 5511HT, Station B
Victoria, British Columbia V8R 6S4
Victoria, Vancouver Island, and the Gulf Islands.
Contact: Maureen Vesey.

Town & Country Bed & Breakfast in British Columbia
Box 46544, Station G
Vancouver, British Columbia V6R 4G6
(604) 731-5942
Vancouver and Victoria.
Contact: Helen Burich.

West Coast Bed & Breakfast
810 West Broadway
P.O. Box 593
Vancouver, British Columbia V5Z 4E2
(604) 276-8616
West Coast.
Contact: Vicki Tyndall.

Alberta Bed and Breakfast
P.O. Box 15477, M.P.O.
Vancouver, British Columbia V6B 5B2
(604) 682-4610
Alberta, British Columbia.
Contact: June M. Brown.

Kingston Area Bed & Breakfast
10 Westview Road
Kingston, Ontario K7M 2C3
(613) 542-0214
C
Kingston and area.
Contact: Ruth MacLachlan.

Metropolitan Bed & Breakfast Registry of Toronto
72 Lowther Avenue
Toronto, Ontario M5R 1C8
(416) 964-2566
Toronto and area.
Contact: Elinor Bolton.

Niagara Region Bed & Breakfast Service
2631 Dorchester Road
Niagara Falls, Ontario L2J 2Y9
(416) 358-8988
Niagara region.
Contact: Monique Wetherup.

A Home Away From Home
1441 Howard Avenue
Burnaby, British Columbia V5B 3S2
(604) 873-4888
Greater Vancouver.
Contact: Irene Finnson and David Myles.

Toronto Bed & Breakfast
Box 269
253 College Street
Toronto, Ontario M5T 1R5
(416) 961-3676
C
Toronto.
Contact: Burke Friedrichkeit and Ken Bosher.

Appendix III: State and Local Tourist Offices

Alabama
State Office
Alabama Bureau of Tourism and Travel
532 South Perry Street
Montgomery 36104
800–252–2266
In Alabama, 800–392–8096

Cities/Towns/Regions
Greater Birmingham Convention & Visitors Bureau
2027 First Avenue, North
Birmingham 35203
(205) 252–9825

Huntsville Convention & Visitors Bureau
700 Monroe Street, Southwest
Huntsville 35801
(205) 533–0125

Convention & Visitor Department
Mobile Area Chamber of Commerce
451 Government Street
P.O. Box 2187
Mobile 36652
(205) 433–6951

Convention & Visitors Division
Montgomery Area Chamber of Commerce
41 Commerce Street
P.O. Box 79
Montgomery 36101
(205) 834–5200

Alaska
State Office
Alaska Division of Tourism
P.O. Box E
Juneau 99811
(907) 465–2010

Cities/Towns/Regions
Anchorage Convention & Visitors Bureau
201 East Third Avenue
Anchorage 99501
(907) 276–4118

Fairbanks Convention & Visitors Bureau
550 First Avenue
Fairbanks 99701
(907) 456–5774

Juneau Convention & Visitors Bureau
City & Borough of Juneau
76 Egan Drive
Suite 140
Juneau 99801
(907) 586–1737

Arizona

State Office

Arizona Office of Tourism
1480 East Bethany Home Road
Phoenix 85014
(602) 255–3618

Cities/Towns/Regions

Mesa Convention & Visitors Bureau
10 West First Street
Mesa 85201
(602) 969–1307

Phoenix & Valley of the Sun Convention & Visitors Bureau
4455 East Camelback Road, Building D146
Phoenix 85018
(602) 952–8687

Scottsdale Chamber of Commerce Convention/Tourism Department
7333 Scottsdale Mall
P.O. Box 130
Scottsdale 85252
(602) 945–8481

Tucson Convention & Visitors Bureau
450 West Paseo Redondo, Suite 110
Tucson 85705
(602) 624–1817

Arkansas

State Office

Arkansas Department of Parks and Tourism
One Capitol Mall
Little Rock 72201
800–643–8383
In Arkansas, 800–482–3999

Cities/Towns/Regions

Convention & Visitors Division
Hot Springs Chamber of Commerce
Convention Boulevard & Malvern
P.O. Box 1500
Hot Springs 71901
(501) 321–1703 or 800–643–1570

Little Rock Convention & Visitors Bureau
Markham & Broadway
P.O. Box 3232
Little Rock 72203
(501) 376–4781

California

State Office

California Office of Tourism
1121 L Street
Suite 600

Sacramento 95814
800–TO–CALIF

Cities/Towns/Regions

Anaheim Area Visitor and Convention Bureau
800 West Katella Avenue
Anaheim 92802
(714) 999–8999

Concord Convention & Visitors Bureau
Salvio Pacheo Square
2151 Salvio Street, Suite N
Concord 94520
(415) 685–1184

Eureka/Humboldt County Convention & Visitors Bureau
1034 Second Street
Eureka 95501
(707) 443–5097

Long Beach Area Convention & Visitors Council, Inc.
Plaza Level
180 East Ocean Boulevard
Long Beach 90802
(213) 436–3645

Greater Los Angeles Visitors & Convention Bureau
505 South Flower Street
Los Angeles 90071
(213) 239–0200

Monterey Peninsula Chamber of Commerce & Visitors & Convention Bureau
380 Alvarado
P.O. Box 1770
Monterey 93942–2198
(408) 649–1770

Oakland Convention & Visitors Bureau
1000 Broadway, Suite 200
Trans Pacific Centre
Oakland 94607
(415) 839–9000

Palm Springs Convention & Visitors Bureau
255 N. El Cielo Road, Suite 315
Palm Springs, California 92262
(619) 327–8411

Pasadena Convention & Visitors Bureau
300 East Green Street
Pasadena 91101
(818) 795–9311

Sacramento Convention & Visitors Bureau
1311 "I" Street
Sacramento 95814
(916) 442–5542

San Diego Convention & Visitors Bureau
1200 Third Avenue, Suite 824
San Diego 92101
(619) 232–3101

San Francisco Convention & Visitors Bureau
201 Third Street, Suite 900
San Francisco 94103
(415) 974–6900

San Jose Convention & Visitors Bureau
One Paseo de San Antonio
P.O. Box 6299
San Jose 95113
(408) 998–7000

Santa Clara Convention & Visitors Bureau
1515 El Camino Real
P.O. Box 387
Santa Clara 95052
(408) 296–6863

San Mateo County Convention & Visitors Bureau
601 Gateway Boulevard
Suite 970
South San Francisco 94080
(415) 347–7004

Colorado
State Office
Colorado Tourism Board
5500 South Syracuse Street
Suite 267
Englewood 80111
800–255–5550

Cities/Towns/Regions
Colorado Springs Convention & Visitors Bureau
801 South Tejon
Colorado Springs 80903
(303) 635–7506

Denver & Colorado Convention & Visitors Bureau
225 West Colfax Avenue
Denver 80202
(303) 892–1112

Vail Resort Association
241 East Meadow Drive
Vail 81657
(303) 476–1000

Connecticut
State Office
State Department of Economic Development
Tourism Division
210 Washington Street
Hartford 06106
800–243–1685
In Connecticut, 800–842–7492

Cities/Towns/Regions
Greater Hartford Convention & Visitors Bureau, Inc.
One Civic Center Plaza
Hartford 06103
(203) 728–6789

New Haven Convention & Visitors Bureau
155 Church Street
New Haven 06511
(203) 787–8367

Delaware
State Office
Director of Tourism Services
Delaware State Travel Service
99 Kings Highway
P.O. Box 1401
Dover 19903
800–441–8846
In Delaware, 800–282–8667

Cities/Towns/Regions
Greater Wilmington Convention & Visitors Bureau

1300 Market Street, Suite 504
P.O. Box 111
Wilmington 19899
(302) 652-4088

District of Columbia
Director of Tourism
Washington Convention and Visitors Association
1575 Eye Street, Northwest
Washington, D.C. 20005
(202) 789-7000

Washington Convention Center
900 9th Street, Northwest
Washington, D.C. 20001
(202) 789-1600

Florida
State Office
Florida Division of Tourism
Department of Commerce
5th Floor
107 West Gaines Street
Collins Building
Tallahassee 32301
(904) 487-1462

Cities/Towns/Regions
Convention & Tourism Division
Daytona Beach Area Chamber of Commerce
City Island Box 2775
Daytona Beach 32015
(904) 255-0981

Broward County Tourist Development Council
201 South East 8th Avenue
Fort Lauderdale 33301
(305) 765-5508

Convention & Visitors Bureau of Jacksonville and its Beaches
33 South Hogan Street
Jacksonville 32202
(904) 353-9736

Kissimmee-St. Cloud Convention & Visitors Bureau
1925 East Space Coast Parkway
P.O. Box 2007
Kissimmee 32741
(305) 847-5000

Greater Miami Convention & Visitors Bureau
4770 Biscayne Boulevard
PH-A
Miami 33137
(305) 573-4300

Miami Beach Convention Bureau
555 Seventeenth Street
Miami Beach 33139
(305) 673-7060

Orlando/Orange County Convention & Visitors Bureau
7600 Dr. Phillips Boulevard
Suite 6
Orlando 32819-8199
(305) 345-8882

Tallahassee Convention & Visitors Bureau
100 North Duval Street
Tallahassee 32302
(904) 224-8116

Tampa Convention & Visitors Bureau
Greater Tampa Chamber of

Commerce
801 East Kennedy
P.O. Box 420
Tampa 33601
(813) 228-7777

Georgia
State Office
Director Tourist Division
Georgia Department of Industry and Trade
P.O. Box 1776
Atlanta 30301
(404) 656-3590

Cities/Towns/Regions
Atlanta Convention and Visitors Bureau
233 Peachtree Street, Northeast, Suite 200
Atlanta 30043
(404) 521-6600

Augusta Convention and Visitors Bureau
600 Broad Street Plaza
P.O. Box 657
Augusta 30901
(404) 722-0421

Jekyll Island Convention & Visitors Bureau
One Beachview Drive
Jekyll Island 31520
(912) 635-3400

Savannah Area Convention & Visitors Bureau
301 West Broad Street
Savannah 31499
(912) 233-6651

Hawaii
State Office
Hawaii Visitors Bureau
1511 K Street Northwest
Suite 415
Washington, D.C. 20005
(202) 393-6752

Cities/Towns/Regions
Hawaii Visitors Bureau
2270 Kalakaua Avenue, Suite 801
Honolulu 96815
(808) 923-1811

Idaho
State Office
State Travel Director
Idaho Travel Council
Capitol Building
Room 108
Statehouse Mall
Boise 83720
800-635-7820
In Idaho, (208) 334-2470

Cities/Towns/Regions
Boise Convention & Visitors Bureau
802 West Bannock, Suite 308
P.O. Box 2106
Boise 83701
(208) 344-7777

Illinois
State Office
Ilinois Tourist Information Center
310 South Michigan Avenue
Suite 108
Chicago 60604
(312) 793-2094
In Illinois, 800-223-0121

Cities/Towns/Regions
Carbondale Convention & Tourism Council
714 East Walnut Street
Carbondale 62901
(618) 529–4451

Chicago Convention & Tourism Bureau
McCormick Place on the Lake
Chicago 60616
(312) 225–5000

Decatur Area Convention & Visitors Bureau
One Central Park East
Decatur 62523
(217) 423–7000
In Illinois, 800–252–3376

Kankakee County Convention & Visitors Association
701 South Harrison
P.O. Box 1967
Kankakee 60901
(815) 935–7390

Mount Vernon Convention & Visitors Bureau
215 Patomac
P.O. Box 2580
Mount Vernon 62864
(618) 242–3151

Peoria Convention & Visitors Bureau
331 Fulton, Suite 625
Peoria 61602
(309) 676–0303

Rosemont/O'Hare Convention Bureau
9291 West Bryn Mawr
Rosemont 60018
(312) 823–2100

Springfield Convention & Visitors Bureau
624 East Adams
Springfield 62701
(217) 789–2360

Indiana
State Office
Indiana Tourism Development Division
Indiana Department of Commerce
One North Capitol
Suite 700
Indianapolis 46204
800–2–WANDER

Cities/Towns/Regions
Clark–Floyd Counties Convention & Tourism Bureau
P.O. Box 608
540 Marriott Drive
Jeffersonville 47131
(812) 282–6654

Evansville Convention & Visitors Bureau
715 Locust Street
Evansville 47708
(812) 425–5402

Fort Wayne Convention & Visitors Bureau
826 Ewing Street

Fort Wayne 46802
(219) 424–1435

Indianapolis Convention & Visitors Association
One Hoosier Dome, Suite 100
200 South Capitol Avenue
Indianapolis 46225
(317) 639–4282

Greater Lafayette Convention & Visitors Bureau
3422 State Road 26 East
P.O. Box 5547
Lafayette 47903
(317) 447–5061

South Bend–Mishawaka Convention & Tourism Division
401 East Colfax Avenue
P.O. Box 1677
South Bend 46634
(219) 234–0051

Terre Haute Convention & Visitors Bureau of Vigo County
Honeycreek Square Complex South
P.O. Box 500
Terre Haute 47808
(812) 234–5555

Iowa

State Office

Visitors and Tourism
Iowa Development Commission
600 East Court Avenue
Des Moines 50309
(515) 281–3100

Cities/Towns/Regions

Cedar Rapids Area Convention & Visitors Bureau
424 First Avenue, Northeast
P.O. Drawer 4860
Cedar Rapids 52401
(319) 364–2591

Des Moines Convention & Visitors Bureau
800 High Street
Des Moines 50307
(515) 286–4968

Iowa City/Coralville Convention & Visitors Bureau
109 East Burlington Street
P.O. Box 2358
Iowa City 52244
(319) 337–9637

Waterloo Convention & Visitors Bureau
221 West Fifth Street
P.O. Box 1587
Waterloo 50704
(319) 233–8431

Kansas

State Office

Travel, Tourism and Film Services Division
Kansas Department of Economic Development
400 West Eighth Street
5th Floor
Topeka 66603
(913) 296–2009

Cities/Towns/Regions
Overland Park Convention & Visitors Bureau
9300 Metcalf, Suite 240
Overland Park 66212
(913) 649–3309

Wichita Convention & Visitors Bureau
111 West Douglas, Suite 804
Wichita 67202
(316) 265–2800

Kentucky
State Office
Kentucky Department of Travel Development
Capitol Plaza Tower
22nd Floor
Frankfort 40601
800–225–TRIP

Cities/Towns/Regions
Bowling Green Tourist Commission
1755–D Scottsville Road
P.O. Box 1040
Bowling Green 42102
(502) 782–0800

Northern Kentucky Convention & Visitors Bureau
Main Strasse Village
605 Philadelphia Street
Covington 41011
(606) 261–4677

Greater Lexington Convention & Visitors Bureau
430 West Vine Street, Suite 363
Lexington 40507
(606) 233–1221

Louisville Convention & Visitors Bureau
501 South Third Street
Louisville 40202
800–626–5646

Owensboro–Daviess County Tourist Commission
326 St. Elizabeth Street
Owensboro 42301
(502) 926–1100

Louisiana
State Office
Louisiana Office of Tourism
P.O. Box 94291
Baton Rouge 70804
800–231–4730
In Louisiana, (504) 925–3860

Cities/Towns/Regions
Baton Rouge Area Convention and Visitors Bureau
Riverside Centroplex
275 South River Road
P.O. Drawer 4149
Baton Rouge 70802
(504) 383–1827

Lafayette Parish Convention & Visitors Commission
310 16th Street
P.O. Drawer 52066
Lafayette 70505
(318) 232–3737

Southwest Louisiana Convention & Visitors Bureau
1211 North Lakeshore Drive
P.O. Box 1912
Lake Charles 70602
(318) 436–9588

Greater New Orleans Tourist & Convention Commission
Louisiana Superdome
Sugar Bowl Drive
New Orleans 70112
(504) 566–5011

West Baton Rouge Tourist Commission
2855 Frontage Road
Port Allen 70767
(504) 344–2927

Shreveport–Bossier Convention & Visitors Bureau
629 Spring Street
P.O. Box 1761
Shreveport–Bossier 71166
(318) 222–9391 or 800–551–8682

St. Tammany Tourist & Convention Commission
2020 First Street
P.O. Box 432
Slidell 70459
(504) 649–0730

Maine

State Office

Maine Publicity Bureau
97 Winthrop Street
Hallowell 04347
(207) 289–2423

Cities/Towns/Regions

Convention & Visitors Bureau of Greater Portland
142 Free Street
Portland 04101
(207) 772–4994

Maryland

State Office

Maryland Office of Tourist Development
Department of Economic and Community Development
45 Calvert Street
Annapolis 21401
(301) 269–3517

Cities/Towns/Regions

Baltimore Convention Bureau, Inc.
One East Pratt Street
Suite 14, Plaza Level
Baltimore 21202
(301) 659–7300

Massachusetts

State Office

Massachusetts Department of Commerce and Development
Department of Tourism
100 Cambridge Street
Boston 02202
(617) 727–3205

Cities/Towns/Regions

Greater Boston Convention & Visitors Bureau, Inc.
800 Boylston
P.O. Box 490, Prudential Plaza
Boston 02199
(617) 536–4100

Convention & Visitors Bureau
Greater Springfield Chamber of Commerce
1500 Main Street, Suite 600
Springfield 01115
(413) 787–1548

Worcester County Convention & Visitors Bureau
350 Mechanics Tower
Worcester 01608
(617) 753–2920

Michigan

State Office

Michigan Travel Bureau
P.O. Box 30226
Lansing 48909
(517) 373–0670
In Michigan, 800–292–2520

Cities/Towns/Regions

Ann Arbor Conference and Visitors Bureau
207 East Washington
Ann Arbor 48104
(313) 995–7281

Metropolitan Detroit Convention & Visitors Bureau
Suite 1950–Tower 100 Renaissance Center
Detroit 48243
(313) 259–4333

Flint Convention & Visitors Bureau
North Bank Center, 400 N. Saginaw Street
Suite 101A
Flint 48502
(313) 232–8900

Greater Grand Rapids Convention Bureau
245 Monroe, Northwest
Grand Rapids 49503
(616) 459–8287

Grand Traverse City Convention & Visitors Bureau
900 East Front Street, Suite 100
Traverse City 49684
(616) 947–1120

Minnesota

State Office

Minnesota Travel Information Center
240 Bremer Building
419 North Robert Street
St. Paul 55101
800–328–1461
In Minnesota, 800–652–9747

Cities/Towns/Regions

Bloomington Convention and Visitors Bureau
9801 Dupont Avenue South, Suite 440
Bloomington 55431
(612) 888–8810

Minneapolis Convention & Visitor Commission
15 South Fifth Street
Minneapolis 55402
(612) 348–4313

Rochester Convention & Visitors Bureau
212 First Avenue, Southwest
Rochester 55902
(507) 288–1122

St. Paul Convention Bureau
Landmark Center B 100
St. Paul 55102
(612) 292–4360

Mississippi
State Office
Mississippi Division of Tourism
P.O. Box 22825
Jackson 39205
800–647–2290
In Mississippi, 800–962–2346

Cities/Towns/Regions
Mississippi Gulf Coast Convention and Visitors Bureau
3800 West Beach
P.O. Box 4554
Biloxi 39531
(601) 388–8000

Jackson Convention & Visitors Bureau
201 South President
P.O. Box 1450
Jackson 39205
(601) 960–1891

Missouri
State Office
Missouri Division of Tourism
P.O. Box 1055
Jefferson City 65102
(314) 751–4133

Cities/Towns/Regions
Columbia Convention & Visitors Bureau
32 North 8th Street
P.O. Box N
Columbia 65205
(314) 875–1231

Convention & Visitors Bureau of Greater Kansas City
1100 Main Street, Suite 2550, City Center Square
Kansas City 64105
(816) 221–5242

Lake of the Ozarks Association
Business 54–A1 Elam–Real Estate Bldg.
P.O. Box 98
Lake Ozark 65049
(314) 365–3371
In Missouri, 800–392–0882
Outside Missouri, 800–325–0213

St. Louis Convention & Visitors Bureau
10 South Broadway, Suite 300
St. Louis 63102
(314) 421–1023 or 800–325–7962

Springfield Convention & Visitors Bureau
320 North Jefferson
P.O. Box 1687
Springfield 65806
(417) 862–5501

Montana
State Office
Department of Commerce
Travel Promotion
1424 Ninth Avenue
Helena 59620
800–548–3390
In Montana, (406) 444–2654

Nebraska
State Office
Nebraska Travel & Tourism Division

Department of Economic Development
P.O. Box 94666
Lincoln 68509
800–228–4307
In Nebraska, 800–742–7595

Cities/Towns/Regions
Hall County Convention & Visitors Bureau
309 West 2nd Street
Grand Island 68802
(308) 382–9210

Convention & Visitors Bureau
Lincoln Chamber of Commerce
1219 N Street, Suite 606
Lincoln 68508
(402) 476–7511

Greater Omaha Convention & Visitors Bureau
1819 Farnam Street, Suite 1200
Omaha 68183
(402) 444–4660

Nevada
State Office
Nevada Commission on Tourism
State Capitol Complex
Carson City 89710
(702) 885–4322

Las Vegas Convention & Visitors Authority
3150 South Paradise Road
Las Vegas 89109
(702) 733–2300

Reno Convention/Visitors Authority
4590 South Virginia
P.O. Box 837
Reno 89504
(702) 827–7600

New Hampshire
State Office
New Hampshire Office of Vacation Travel
P.O. Box 856
Concord 03301
(603) 271–2666

New Jersey
State Office
New Jersey Division of Travel and Tourism
Dept. of Commerce and Economic Development
CN 826
Trenton 08625
(609) 292–2470

Cities/Towns/Regions
Atlantic City Convention and Visitors Bureau
16 Central Pier
Atlantic City 08401
(609) 345–7536

New Mexico
State Office
New Mexico Tourism and Travel Division
Economic Development and Tourism Department
Bataan Memorial Building
Santa Fe 87503
800–545–2040
In New Mexico, (505) 827–6230

Cities/Towns/Regions
Albuquerque Convention and Visitors Bureau, Inc.
202 Central Southeast, Suite 301
P.O. Box 26866
Albuquerque 87102
(505) 243-3696

Las Cruces Convention & Visitors Bureau
311 North Downtown Mall
Las Cruces 88001
(505) 524-8521

New York
State Office
Division of Tourism
New York State Department of Commerce
One Commerce Plaza
Albany 12245
(518) 474-4116

Cities/Towns/Regions
Albany County Convention and Visitors Bureau
600 Broadway
Albany 12207
(518) 434-1217

Buffalo Area Chamber of Commerce
Convention and Tourism Division
107 Delaware Avenue
Buffalo 14202
(716) 849-6609

New York Convention & Visitors Bureau
Two Columbus Circle
New York 10019
(212) 397-8200

Niagara Falls Convention & Visitors Bureau
345 Third Street, Carbarundum Center
Suite 101
Niagara Falls 14303
(716) 278-8010 or (716) 285-2400

Rochester/Monroe County Convention & Visitors Bureau
120 East Main Street
Rochester 14604
(716) 546-3070

Syracuse Convention & Visitors Bureau
100 East Onondaga Street
Syracuse 13202
(315) 470-1343

North Carolina
State Office
North Carolina Travel and Tourism Division
430 North Salisbury Street
Raleigh 27611
800-VISIT-NC

Cities/Towns/Regions
Asheville Area Convention and Visitors Bureau
151 Haywood Street
P.O. Box 1011
Asheville 28802
(704) 258-3916

Charlotte Convention & Visitors Bureau, Inc.
One Independence Center
Suite 1290
Charlotte 28246
(704) 334–2282

Winston–Salem Convention & Visitors Bureau
Greater Winston–Salem Chamber of Commerce
2640 North Marshall Street
P.O. Box 1408
Winston–Salem 27102
(919) 725–2361

North Dakota
State Office
North Dakota Tourism Promotion
Liberty Memorial Building
State Capitol Grounds
Bismarck 58505
800–437–2077
In North Dakota, 800–472–2100

Ohio
State Office
Travel Information
Ohio Office of Travel and Tourism
Department of Development
P.O. Box 1001
Columbus 43216
800–BUCKEYE

Cities/Towns/Regions
Akron/Summit Convention and Visitors Bureau
Cascade Plaza
Akron 44308
(216) 376–4254

Stark County Convention & Visitors Bureau
229 Wells Avenue, Northwest
Canton 44703
(216) 454–1439

Greater Cincinnati Convention & Visitors Bureau
200 West Fifth Street
Cincinnati 45202
(513) 621–2142

Convention & Visitors Bureau of Greater Cleveland
1301 East Sixth Street
Cleveland 44114
(216) 621–4110

Greater Columbus Convention & Visitors Bureau
50 West Broad Street, 16th Floor
Columbus 43215
(614) 221–6623

Dayton/Montgomery County Convention & Visitors Bureau
1880 Kettering Tower
Dayton 45423–1880
(513) 226–1444

Trumbull County Convention & Visitors Bureau, Inc.
650 Youngstown
Warren Road, Suite 1
P.O. Box 608
Niles 44446
(216) 544–3468

Toledo Area Convention & Visitors Bureau

218 Huron Street
Toledo 43604
(419) 243-8191

Oklahoma

State Office

Oklahoma Tourism and Recreation Department
Literature Distribution Center
215 North East 28th Street
Oklahoma City 73105
In Oklahoma, 800-522-8565
Out of State, (405) 521-2409

Cities/Towns/Regions

Convention & Tourism Division
Oklahoma City Chamber of Commerce
4 Sante Fe Plaza
Oklahoma City 73102
(405) 232-2211

Tulsa Convention & Visitors Bureau
616 South Boston Avenue
Tulsa 74119
(918) 585-1201

Oregon

State Office

Tourism Division
Oregon Economic Development Department
595 Cottage Street Northeast
Salem 97310
800-547-7842
In Oregon, 800-233-3306

Cities/Towns/Regions

Eugene-Springfield Convention & Visitors Bureau
305 West Seventh Street
P.O. Box 10286
Eugene 97440
(503) 484-5307

Greater Portland Convention & Visitors Association
26 Southwest Salmon
Portland 97204-3299
(503) 222-2223

Pennsylvania

State Office

Pennsylvania Bureau of Travel Development
Department of Commerce
416 Forum Building
Harrisburg 17120
800-VISIT-PA

Cities/Towns/Regions

Philadelphia Convention & Visitors Bureau
Three Penn Center Plaza
Philadelphia 19102
(215) 636-3300

Pittsburgh Convention & Visitors Bureau
4 Gateway Center
Pittsburgh 15222
(412) 281-7711

Valley Forge County Convention & Visitors Bureau
One Montgomery Plaza, Suite 611
P.O. Box 311
Norristown 19404
(215) 278-3558

Puerto Rico
Commonwealth of Puerto Rico
Puerto Rico Tourism Company
1290 Avenue of the Americas
Room 2230
New York, New York 10104
800–223–6530
In New York City, (212) 541–6630

Cities/Towns/Regions
San Juan–Puerto Rico Convention Bureau
1120 Ashford Avenue
San Juan 00907
(809) 725–2110

Rhode Island
State Office
Rhode Island Division of Tourism and Promotion
Seven Jackson Walkway
Providence 02903
(401) 277–2601

Cities/Towns/Regions
Greater Providence Convention & Visitors Bureau
10 Dorrance Street
Providence 02903
(401) 274–1636

South Carolina
State Office
South Carolina Tourism Division
P.O. Box 71
Columbia 29202
(803) 758–2279

Cities/Towns/Regions
Charleston Convention & Visitors Bureau
172 Meeting Street
P.O. Box 834
Charleston 29402
(803) 723–7641
Outside South Carolina, 800–845–7108

Columbia Convention & Visitors Bureau
1527 Senate Street
Columbia 29201
(803) 254–0479

Greater Greenville Convention & Visitors Bureau
24 Cleveland Street
Greenville 29603
(803) 233–0461

Hilton Head Island Visitor & Convention Bureau
1 Chamber of Commerce Drive
P.O. Box 5647
Hilton Head Island 29938
(803) 785–3673

Myrtle Beach Area Convention Bureau
1301 North Kings Highway
P.O. Box 2115
Myrtle Beach 29578
(803) 448–1629

South Dakota
State Office
Department of State Development
Capitol Lake Plaza
711 South Wells
Pierre 57501
800–843–1930
In South Dakota, 800–952–2217

Cities/Towns/Regions
Rapid City Area Convention & Visitors Bureau
444 Mount Rushmore Road North
P.O. Box 747
Rapid City 57709
(605) 343-1744

Tennessee
State Office
Tennessee Department of Tourist Development
P.O. Box 23170
Nashville 37202
(615) 741-2158

Cities/Towns/Regions
Chattanooga Area Convention & Visitors Bureau
1001 Market Street
Chattanooga 37402
(615) 756-2121

Gatlinburg Tourist & Convention Bureau
520 Parkway
P.O. Box 527
Gatlinburg 37738
(615) 436-4178

Johnson City Conventions & Visitors Bureau
603 East Market Street
P.O. Box 1674
Johnson City 37601
(615) 926-2141

Knoxville Area Council for Conventions & Visitors
500 Henley Street
P.O. Box 15012
Knoxville 37901
(615) 523-7263

Memphis Convention & Visitors Bureau
203 Beale Street
Suite 305
Memphis 38103
(901) 526-1919

Nashville Area Chamber of Commerce
161 Fourth Avenue, North
Nashville 37219
(615) 259-3900

Texas
State Office
Texas Tourist Development Agency
P.O. Box 12008
Capitol Station
Austin 78711
(512) 463-7400

Cities/Towns/Regions
Amarillo Convention and Visitors Council
1000 South Polk
P.O. Box 9480
Amarillo 79101
(806) 373-7800

Arlington Convention and Visitors Bureau
1908 East Randol Mill Road
Suite 204
Arlington 76011
(817) 265-7721

Austin Convention and Visitors Council

901 West Riverside
P.O. Box 1967
Austin 78767
(512) 478–9383

Convention and Visitors Bureau
Beaumont Chamber of Commerce
595 Orleans Street
P.O. Box 3150
Beaumont 77704
(409) 838–1424

Corpus Christi Area Convention & Tourist Bureau
1201 North Shoreline
P.O. Box 2664
Corpus Christi 78403
(512) 882–5603

Convention & Visitors Bureau
Dallas Chamber of Commerce
1507 Pacific Avenue
Dallas 75201
(214) 954–1111

Denton Convention & Visitors Bureau
414 Parkway
P.O. Drawer P
Denton 76202
(817) 382–9693

El Paso Convention & Visitors Bureau
5 Civic Center Plaza
El Paso 79999
(915) 534–0600

Fort Worth Convention & Visitors Bureau
700 Throckmorton
Fort Worth 76102
(817) 336–8791

Grapevine Convention & Visitors Bureau
909 South Main Street
Grapevine 76051
(817) 481–0954

Greater Houston Convention & Visitors Council
3300 Main Street
Houston 77002
(713) 523–5050

San Angelo Convention & Visitors Bureau
500 Rio Concho Drive
San Angelo 76902
(915) 653–1206

San Antonio Convention & Visitors Bureau
121 Alamo Plaza
San Antonio 78205
(512) 299–8123

Victoria Convention & Visitors Bureau
1106 East Rio Grande
P.O. Box 2465
Victoria 77902
(512) 573–5277

Utah

State Office

Utah Travel Council
Council Hall
State Capitol

Salt Lake City 84114
(801) 533-5681

Cities/Towns/Regions
Salt Lake Convention & Visitors Bureau
180 South West Temple
Salt Lake City 84101
(801) 521-2822

Vermont
State Office
Vermont Travel Division
134 State Street
Montpelier 05602
(802) 828-3236

Virginia
State Office
Virginia Division of Tourism
202 North Ninth Street
Suite 500
Richmond 23219
800-VISIT-VA

Cities/Towns/Regions
Alexandria Tourist Council
221 King Street
Alexandria 22314
(703) 549-0205

Norfolk Convention & Visitors Bureau
Monticello Arcade
208 East Plume Street
Norfolk 23510
(804) 441-5266

Metropolitan Richmond Convention & Visitors Bureau
300 East Main Street, Suite 100
Richmond 23219
(804) 782-2777

Virginia Beach Convention Bureau
1000 19th Street
P.O. Box 136
Virginia Beach 23458
(804) 428-8000

Williamsburg Area Tourism & Conference Bureau
901 Richmond Road
P.O. Drawer G-B
Williamsburg 23187-3620
(804) 253-0192

Virgin Islands
United States Virgin Islands Division of Tourism
1667 K Street, Northwest
Suite 270
Washington, D.C. 20006
(202) 293-3707

Washington
State Office
State of Washington Tourism Development Division
101 General Administration Building
Olympia 98504
800-541-9274
In Washington, 800-562-4570

Cities/Towns/Regions
Seattle/King County Convention & Visitors Bureau
1815 Seventh Avenue
Seattle 98101
(206) 447-7276

Spokane Area Convention & Visitors Bureau
West 301 Main
Spokane 99201
(509) 624–1341

West Virginia

State Office

West Virginia Department of Commerce
Tourism Division
State Capitol
1900 Washington Street, East
Charleston 25305
800–CALL–WVA

Cities/Towns/Regions

Charleston Convention & Visitors Bureau
200 Civic Center, Suite 002
Charleston 25301
(304) 344–5075

Wisconsin

State Office

Wisconsin Division of Tourism
P.O. Box 7606
Madison 53707
(608) 266–2161

Cities/Towns/Regions

Eau Claire Area Convention & Tourism Bureau
Wagner's Complex
2127 Brackett Avenue
Eau Claire 54701
(715) 836–7680

Fond du Lac Convention & Visitors Bureau
207 North Main Street
Fond du Lac 54935
(414) 923–3010

Green Bay Area Visitor & Convention Bureau, Inc.
1901 South Oneida Street
P.O. Box 10596
Green Bay 54307–0596
(414) 494–9507

LaCrosse Area Convention & Visitor Bureau
P.O. Box 1895, Riverside Park
LaCrosse 54601
(608) 782–2366

Lake Geneva Area Convention & Visitors Bureau
201 Wrigley Drive
Lake Geneva 53147
(414) 248–4416

Greater Madison Convention & Visitors Bureau
425 West Washington Avenue
Madison 53703
(608) 255–0701

Greater Milwaukee Convention & Visitors Bureau
756 North Milwaukee Street
Milwaukee 53202
(414) 273–3950

Greater Racine Area Convention &
Visitors Bureau
300 Fifth Street
Racine 53403
(414) 634–3293

Wyoming

State Office

Wyoming Travel Commission
Travel Center
I–25 and College Drive
Cheyenne 82002
800–CALL–WYO
In Wyoming, (307) 777–7777

Index

absentee hosts, 46, 47, 168–69
advertising, 79, 82, 83, 131–32, 139, 166
air conditioning, 33–34, 58, 172
alcohol, 182, 225, 231
allergies, 32, 137, 145, 209
amenities, 66–74
  checklist, 73–74
American Bed & Breakfast Association, 85, 94, 124, 228
American Historic Homes, 92
Anchor Hill Lodge, 7, 45, 109, 152
Arndt McBee Insurance Agency, 232
arrivals, 46–48, 140–41, 144, 167–74, 243
Association of Bed & Breakfast Innkeepers of San Francisco, 97
Association of Massachusetts B&B Reservation Services, 98
atmosphere, 12, 34–35, 155, 172, 197, 199
attire, 41–42

B&B Ski America & Canada, 92
B&B Suncoast Accommodations, 32, 86, 141, 170
B&G's B&B, 46
babysitting, 75, 154
bathrooms, 60–66, 136–37, 163–64, 233–34
  checklist, 65–66
Bay Hosts, 92
Be Our Guest, 67, 70, 172, 219, 233, 234
Beach House, 71
bedrooms, 50–59, 163
  checklist, 59
beds, 50–56, 144, 152–53
Bed & Breakfast Adventures, 104
Bed and Breakfast Associates Bay Colony, Ltd., 50, 80–81, 89, 142, 151, 184, 185, 233
Bed & Breakfast Association of the Delaware River Valley, 98
Bed & Breakfast Association of Napa Valley, 97
Bed & Breakfast Association of Western New York and Northwestern Pennsylvania, 98, 99
Bed & Breakfast Atlanta, 33, 83, 236
Bed and Breakfast Brookline/Boston, 17, 34, 81, 104, 174
Bed and Breakfast Center City, 46, 48, 69, 78, 79, 81, 161, 179, 204, 221
Bed and Breakfast Colorado, 50, 170, 239
Bed & Breakfast Down East, 71, 83, 143, 195
Bed & Breakfast Exchange, 13, 142, 240
Bed & Breakfast of the Florida Keys, 20
Bed & Breakfast Guest Homes, 142
Bed & Breakfast Innkeepers Guild of Santa Barbara, 97
Bed & Breakfast Innkeepers of Northern California, 97

Bed & Breakfast Innkeepers of Southern California, 97
Bed & Breakfast Inns of Amador County, 97
Bed and Breakfast Inns of Connecticut, 98
Bed & Breakfast Inns of Gold Country, 97
Bed & Breakfast Inns of Humboldt County, 97
Bed & Breakfast Insurance Services, 232
Bed & Breakfast International, 81, 89, 142
Bed & Breakfast League, 50, 68, 142
Bed and Breakfast Ltd. (CT), 138, 142
Bed 'n' Breakfast Ltd. (DC), 5, 141, 186
Bed and Breakfast of Maine, 10, 71, 74, 77, 178, 179, 195, 233
Bed & Breakfast in Marblehead and North Shore, 79, 104
Bed & Breakfast: The National Network, 84
Bed 'n Breakfast in Phoenix, 246
Bed and Breakfast Pocono Northeast, 110
Bed & Breakfast Registry, 76, 143, 146, 233, 239
Bed & Breakfast Reservation Services World-Wide, 84, 232
Bed & Breakfast of Rhode Island, 7, 8, 21, 35, 43, 50, 81, 86, 104, 133, 233, 235
Bed & Breakfast Rochester, 40, 79, 82
Bed & Breakfast Rocky Mountains, 38, 50, 71, 81, 104, 142, 191
Bed & Breakfast Service (BABS), 67
Bed & Breakfast Society of Houston, 68, 81, 82, 218
Bed & Breakfast of Southeast Pennsylvania, 17, 38, 87
Bed & Breakfast Texas Style, 20, 142
Bed & Breakfast, The National Network, 84, 232
Bed & Breakfast of Tidewater, Virginia, 8, 11, 79, 83, 156
Bed & Breakfast Tropical Florida, 161
Bed and Breakfast U.S.A., Ltd., 71, 105
Bed & Breakfast of Waterville, 250
Betsy's Bed & Breakfast, 110
Blue Ridge Bed and Breakfast, 20, 37, 66, 82
Blue Wax Farm, 176
book exchange, 201–202
Boston Bed & Breakfast, 92
Bowling Green Bed & Breakfast, 48
Brinley Victorian Inn, 67
brochures, 83, 107–14, 116–18, 160, 161, 166, 218
business cards, 107, 114

Camel Lot, 109, 207
cancellations, 90, 141, 145
car rentals, 73, 118, 135, 145
Carolyn's Bed & Breakfast Homes, 81
Caroyl's B&B, 248
centerpiece, 208–11
chamber of commerce, 16, 85, 90, 118, 175
check-in (*see* arrivals)
check-out (*see* departures)
Cherry Valley Ventures, 78, 84, 86
children, 31, 76, 136, 144, 152–56, 211–13, 224, 225–26, 230–31, 235
Chinguague Compound, 8, 30, 68, 70
Christian Bed & Breakfast, 93
Christian Hospitality Bed & Breakfast, 70, 93
City Lights Bed & Breakfast, 11, 181
cleaning, 4, 35–40
  checklist, 39–40
coffee, 213–17
Commissioned Host & Toast, 92

community, 15–17, 118–19, 170, 175–76, 228, 229–30
consultants, 102–105
Corner House, 15, 69
Cottage, The, 8, 12, 45, 104, 204
Countryside, 10, 47–48, 69, 109–10, 204
Covered Bridge Bed and Breakfast, 79, 179–80
Cozy Acres, 23, 70

Dairy Hollow House, 10, 15, 45, 72, 218–19
decorating, 12, 81, 150, 208
departures, 47–48, 144, 181, 190–92
deposits, 79, 90, 140–41, 145
diet restrictions, 137, 145
disabled guests, 137, 162–66, 231
disabled hosts, 13, 166
discrimination, 140, 153

Eastwood House, 249
Educators Inn, 91
Educators' Vacation Alternatives, 91
emergencies, 11–12, 182, 235–36
evaluations, 193–95
  sample form, 194
Evergreen Club, 93
expenses, 20, 90–91, 237–38, 241–42
Eye Openers Bed & Breakfast Reservations, 17, 104, 143, 153, 233

Finger Lakes Bed & Breakfast Association, 98, 220
Fireacre Farm, 132
Folkstone Bed & Breakfast, 42–43, 50, 79, 85, 179, 234
foreign visitors, 160–62
Friends We Haven't Met, 5

Gates Hill Homestead, 29, 70
gifts, 155, 190–91, 209, 213
Greater Boston Hospitality, 4, 22, 38, 68, 86, 186, 219
Green Meadow Ranch, 23
Guest House Association of Newport, 99
guest register, 242
guidebooks, 82, 115, 120–29, 139, 174, 177
Gull House, 7, 12, 70
Gwen's Guest Home, 113

Hampshire Hills B&B Association, 98
health and safety, 61, 106, 151, 153, 158–59, 164, 225, 227, 232–36
heat, 33–34, 58, 172
Helping Hands Network, 99–101, 116
  listing, 246–53
Hidden Brooks Bed & Breakfast, 68
High Tide, 70
Historian Bed & Breakfast, 249
Historic Charleston Bed & Breakfast, 67, 195
Historic Country Inns of the Mother Lode, 97
historic homes, 16
Homecomings, 93
host contract, 89–90
Host Homes of Boston, 9, 20
House of Amacord, 6, 104, 157
House Guests Cape Cod, 41, 67, 167
house rules, 178–84
House of Snee, 17, 110
Hunt's Hideaway, 45, 109

income, 17–21, 236–39
  worksheet, 19
  see also pricing
Inn Reference, 96
Inn Transition, 105
Innkeepers of Santa Cruz, 97
Inns of the Central Sierra, 97
Inns of Point Reyes, 97
insurance, 81, 107, 227, 230–32

Internal Revenue Service, 228, 236, 239
Ivy Chimney, 71

keys, 173, 179, 234–35
Kingston Area Bed & Breakfast, 81, 160, 234
kitchen privileges, 68–69

Lakeside Farm, 44, 190, 191
Lamplight Inn B&B Guesthouse, 248
laundry, 72, 73, 182
League of Women Voters, 94
Leatherstocking Bed & Breakfast, 87, 152, 233
Leavenworth Country Inns & Recreation Association, 99
Leftwich House, 37, 67, 70, 148, 152, 241
Legislation Kit, 228
lifestyle, 40–44
Linden Lodge, 65
location, 4, 22–27, 74, 76, 80, 109, 135, 144, 197
  checklist, 26–27
London and Area Bed & Breakfast Association, 99
Longswamp Bed and Breakfast, 12, 110
lost items, 191–92

Maine Innkeepers Association, 98
Marjon Bed & Breakfast Inn, 16, 71, 205
Mayflower Bed and Breakfast, 110
Meadow Spring Farm, 110
Meadowview Guest House, 154
meals, other than breakfast, 68–69, 73, 176, 224–25, 235
Mendocino Coast Innkeepers Association, 97
menus, 217–21, 225–26
Mi Casa–Su Casa, 186, 233, 234
Monterey Peninsula Bed & Breakfast Association, 98
Mrs. K's Bed & Breakfast, 110, 197

naming your B&B, 109, 196–97
national B&B groups, 84–85, 94–96
  listing, 94–96
National Bed & Breakfast Association, 95, 120
neighborhood, 34, 203, 228, 230
  see also community
neighbors, 46, 169, 203–205
networking, 85–86, 118–19, 204–205
  see also Helping Hands Network
newsletters, 82, 102, 200
  listing, 102
noise, 28–31, 173, 180, 204, 230
nondiscrimination, 4–5, 140
Northwest Bed & Breakfast, 20
no-shows, 141
Nutmeg Bed & Breakfast, 82, 104

Oates & Hyde, 103
Ocean View House, 247
Ohio Valley Bed & Breakfast, 234
one-night guests, 76, 148–49
orientation, 12–13, 171, 174–78
  checklist, 177–78
Orleans Bed & Breakfast Associates, 81, 90, 146, 156

Pacific Bed & Breakfast, 16–17, 50, 81, 142, 161, 186
parking, 145, 164, 171, 204, 230, 234
Parsonage 1915, The, 170
payment, 140–41, 145, 173–74, 192
Penury Hall, 5, 218
pets, 32, 76, 136, 137, 144, 156–60, 173, 182, 231
Pineapple Hospitality, 142, 152
Pittsburgh Bed and Breakfast, 9, 25, 50, 234
press releases, 129–31
pricing, 74–77, 148, 149–50, 157, 221, 225
Prince George Inn B&B, 15, 43, 68, 137, 229

privacy:
  of guest, 58–59, 61, 142, 187
  of host, 14–15, 79, 107, 187
Prospect Hill B&B, 253

RCA Bed & Breakfast Publications, 93
real estate, 102–103
record keeping, 13, 82, 240–45
references, 139, 142, 144
refunds, 141, 145, 171
regional B&B groups, 96–99
  listing, 97–99
renovations, 64–65, 162–66, 241–42
repeat guests, 86–87, 89, 146, 195–203
reservation service organizations, 25, 38–39, 78–91, 141–43, 146–47
  listing, 254–70
reservations, 78, 113, 135, 140–41, 143, 146
Rest & Repast Bed & Breakfast, 11, 24, 58, 81, 83, 87, 146
RMF Bed & Breakfast, 15, 45, 71, 233, 241
Rockland Farm Retreat, 12, 205
Royal Carter House, 250

Sacramento Innkeepers Association, 98
safety (*see* health and safety)
sales tax, 238–39
SCORE, 228
screening, 82, 134–47
  checklist, 144–45
Seafield House, 250
seasonal business, 14, 24, 76, 87, 132–33, 243
Seattle Bed & Breakfast Association, 99
Servas, 93
Shaw House, 67, 69
Shir-Will Farms, 67
single travelers, 146, 148–52
Singleton House, 70, 199
Small Business Administration, 228, 239, 245
smoking and nonsmoking, 32–33, 137, 145, 181–82, 233
snacks, 67–68, 172–73, 179, 224, 235
Social Security, 238
Southern B&B Reservations Service, 44
Southern Comfort Bed & Breakfast, 21, 83, 166, 187, 233, 235
special-focus B&B groups, 91–94
Spindrift Bed & Breakfast, 70, 110, 153, 164, 234
stationery, 107, 114–16
Strawberry Castle, 7, 46, 72
Summerwood, 152, 191, 198, 205
Sycamore Haven Farm, 44–45, 71

table setting, 206–13
tea, 217
Teacher's Co-Op Travel Club, 92
telephone, 45, 106, 113, 135, 139, 140, 141, 180–81
Terrace Townehouse, 41, 67, 68
3B's Bed and Breakfast, 67, 152–53
tourist bureaus, 85, 90, 118–19, 175
  listing, 271–92
Tourist House Association of America, 95, 120, 232
Trade Winds, 4, 161
Traditional Bed & Breakfast Association of New Hampshire, 98
transportation:
  provided by host, 69, 73, 140, 144–45, 232, 244
  public, 135, 145
Traveler in Maryland, The, 5, 142
Traveler's Information Exchange, 93, 148
Turkey Nest Rest, 154

University Bed & Breakfast, 92
Urban Ventures, 47, 142

Valley View Farm, 5, 23, 45, 160, 184
ventilation, 33–34, 58, 62

Watercourse Way Bed & Breakfast, 156
Wedgewood Inn, 105
Wheeler's Bed & Breakfast, 250
Whidbey Island Bed & Breakfast Association, 99
Wild Rose of York, 110
Wildwood Inn, 105
Wine Country Inns of Sonoma County, 98
Woodruff House, 8, 12, 41, 70, 72, 204
Woody Hill Guest House, 6, 13, 72, 87–88, 154, 170
working hosts, 13, 44–49
workshops, 103–105

Yellow Pages, 83, 131

zoning, 107, 205, 227, 228–30

About the Author

An avid traveler all her life, Jan Stankus has accumulated a veritable gold mine of information to help people get the most out of their travels. Her offices both at home and at the Traveler's Information Exchange, where she has been director since 1982, are filled with books and clippings about places all over the world. She enjoys writing and lecturing about any aspect of travel, her passion.

Included among her favorite adventures are working on an archaeological dig in Spain, cruising down the Amazon River through the jungle to the "Wedding of the Waters," and looking for lost luggage in Egypt. She resides in Boston, which, she says, is a trip in itself. She is a co-author of the Boston edition of *How to Become Happily Employed*.